AMERICA'S UTOPIAN EXPERIMENTS

D0770532

THE NELSON A. ROCKEFELLER SERIES

in Social Science and Public Policy

BRIAN J. L. BERRY

America's Utopian Experiments

COMMUNAL HAVENS FROM

LONG-WAVE CRISES

DARTMOUTH COLLEGE

Published by University Press of New England / Hanover and London

DARTMOUTH COLLEGE

Published by University Press of New England, Hanover, NH 03755

Printed in the United States of America 5 4 3 2 1

CIP data appear at the end of the book

In memory of

HENRY CLIFFORD DARBY,

who first taught me

historical geography,

and to

BILL MEAD,

who aided and abetted

With the assistance of

Thelma W. Byrne

Bill Fountain

Thelma A. Guseh

Hak-Min Kim

Heja Kim

Rebecca A. Nelson

Zhiying Qi

Phillip S. Rotman

Dorothea Weir

CONTENTS

ILLUSTRATIONS

Figure

In the last decade of the twentieth century, as the global community faces a growing array of complex and interrelated social problems, public policymakers increasingly will turn to scholars and practitioners for guidance. To chronicle and disseminate the substance of the compelling discussions that will result, the Nelson A. Rockefeller Center for the Social Sciences at Dartmouth College, in collaboration with University Press of New England, has inaugurated this series of books.

Rockefeller Series books will be disparate in content but united in a common approach: presenting ways in which social scientific expertise is brought to bear on public policy issues of current or historic importance. The specific topics addressed will be as diverse as were the interests and work of U.S. Vice-President Nelson A. Rockefeller, which included state and local government, the environment, Third World economic development, publicly funded art, racism and intergroup conflict, and the functioning of communities. Authors will assess historical or existing policies, as well as the need for new or adjusted policies, in a search for viable solutions to pressing social, political, and economic problems.

The Rockefeller Series draws upon two sources for its books, the annual Nelson A. Rockefeller Monograph Competition, and works generated from Rockefeller Center research programs or Center-sponsored conferences. Included in the latter are scholarly works originating in one or more of the eight social science departments associated with the Center.

The overriding goal of the Nelson A. Rockefeller Series is to stimulate academics, policymakers, practitioners, and the public to think about and understand societal processes and the public policy implications associated with them. It is our fondest hope that these volumes will promulgate innovative and useful ideas, for as P. W. Bridgman notes, "There is no adequate defense, except stupidity, against the impact of a new idea."

George J. Demko, Director of the Rockefeller Center

INTRODUCTION

This book is neither a historian's history, based on careful interpretation of original sources, nor is it a sociologist's sociology, based on statistical analysis of community characteristics and trends. Rather, what I offer is a speculative essay that suggests relationships between economics, religion, and politics in the development of utopian communities on the American frontier.

The central hypothesis is that utopian surges, embedded within upwellings of millenarian excitation, have been triggered by the long-wave crises that periodically have affected American economic development. A corollary is that the utopias that have been built have been critical reactions to the moving target of capitalism; as capitalism has been transformed, so have the utopian alternatives. If this ultimately sounds like determinism, so be it. The correlations between utopian rhythms and long waves are as clear as they are powerful.

My attention was drawn to the successive bursts of development of utopian communities in America by Michael Barkun's 1984 paper "Communal Societies as Cyclical Phenomena" when I was working on *Long-Wave Rhythms in Economic Development and Political Behavior* (1991). To summarize Barkun's argument: The United States has experienced four brief but intense periods of communal activity, in the 1840s, the 1890s, the Great Depression, and the 1960s; these coincided with upswings of millenarian expectation. The first three came at or near the troughs of successive Kondratiev waves. What is strongly suggested, Barkun said, is a utopian cycle with moderately predictable rhythms that are so related to other episodic phenomena that there is the possibility of a theory of utopian growth and decline.

Spurred on by Barkun's paper, I studied the inventory of communal and utopian societies in the United States from 1787 to 1919 compiled by Otohiko Okugawa (1980) and examined information on such developments 1920–1990. I discovered a closer relationship to the long wave than Barkun intimated in his essay. Not only did there appear to be concentrations of communal and utopian experiments in the deflationary depressions of the 1840s and the 1890s; episodes of lesser magnitude were associated with the primary troughs into which prices plunged in the 1790s, the 1820s, and the 1870s. The rhythms have continued since. The federal government took the lead in alternative community development during the New Deal, following the primary trough that ill-advised federal intervention turned into the Great Depression (Berry, 1991, pp. 31–34). There also was a rush to "backwoods utopias" during the 1960s.

I decided that a closer look was warranted. Seven graduate students in the political economy program at the University of Texas at Dallas joined me for a graduate-level seminar, and we worked together during the spring semester of 1990. Several sections of this book had their origins in the raw materials gathered by the group.

Subsequently, aided by research assistant Bill Fountain and spurred on by the need to stay sane while bed-bound with a pair of herniated lumbar disks, I worked on a first draft of the book, completing it by October 1990. After Giselle Nunez had committed my scribble to the word processor, I circulated the draft to a number of colleagues and friends for their critical assessment. Robert McC. Adams, Simon Fass, Harvey Graff, Edward Harpham, Maury Seldin, and Henry Tom were all most helpful in forcing me to evaluate my arguments critically and to tighten the logic of my presentation. Aided by Heja Kim, who reconstructed the most critical graphics, I redrafted the manuscript. I was quite pleased to learn that the result of my efforts had been awarded first place in the first Nelson A. Rockefeller Monograph Series Competition.

Review of the second draft by a thorough and thoroughly critical Lawrence Foster for the University Press of New England resulted in an additional set of refinements, including both organizational improvements and more effective treatments of Transcendentalism, Theosophy, and the New Age Paradigm, as well as consistent reference to and reliance upon what he considered to be the most important secondary sources on the nineteenth-century movements. Once these improvements were complete, Cynthia Keheley made sure that the revised diskettes were what the publisher needed.

My conclusions will be uncomfortable to many. I do find clear and persuasive relationships to the long wave. But this should not really be any great surprise; communal experimenters have shared an intense concern with social disorder (Foster, 1981, p. 245). In crisis conditions that depress asset values, destroy wealth, and produce social disruption, there have been surges of millenarian expectation. While many have prepared for the Last Judgment by choosing salvation over original sin, some have sought perfection in communities where heterodox views of the economic system and of the role of the individual, women, the family, and the institution of private property were translated into experimental utopias.

In *The American Ethos*, Herbert McCloskey and John Zaller (1984) argue that tension between capitalist and democratic-egalitarian values is central to understanding American political attitudes. Nowhere has this tension been more apparent than during long-wave crises, when capitalism has seemed to falter. With a sinful and imperfect world perceived to be collapsing around them, utopians have sought to detach themselves from the mainstream, establishing communities offering a contrasting social order and economic organization, believing that by their pursuit of perfection they might anticipate the arrival of New Jerusalem.

Some will object that the tie to religious millenarianism confounds my analysis of the later emergence of secular and socialist utopias. This could not be further from the truth. In "The Religious Basis of Western Socialism," Albert T. Mollegen argues that Marx, from whom the concept of "critical utopias" derives, "was a Jewish Christian Apocalyptist in spirit, a Hegelian in methodological thinking, and an empiricist in gathering data for his philosophy of history. He inverted the Hegelian dialectic so that the Spirit does not move history, but changing economic relations which move history create the expressions of Spirit . . . Hegel rationalized divine providence and Marx materialized Hegel's rationalization" (quoted in Egbert and Persons, 1952, p. 109). I share this belief in economic triggers. "Downwave" conditions elicit a millenarian response that leads some to detach themselves from the economic mainstream so as to be able to construct idealized alternatives to it. Paired with capitalist crises have been communal, later socialist, responses.

In what follows, I first develop my hypothesis and then explore the links to long-wave crises by telling the stories of America's many utopian experiments. In so doing I cannot hope to provide the treatment that a group of utopian historians, each an expert on a particular movement, has provided editor John Pitzer for his forthcoming seventeen-chapter volume, *America's Communal Utopias*. Based on extensive primary research, one of the contributors says that this new book will be the "definitive scholarly introduction for those seriously interested in understanding the major communitarian experiments in America's history. Nothing of its scope has ever been published in the field." I seek in this book to provide a briefer overview that links each movement to the long-wave theme.

Chapter 1 deals with the facts of place, establishing that before Reconstruction utopian communities were built only within the regions settled by a northern culture predisposed to millenarian excitation. Chapter 2 deals with the facts of time, establishing that utopian surges have occurred in each successive primary trough and deflationary depression formed by the long-wave rhythms of prices that have helped shape the nation's economic history.

The next sixteen chapters are devoted to the successive utopian movements, from the Shakers to the communards of the 1960s. The long-wave triggers are identified as the individual stories are told. I make no apologies for these stories, which paraphrase earlier movement-specific monographs. I hope that I have used the most authoritative secondary sources, but the literature on utopianism is immense, and there is no consensus among the utopian historians. Certainly, someone's favorites will have been missed. That being said, I find it useful to have what I hope is a reasonable and informative summary in a single place, particularly one that includes what has happened since World War I.

The book concludes with two chapters that build on Barkun's theory of utopian development and that examine the currently unfolding utopian wave. The theory goes beyond the one Barkun suggested was within reach by incorporating both economic triggers and the social transformations that parallel such transformations in the economic sphere. These social transformations give rise to the successive critical utopias that Marx envisioned to be revolutionary alternatives to the "moving target" of capitalism. I bring them up to the present and project them beyond.

AMERICA'S UTOPIAN EXPERIMENTS

The Spatial Pattern and
the Cultural Matrix

Sir Thomas More's *Utopia* was an ironic dialogue, an indictment of the economic and social conditions prevailing in early-sixteenth-century Europe and the presentation of an idealized alternative that was simultaneously *ou-topos* ("no place") and *eu-topos* (the "good place"). The island of Nowhere was to More a vision to be contemplated, not a practical goal to be achieved. His alternative to Europe's ills was a communal society in which all citizens participated with full equality in activities related to food, housing, education, and government. A common denominator for full citizenship was a belief in a God who rules the world, meting out reward or punishment in an afterlife of immortality.

More's utopian vision was to assume significance as Reformation thinkers reversed the Augustinian interpretation of history later in the sixteenth century. To Augustine, the world was cursed by the ubiquitous power of evil; and humankind, by original sin. Only with the final triumph of good over evil would this burden be lifted (Tuveson, 1968). Those in the world of action were not to live in the City of God until the Last Judgment ends history. Instead of this pessimism about the possibility of happiness on an earth beset by original sin there emerged during the Reformation a new optimism about the future of humanity. Revelation 20:4–6 predicts that after his Second Coming, Christ will establish a messianic kingdom on earth and will reign over it for a thousand years before the Last Judgment. Perhaps, Reformation thinkers said, this prediction was not an allegory but a literal foretelling of an *earthly* utopia, an age at the end of history when Christian principles would be triumphant on earth rather than in the City of God.

There emerged a variety of millenarian religious movements inspired by the belief in a salvation that was to be *collective*, in that it is to be enjoyed by the faithful as a group; *terrestrial*, in that it is to be realized on earth; *imminent*, in that it will come soon and suddenly; *total*, in that it will completely transform life on earth; and *supernatural* in that it will be accomplished by nonhuman agencies. "Premillennialists" supposed that Christ's appearance was necessary for a thousand years of peace to begin and that fiery and catastrophic events would signal his arrival. "Postmillennialists" conceived of the millennium as a new golden age in history that would prepare the way for Christ's Second Coming and the descent of New Jerusalem on some specifically prepared locality on earth (Smith, 1965, pp. 538–39).

It was not long before Old World corruption was contrasted with the possibility of redemption amid New World innocence. Many believed that America would become an "Earthly Paradise" (Eliade, 1966, p. 265). This pursuit of redemption was central to the earliest Puritan settlement of New England. "Puritanism was a revitalization movement within English society" (McLoughlin, 1978, p. 238): "the counterculture, the 'new light' to the Anglican 'old light' " (ibid., p. 23). The settlers fled conditions that had grown intolerable in England, as attempts were made to repress dissent. During the years 1629–40, Charles I tried to rule without a Parliament, and Archbishop William Laud purged the Anglican church of its Puritan members and forced the Separatists out of the country. The eleven years also were an era of depression and of epidemic disease. John Winthrop felt that England had "grown weary of her Inhabitants" and determined to establish a new society in the New World.

Following the Winthrop Fleet of 1630, some two hundred ships brought close to twenty thousand emigrants in the first Great Migration. Winthrop and the Cambridge Divines who joined him called on their flocks to be worthy of the mission for which they had been predestined. They had covenanted with God on a special errand into the wilderness. Their purpose, Winthrop said in his speech on the *Arbella* in 1630, was to establish ideal communities that would be "a light unto the world, a city upon a hill." In Winthrop's Boston, Samuel Sewall preached that American soil would most likely be the location of the New Jerusalem. Cotton Mather acknowledged his indebtedness to Sewall in *Theopolis Americana* (1710), which promoted America as the prophetic locale for the appearance of a millennial paradise.

In preparation, the early Puritan settlements were given cohesion by the commitment of the émigrés, by their strong moral code, by their belief in predestination, by a strict patriarchal social order, and by the acceptance of authority. They were economically independent and were committed to mutual self-help—the antithesis of the "popish idolatry" that the Puritans felt was visiting the wrath of God upon England through wars, famine, and the plague. After reinvigoration by the First Great

Awakening (1730–60), there emerged from these beginnings a cultural milieu that fostered the idea of the United States as a "redeemer nation" committed to the war of good (progress) over evil (reaction) (Tuveson, 1968). The Second Great Awakening, following the turmoil of the Revolution, added, at microscale, utopian communities whose later surges coincided with periods of social and economic crisis. The earliest utopian communities were built in "backwoods" locations (Bestor, 1950) close to the expanding frontier of settlement (Porter and Lukermann, 1976). Later development was back from the frontier, in areas where the settlement system was maturing (Cross, 1950); and by the 1840s, the location of the Fourierist communes mirrored the configuration of the emergent northeastern industrial belt, belying Turnerian "frontier" hypotheses of utopian development advanced by Tyler (1944).

The first examples of utopian communities in America were built by Separatists and Pietists soon after Winthrop settled in Boston. In 1663, Peter Cornelius Plockhoy established a Dutch Mennonite community in Delaware that was looted and destroyed when the British conquered the area in 1664. The first Labadist colony in America was established in 1683, when followers of the French Separatist Jean de Labadie (1610–74) acquired 3,750 acres on an estate they called Bohemia Manor, which was located on the remote periphery where Maryland, Pennsylvania, and Delaware touch. The Labadists sought isolation from existing society to be able to purify themselves for the millennium. The concept was monastic. Members lived in cells in a communal dwelling, men apart from women. Celibacy was thought to be an important component of perfection. Because history would soon end, there no longer was any need to reproduce. Work was shared equally between the sexes. Living conditions were spartan. Deliberately, meals were tasteless. There was no heat, even in midwinter. But in a pattern that was to repeat itself throughout American utopian history, the 125-member community splintered after the first decade. A few maintained the communal way of life until the 1720s. Others, led by Bishop Peter Sluyter, privatized their farms to produce tobacco for the market, using imported slave labor. For Sluyter's majority, as in many of the movements that followed, the prospect of material gain outweighed the promise of salvation.

A second pre-Revolution example was the settlement called "The Woman in the Wilderness." Mystic Jacob Zimmerman, a lecturer in mathematics at Heidelberg University, calculated that the millennium would arrive in the autumn of 1694. Persecuted by the Lutheran church, he attracted a following among the German Pietists at Ehrfurth, largely students and university graduates to whom Pietism, with its emphasis on personal faith, was attractive. The group decided to emigrate to the American wilderness, but Zimmerman died in Rotterdam on the day they were due to depart. His place was taken by twenty-year-old Johann Kelpius. Arriving in America forty strong, the group acquired a 175-acre tract at Germantown, Pennsylvania, where they constructed a tabernacle containing forty cells, organized for communal living. On the roof was an observatory to enable them to watch the skies for the biblical portents of the millennium. The local Germans dubbed them *Das Weib in der Wuste*—"The Woman in the Wilderness"—following the Revelation to John. They practiced communal production and consumption, suppressing individualism by both self-discipline and mortification. Unfortunately, the date set for the arrival of the millennium came and passed. Kelpius tried to change the appointed time, but disaffected intellectuals left. For a while the community maintained its strength by recruiting other German Pietists, but the appeal waned and the settlement withered. Kelpius became a progressively more isolated hermit. In 1741 the community was dissolved and the estate was sold.

In 1720 another group of the German Pietist Brethren arrived to join the Woman in the Wilderness but were unhappy when they saw the disaffection and decay. This was no place to purify themselves. They formed their own congregation of Baptists in the Germantown area of Pennsylvania, spreading to twenty-eight congregations along the Atlantic seaboard by 1770. They were commonly called the Dunkers or Dunkards. One offshoot group accompanied Johann Conrad Beissel (1690–1768), a Pietist from the Palatine, to an isolated section of Conestoga County, Pennsylvania, where he established a utopian community. Active missionary activity drew in a following among the German Baptists of southern Pennsylvania, who were experiencing a religious revival in the years 1722–24. A schism occurred among these Baptists in 1728. Beissel and his followers seceded and established their own group, the Seventh-Day Church. Conflict and persecution followed—their seventh day differed from that of the established church—until Beissel retreated to seclusion north of Conestoga and developed a community of hermits. Later this community was called Ephrata, the third of the post-Pilgrim utopias. Other followers established private farms in the area, surrounding the core of ascetic hermits with a supporting community of "brothers" and "sisters."

Communal living arrangements were developed after a group of intellectuals led by Peter Miller joined the community in 1735. Brothers and sisters lived in a single community house. The sexes were segregated, and the group functioned as a commune. Private property was abolished. Life was austere. Clothes were crude and simple. The "perfect" group of hermits was celibate. New candidates were tested physically and spiritually for a year before they were accepted into the inner group that devoted its life to preparation for entering the gates to the Kingdom of Heaven. Individualism and materialism were suppressed. Members were expected to purge themselves of their former ego and to experience rebirth on entering the commune, taking on a new biblical name and identity. The group's missionaries sparked religious revivals and brought new members to the community, where they too could prepare themselves for the millennium. Music was central to the religious life, as it was in many other utopian communities, a means of establishing a bridge between the world of the commune and the Kingdom of Heaven. The whole was presided over by an autocratic Beissel.

The first challenge to his leadership came from a sect called the Zionitic Brethren, who joined Ephrata in 1739. Prior to their arrival, Ephrata's economy was austere and marginal at best. Israel Eckerling of the Brethren quickly converted the community into a productive agricultural and handicraft enterprise that flourished by marketing its product in the cities. By 1745 this new corporate prosperity so threatened the older ascetic religious fervor that Beissel ousted Eckerling and disbanded the Brethren. Ephrata's economy collapsed. Although boosted by arrival of new Pietists, Beissel's control was, however, eroded as he grew older. The missionary zeal vanished, and the vital spark of commitment to ideals was dampened. After Beissel's death his successor, Peter Miller, was unable to stem the deterioration. The community aged, unable to recruit the young. During the revolutionary war, General Washington used Ephrata as a hospital, knowing that the group's commitment to caring guaranteed that they would look after his wounded, but a typhoid epidemic took not only many of the wounded soldiers but many of the community's leading members as well. Ephrata deteriorated further, both physically and spiritually. Finally, in 1786 private ownership was allowed. Once again the economic mainstream prevailed.

Ephrata left one offshoot, Snow Hill, founded in a Sabbatarian farming area established by Beissel's missionaries in the 1750s. By 1788, Peter Miller (who died in 1791) realized that Ephrata was disintegrating and sent his most trusted associate, Peter Lehmann, to organize an Ephratan commune at Snow Hill. This was the only physical vestige of pre-Revolution utopianism to survive into independence. The Snow Hill Nunnery, or Seventh Day Baptist Church at Snow Hill, was formally organized in 1798. No vows of celibacy were taken, but those who married had to live outside the cloister in the surrounding area, as did secular members. Snow Hill flourished until the 1840s, when alternative communities captured the imagination of those seeking refuge from economic crisis amid escalating millenarian expectations.

There were several common threads in these pre-Revolution settlements. All were transatlantic transplants that left behind the evils and persecution of the Old World, looking to the New World as a place to build celibate, communal settlements in frontier locations isolated from worldly sin. Following the Labadists, each had a Germanic origin and was drawn to the frontier of active German settlement in Pennsylvania. Life in these settlements, it was thought, would prepare their residents for the millennium. Ephrata and Snow Hill, the communes that lasted beyond a generation, transmitted to post-Revolution America a heritage that included personal preparation for the Last Judgment, communal organization, separation of the sexes, celibacy, and rituals to link the worlds of man and God.

Between the Revolution and World War I more than 270 additional communal and utopian communities were built in the United States (Okugawa, 1980—his list is incomplete; utopian historians continue to discover new cases). Before 1840 the new utopian settlements were built within one hundred miles of the frontier, although exceptions can always be found. As the frontier moved westward, so did the locus of utopian development. The important criterion was that communities be developed at the greatest possible remove from worldly temptation. So much is already well documented (Porter and Lukermann, 1976).

After 1840 the locus of development shifted, delineating what subsequently became the American manufacturing belt; and indeed, if the locations of the utopian settlements on Okugawa's list that were established prior to Reconstruction and those built between 1870 and 1919 are plotted on a pair of maps, as in Figure 1, a distinctive spatial pattern is revealed: *before Reconstruction the utopians avoided the South*. Indeed, before 1890 there were only two short-lived ventures in that region. The first was the Warm Springs Colony, created in 1871 by fifty colonists from New York City, who purchased fifteen hundred acres in western North Carolina but found themselves in debt even before they had set up communal housekeeping. The community lasted less than a year. The second experiment was equally brief. The Social Freedom Colony was set up in Chesterfield County, Virginia, in 1874. With only half a dozen members and no converts, it quickly vanished.

Even in the next three decades, 1890–1919, only a few additional utopian experiments occurred in the South, all during the depression of the later 1890s. These included Narcosee, Florida, 1894–1912, established in Osceola County by a group of Shakers from the Watervliet, New York, and dissolved when the settlers grew old; the Willard Cooperative Colony, set up by fifty prohibitionists in Harriman, Tennessee, in 1895, which lasted a year; the Fairhope Industrial Association, which was established to implement Henry George's single tax ideas in Fairhope, Alabama, in 1895

Figure 1. Spatial Patterns of Utopian Community Development before and after 1870. Before Reconstruction utopian communities avoided the South. After 1870 the most intense utopian activity shifted to the Great Plains and the Pacific Coast, although utopians did begin to move into the South as well.

and which has survived as a cooperative organization; White Oak, Georgia, 1898–1902, the last of the Shaker colonies, an unsuccessful venture of a small group of Shakers from Union Village, Ohio; Freidheim, a Virginian communistic society that lasted only from 1899 to 1900; and Lystra, a religious commune, also in Virginia, 1899–1902.

Why was the South such infertile ground for utopian seed? The answer to this question resides, I believe, in the cultural matrix, the different sets of values, beliefs, and behaviors embedded in southern society. Indeed, with the exception of temperance and revivalism, the South was devoid of all social reform movements, not simply communal experiments. It was northern culture that fostered the millenarian beliefs within which episodic utopian surges were embedded.

Several types of society were planted in the New World. In the better parts of his treatise, David Hackett Fischer (1989) writes, in *Albion's Seed: Four British Folkways in America*, that fundamental differences in values and folkways were set in place by the migration of John Winthrop's Puritans to Massachusetts Bay in the 1630s and the movement of a Royalist elite and their indentured servants to Virginia in the 1640s.

The Puritans organized corporate towns with a strong sense of community and a belief in collective order. Liberty was not something that belonged to an individual but to the entire community. Such collective or "publick" liberty enabled towns to regulate the behavior of their individual members in a variety of ways, but it also meant that deviants were invited to leave. Boorstin (1958, p. 7) quotes Nathaniel Ward's declaration, in the *Simple Cobler of Aggawam* (1647), that "I . . . proclaime to the world, in the name of our Colony, that all Familists, Antinomians, Anabaptists, and other Enthusiasts, shall have free Liberty to keep away from us, and such as will come to be gone as fast as they can, the sooner the better."

Boston's Puritan theologians initially contested the anti-Calvinist ideas of Arminianism, with its concept of freedom of the will and individual responsibility, and Antinomianism, the notion that individuals are not fundamentally depraved but have the potentiality to achieve personal salvation (Erikson, 1966). Despite their attempts to suppress deviance, both ideas ultimately were to prove important in the evolution of the northern culture, however, as northerners came to believe that the elect were not prechosen, that individuals could cast off the shackles of original sin, and that a righteous life and good works would lead to personal success and to salvation (Mandelker, 1984, p. 43), all ideas that took hold on the edges of the Puritan ecumene and came back to transform it in the Great Awakenings.

In the emergent southern society, order did not inhere in the community but in the hierarchical social structure. Disorder implied confused social hierarchies and was punished with severity. Deviants, interlopers, and others who threatened the social order were punished and suppressed. Liberty was an elite concept: the liberty to rule, the freedom to be an individual. The "idea of natural liberty was not a reciprocal idea. It did not recognize the right of dissent or disagreement. Deviance from cultural norms was rarely tolerated; opposition was suppressed by force" (Fischer, 1989, p. 781). The cultural ethic was libertarian, ultimately placing the highest value in the concept of the autonomous individual. There was no room in such a system for social reform generally or for communal utopias specifically.

Americans were well aware of the contrasts between the northern and southern cultures, just as American historians have been since. Some of the behavioral differences between northerners and southerners were captured by Thomas Jefferson in 1785 in a letter he wrote to the Marquis de Chastellux. He set forth a table of the differences (quoted in O'Brien, 1979, p. 3):

In the North they are	*In the South they are*
cool	fiery
sober	voluptuary
laborious	indolent
independent	unsteady
jealous of their own liberties, and just to those of others	zealous for their own own liberties, but trampling on those of others
interested	generous
chicaning	candid
superstitious and hypocritical of their religion	without attachment or pretensions to any religion but that of the heart

The utopian vision of deliberate replacement of an existing social structure was inconceivable in a society in which status is ascribed at birth and in which values, customs, and behavior patterns are endowed with the sanctity of tradition. Utopian conceptions can arise only where there exists an awareness and belief in the mutability of social institutions and a perception of the importance of the social structure for the behavior of the individual (Whitworth, 1975, p. 212). This was in northern, not southern, society.

The spatial pattern of utopian communities built before Reconstruction, mapped in Figure 1, thus mirrors that of the spread of northern culture. Only after the southern planter aristocracy had been destroyed in the Civil War did the southern cultural matrix begin to change, and along with it the possibility for utopian development in that region. Even then, utopian experiments were few and short-lived until the federal government took over utopian community building during the New Deal.

Utopian development did not begin in earnest in the North either until society was disrupted by the Revolution. By then, Puritanism had been transformed into "a spiritual centrifuge, the disparate elements separating into sectarianism" (Mandelker, 1984, p. 27). "As early as 1650 Congregationalism, Presbyterianism, Anabaptism, and Arminianism were split on fundamental religious questions such as free will, the calling, predestination, and preparation for salvation" (ibid.).

It was during the First Great Awakening of 1730–60, a religious revival that relegitimated emotional religiosity, that the major figure, Jonathan Edwards, gave millenarian thought a distinctive American tone. At center stage was the Puritan belief that America represented a postmillennial beginning, the special mission of its church to craft a golden age and lead the world to salvation. Edwards preached that liberty went to the person from whom the fetters of original sin had fallen. New institutions, such as the revival, where the required conversions would take place under the guidance of evangelical preachers, brought significant changes to American religious life. There was a sense of the possibility of general salvation, to be achieved in a regenerated America. But rather than reestablishing a Puritan consensus, as some of the revivalists thought they might, these changes "furthered the fragmentation of the social order by aggravating sectarian differences and pitting adherents of the new against adherents of the old" (Mandelker, 1984, p. 29). By substituting conversion for predestination, the First Great Awakening reinforced the doctrine of freedom of the will by providing individuals with the opportunity to choose salvation over sin. For many, being "saved" was enough to prepare for the Last Judgment.

By the revolutionary period the strain between individual freedom and social order assumed the form of tension between a *Protestant ethic* that urged individuals to work hard and to succeed (for clearly, material success was evidence of God's grace) and a *Puritan ethic* that preached social responsibility, the joining of callings in a communal effort. In the economic mainstream of the North, individual pursuit of material gain prevailed, rationalized as God's will. It was in utopian experiments that the Puritan ethic preserved the idea of communal order.

The discontinuities of the revolutionary period produced a Second Great Awakening, which lasted from 1800 to 1830 (McLoughlin, 1978). Already accepting of revival-oriented evangelical Protestantism, the revivals achieved their greatest intensity in the "West," where the first settlement phase was just ending. The fundamental strain was between the Calvinists' belief in humankind's depravity and new Enlightenment belief in innate goodness and free will (ibid., p. 99). Essential to the Second Great Awakening was the idea that if conversion is possible by an act of will, then all things are possible: not only the individual spirit can be renovated; society at large can be regenerated by the power of human will in harmony with God's will (Mandelker, 1984, p. 45). Thus, the demo-cratic doctrine of the free individual was harmonized with the religious notion of personal and universal salvation as religious and secular ideals converged. The result in northern society was not simply increasing ma-terialism and growing secularization; it also involved the emergence of the notion of a "redeemer nation" with a millennial destiny in which good (progress) will triumph over evil (reaction) as the benefits of liberty, democracy, and individual enterprise are spread with missionary zeal (Tuveson, 1968, pp. vii–ix). At the same time, the Second Great Awaken-ing added a strand to utopian thought: The utopians came to think that their settlements were not merely places of refuge where perfection might be sought; they could serve as models for the redemption of mankind. Utopian communities became the locus of social experimentation.

As the cultural mainstream centering on individual liberties and com-petitive struggle strengthened, important distinctions emerged between what Tuveson (1968) has termed the *millennialists* and the *millenarians*. Millennialists, heirs to the scholarly traditions of the seventeenth-century scholars and Cambridge divines (Harrison, 1979, p. 6), subscribed to an idea of progress that combines the religious and the secular and reinforces the mainstream: Human history, under divine guidance, will bring about the triumph of Christian principles; society at large will be transformed into a holy utopia. God, it is thought, operates through the laws of nature—through confrontation and conflict between the righteous and the wicked—to produce progress toward this utopia. Millenarians, whose popular, largely self-educated adventism derives from the radical sects of the English revolution (ibid.), preserved an older view of St. John's Revelation, subscribing to the literal idea of the Apocalypse: following calamitous portents, Christ will return, and good will triumph over evil as history as we know it ends.

Two groups of millenarians can be distinguished. *Apocalyptic or pre-millenarians* believe that the advent is ahead, that it is predictable, that it will come down from the heavens in an overwhelming manner, that it will be instantaneous, and that it requires the choice of salvation by those who are to be accepted into the Kingdom of God. *Progressive or postmillenari-ans* believe that the advent has already occurred, that there are prophets to whom divine wisdom has been revealed, and that these prophets will lead in the gradual construction of communities where perfection might be sought. When perfection is achieved, history will end.

Apocalyptic millenarianism appeared most graphically in the Millerite

mass movements that occurred in the "Burned-Over District" first discussed by Whitney Cross (1950) and described so eloquently by Michael
Barkun (1986) in his *Crucible of the Millenium*. This district is the section of
upstate New York along the route of the Erie Canal that experienced wave
after wave of religious revivals after initial settlement. These upheavals
reached a maximum in the Millerite movement of the 1830s. The region
was part of a "Second New England" created by migration of people of
Yankee heritage, impelled by land shortages and the decreasing quality
of rural life as population pressures mounted in the hill country of New
England. Fathers could no longer subdivide their land and provide their
sons with adequate livings. Open spaces were no longer available for new
settlements to be planted. The new inhabitants brought with them religious patterns in which millennial themes and emotional excitation were
already present, especially the Vermonters, who preserved the spirit of
the First Great Awakening. Barkun (1986) writes: "The millenarian ferment that reached its climax in the Millerite debacle was an intellectu-
ally respectable feature of New England Protestantism, which grew from
English roots" (p. 21; for recent works on the Millerites, see Doan, 1987;
and Numbers and Butler, 1987).

William Miller (1782–1849), a farmer from Vermont and a U.S. officer in
the War of 1812, concluded, after undergoing a religious conversion, that
the Second Advent of Christ would come on 21 March 1844. He gave his
first sermon in 1831 and thereafter preached both widely and eloquently
that that the Kingdom of God was at hand, stressing that Christ would arrive in a fiery conflagration. In preparation for the Last Judgment, people
should choose salvation. His imagery of the portents of the Apocalypse
included both political upheavals and natural disasters and appeared to
have been confirmed by the Crisis of 1837 and its aftermath as the economy slid toward depression. Between August and October 1844, fifty
thousand to one hundred thousand Adventist followers, drawn in particular from the more conservative populations of remote rural areas and
small towns, withdrew from their churches, many selling their property,
and awaited the Second Coming (Harrison, 1979, p. 194).

Unfortunately, the appointed day came and went, and the Millerite
cause fell into disrepute, becoming the "Great Disappointment." Miller
admitted his incorrect chronology but continued to expect the imminent
end of the world. He and those who stayed with him later took the name
Advent Christians. Some insisted the Second Advent had occurred in a
"spiritual" sense. They joined other movements, including the Shakers. A
third group concluded that 1844 was indeed the date that Christ entered
the sanctuary to judge the sins of those both living and dead but that
the sanctuary was in heaven, not on earth, and the final phase of human

history had indeed begun. These Millerites went on to found a number of other Adventist churches and movements. Ellen G. White, for example, codified the new doctrine for what became the Seventh-day Adventist Church (Schwartz, 1970, pp. 91ff.). Among the later manifestations were the Church of God movement, which rejected Ellen White's visions, and Charles Taze Russell's Millennial Dawn Bible Students—later the Jehovah's Witnesses—an offshoot of the Advent Christian Church, who consider it their responsibility to announce the Second Coming of Christ, which will be marked by the battle of Armageddon in which Satan will be defeated, the wicked annihilated, and the faithful rewarded. (For a discussion of these and other Adventist movements, see J. Gordon Melton's [1989] *Encyclopedia of American Religions*).

Amid the economic crisis of the early 1870s, resurgent interest in the imminent return of Christ was built into a later apocalyptic movement via the Niagara Bible Conference, initiated by James Inglis (d. 1872) and continued by James H. Brooks (1830–97), editor of the millenarian publication *The Truth*. The group held conferences in major cities beginning in 1878, growing in strength as Protestant Yankees expressed concern about an American future afflicted by labor unrest and Catholic immigration. Their millenarianism was driven by what were believed to be signs of degeneracy and decay and found expression both in the later upsurge of populism, progressivism, and liberal Protestantism during the Third Great Awakening of 1890–1920, as well as in the Fundamentalist reactions to it (McLoughlin, 1978).

A few apocalyptic millenarians did develop utopian communities (Okugawa, 1980):

(1.) *The Mountain Cove Community*, in Fayette County, West Virginia, organized in 1851 as a hundred-member spiritualist community of the Apostolic Circle, gathered in Auburn, New York, by Thomas Lake Harris[1] and James L. Scott. The group believed they would witness the Second Coming of Christ at Mountain Cove, but Christ did not oblige, and the commune disintegrated in 1853 as a result of a property quarrel.

(2.) *The Germania Company*, in Marquette County, Michigan, founded by a Millerite group of Second Day Adventists in 1855. It was small— six families and five unmarried women—and it prospered. When their leader, Benjamin Hall, died in 1879, the group divided the property.

(3.) *The Adonia Shomo Company*, or Community of Fullerites, at Petersham in Worcester County, Massachusetts. This community originated at a Groton meeting, and was led by ex-Quaker Frederick T. Howland. Initially the group, mainly women, settled at Leonard Fuller's home in Athol in 1861. In 1864, with thirty members, they moved to a large farm at Petersham. The community dissolved amid litigation in 1897.

(4.) *Celesta*. In 1852, Second Adventist preacher Peter Armstrong set out to create a Heavenly Celestial City of 144,000 saints at the top of the Allegheny Mountains in Sullivan County, Pennsylvania. After eleven years, in 1863, despite widespread recruiting through his paper *The Day Star of Zion*, he recruited only dozen families. The community fell apart the following year.

These few examples notwithstanding, it was the progressive millenarians who developed the utopian communities. The progressives thought that the millennium would arrive once perfection had been achieved, according to the plans revealed by God to his prophets. This was the concept that was transmitted to the utopian community builders in the Second New England as the frontier swept westward. Barkun (1986) comments that in the Burned-Over District "religious millenarianism and utopian experimentation coexisted in time and space . . . manifestations of a regional ethos that encouraged radical religious and social experimentation" (pp. 3–4). The differences between the two in the 1840s were as follows:

Apocalyptic	*Progressive*
Militancy	vs Withdrawal
Mass movements	vs Small insular communities
Focus on salvation	vs Search for perfection
Venerable language of religion	vs Embryonic language of secularism
Awaiting the millennium in macrocosm	vs Construction of millennium in microcosm

Thus, the Church of Jesus Christ of Latter-day Saints (The Mormon Church), which had its origins in the Burned-Over District, maintains a progressive millenarian doctrine: the function of the elect is to prepare the way for Christ's Second Advent by building, somewhere in the American West, a holy city called Zion, the precursor to New Jerusalem. There, perfection may be achieved.

In each utopian upwelling there has reappeared the theme of economic and social crises and natural disasters portending the Apocalypse. And to each major economic crisis there appears to have been a dual response: that of the mass-movement salvationists and that of the community-building perfectionists. The construction of utopian communities thus has been

Based in religious radicalism—the roots of American communalism were in the European religious dissent that was brought to the northern colonies, not to the South.

Drawn to the locations where it was easiest to separate from society, to achieve perfection.

Defensively structured, exercising the right to separation without political ambitions, avoiding challenges to the prevailing structures of power.

Triggered by crisis. "Catastrophic stress plays a pivotal role in inducing people to abandon old loyalties in favor of imminent millenium" (Barkun, 1986, p. ix).

It is to the triggering mechanism of economic crises that we now turn, crises that have produced long-wave rhythms of utopian development, as subjective perceptions of an impending apocalypse have been reinforced by economic distress. Long-wave rhythms have been an integral feature of American economic development, but as they have occurred, the nature of the economic system has changed and along with it the nature of the periodic crises. The rest of the book thus is devoted to the history of the successive utopian alternatives that have evolved in reaction to the changing nature of capitalism and its crises. At each critical juncture in capitalist development, when the economy has seemed to falter, utopian communities have emerged to offer life-styles and values running counter to those of the mainstream, translating into action heterodox social beliefs about property, the organization of work, the family, sex, and the role of women.

CHAPTER TWO

Contrapuntal Long-Wave
Rhythms

Utopian community building occurred episodically between the Revolution and World War I, according to Okugawa's (1980) admittedly incomplete inventory of the more than 270 communal and utopian communities that were built in the United States between 1787 and 1919. Another 99 communities were built by the federal government between 1933 and 1937, and a very large but uninventoried number of communes were started by a diversity of groups between 1965 and 1973.

Figure 2 charts the number of communities started in each 5-year interval of the 132-year time span covered by Okugawa. Some were built by immigrants for immigrants, their timing a response to forces in their country of origin rather than to American crises (Fig. 3). The utopian communities started for American settlers are plotted in Figure 4. Clearly, the fluctuations seen in Figure 2 are a product of the domestic rhythms graphed in Figure 4. Figure 3 reveals a steady rate of foreign imports until the 1850s, when the Ebenezer settlements were established, and the 1875–85 decade, when the Hutterites arrived and settlements were built for Jewish émigrés from the Russian Pale.

Figure 2, according to Michael Barkun's (1984) paper "Communal Societies as Cyclical Phenomena," shows brief but intense periods of communal activity in the 1840s and 1890s that coincide with upswings of millenarian activity. Rather than Figure 2, it is better to use Figure 4 to explain America's utopian rhythms, however. The timing of the immigrant communes was dictated by circumstances *external* to the United States, even if their later fortunes were responsive to the U.S. economic cycles. It is both necessary and desirable to separate the external from the internal initiatives.

Figure 4 shows that the domestic rhythms of communities whose genesis before World War I was *internal* to the United States were composed

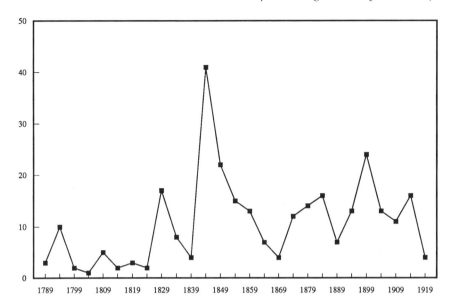

Figure 2. Utopian Rhythms: Timing of Construction of Utopian Communities in the United States, 1787–1919. Dramatic surges of utopian activity are evident in this graph, which charts numbers of communities established in each five-year time period that ends in the stated years (e.g., 1845–46–47–48–*1849*) on the vertical axis. The greatest peaks are in the depressions of the 1840s and 1890s.

not simply of the major surges in the 1840s and the 1890s noted by Barkun but also of lesser surges in the 1790s, the 1820s, the 1870s, and the years before the outbreak of war in Europe. Not shown in the figure are the later surges of the 1930s and the period following World War II because they were not parts of Okugawa's (1980) inventory.

What might explain these fluctuations in the rate at which Americans formed communes and the millenarian surges that accompanied them? J. M. Powell (1971) argues that "the triggering mechanism [of this millenarianism] has not yet been explained" (p. 609). I believe that the answer lies in the long-wave rhythms that have characterized American economic development.

The long-wave concept was introduced by the Russian economist Nikolai D. Kondratiev (1926/1935). His work is reviewed in detail in my book *Long-Wave Rhythms in Economic Development and Political Behavior* (1991), where I provide new and compelling evidence that there have been fifty- to fifty-five-year accelerations and decelerations of prices (Kondratiev waves) within which there have been embedded pairs of twenty-five- to thirty-year accelerations and decelerations in the rate of real per capita

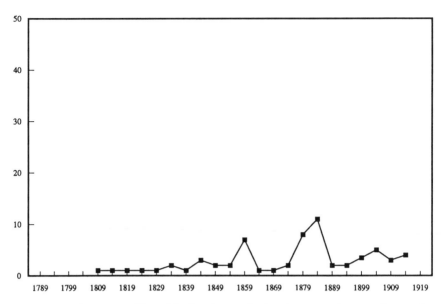

Figure 3. Communes Planted by Immigrants for Immigrants, 1787–1919. Among the communities charted in Figure 2 is a steady stream built by and for immigrants. There was one pulse in the 1850s, but the greatest peak, that of 1875–85, was produced by the arrival of the Hutterites and by the resettlement of Jews from the Eastern European Pale.

economic growth (Kuznets cycles). The price and growth cycles were synchronized by stagflation crises (1814–15, 1864–65, 1919–20, 1980–81), when inflation rates were at their maximum and the economy was in deep decline, and by deflationary depressions (the 1840s, the 1890s), when both prices and growth were at their lowest ebb.

Barkun (1984) hypothesizes that utopian surges occur at or near the troughs of successive fifty-five-year Kondratiev waves (i.e., during deflationary depressions). This hypothesis is correct only in part. The lesser utopian surges also are correlated with long-wave crises. I hypothesize, and hope to demonstrate in the chapters that follow, that it is the long-wave crises that trigger millenarian responses and that one set of responses, that of the progressive millenarians, has involved withdrawal to the periphery to build alternative communities structured antithetically to the values prevailing in the economic and social mainstream.

Let us begin by reviewing the long-wave concept. Working with wholesale price levels in England, France, Germany, and the United States, Kondratiev said that he had detected "waves of an average length of 50 years" running from trough to peak to trough as follows: 1789–1814–1849; 1849–1865(U.S.)/1873(Europe)–1896; 1896–1920–? Writing in 1925, he predicted that a plunge in commodity prices was ahead. Before and during

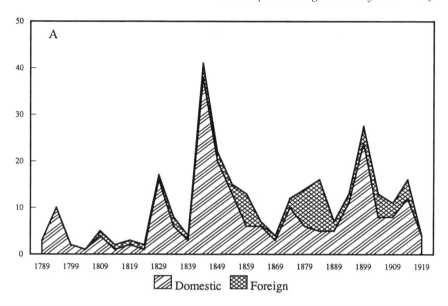

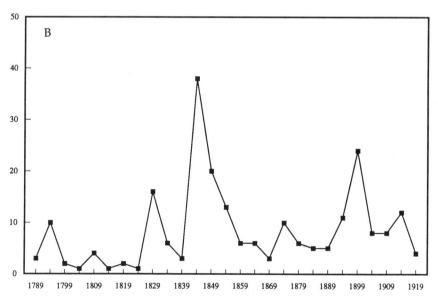

Figure 4. Domestic Utopian Rhythms, 1787–1919. By subtracting the immigrant activity reported in Figure 3 from the total utopian activity shown in Figure 2, as in the upper graph (*A*), we are left with the domestic utopian rhythms in the lower graph (*B*). The contrast between depression-era surges (the 1790s, 1840s, and 1890s) and the increased activity associated with primary deflationary troughs (the 1800s, 1820s, and the 1870s) is sharpened.

the beginning of the rising part of the upwave, he said, society's economic life undergoes considerable shifts in production and exchange, precipitating radical social change as the rising wave runs its course. On the other hand, downward waves of the long cycle are characterized by prolonged and serious depressions in agriculture. It is also, he said, during the downswings that the important scientific discoveries and inventions in production and communication have been made. These discoveries are diffused in the next wave's upswing, transforming the economic system. The historical material relative to the development of economic and social life as a whole, he said, conforms to the hypothesis of long waves: prosperity and depression, with all of their profound social implications, are tied to the upswings and downswings of the long waves.

Kondratiev's innovation-led theory of long waves has received considerable support. Joseph A. Schumpeter (1939) explored the notion of clusters of innovations that periodically transform capitalism by releasing "gales of creative destruction." Mensch (1979) placed these clusters in the downwaves that have followed "technology stalemates" (his term for stagflation crises, when old technologies reach market saturation). Further support has been lent to the idea by such contemporary neo-Schumpeterians as Van Duijn (1983) and Ayres (1990). Freeman and Perez (1990) sketch the principal technological and organizational characteristics of successive long waves, viewed as modes of economic growth.

Robert Beckman (1983, 1988), among others, has focused on the social accompaniments of long-wave rhythms. The causes, Beckman says, lie deep within the psyche of our human race. We can look at inflation, wars, political trends, speculative manias, and the like, but those are not causes. They are the effects of mass psychological phenomena involving long-term swings of pessimism and optimism.

Upwaves, says Beckman, begin in depressions, when confidence is at its nadir. They are "up" waves because they are periods in which both prices and growth increase after their long slide into the depression. Expectations rise as the economy becomes more prosperous. Attitudes shift from fear to optimism. People become willing to assume more risk, and as prosperity increases, they become more outgoing and gregarious.

Mass psychology is at work: attitudes and behavior diffuse and intensify. Progressively, a consumer mentality comes to dominate. Fashion, music, literature, theater, and dance all fall under the influence of the upwave. There is greater hedonism and a quest for pleasure, leisure, and freedom of individual expression. As the upswing progresses further, liberty turns to self-indulgent license. Clothing becomes extreme, even bizarre. Sex life turns libertarian.

With continuing expansion, economy and society are primed for an inflationary orgy. A generation learns that wealth can be acquired by debt, fed by an expansion of bank credit that enlarges the money supply—easy money that encourages people to speculate beyond their means in an atmosphere of accelerating inflation. Credit produces demand for goods or financial assets that are in short supply; prices increase and produce new profit opportunities, drawing in new investors. Positive feedback drives an upward price spiral: investment increases incomes, higher incomes increase investment, further investment increases incomes. Feverish speculation ensues; there is a manic desire to "get rich quick." A nouveau riche emerges, their affluence a product of such speculative gain. Thus, Beckman argues that the upwave spans a period of psychological desolation to a period of excessive optimism, covering the full spectrum of people's fear and greed.

An impending bursting of the speculatory bubble is sensed by the more knowledgeable insiders, who become queasy about get-rich-quick schemes and decide to take their profits and withdraw. As others follow, a rush for liquidity begins, and the prices of assets—goods, securities, land—drop. As the asset base falls, both individuals and firms are unable to cover their liabilities. Frequently, the crisis is signaled by the failure of an overextended bank or the revelation of a swindle. The bubble bursts, bank failures multiply, and a general panic ensues.

Greed turns to fear; the crowd seeks security. A downwave begins, and the "world is turned upside down" (Beckman, 1983 p. 67). Optimism turns to pessimism. Security rather than risk becomes the order of the day. Investment slackens, and the economy slows down.

Recession turns to depression when slowdown becomes a self-reinforcing downward spiral: lack of investment means cutbacks in employment, loss of income, falling demand, and reduction of investment opportunities. As the vortex pulls the economy downward, mass bankruptcies in industry occur, capital markets collapse, and land and property values decline. Businessmen respond to the profit and price squeeze by cutting wages and attempting to reduce competition. Some who find it difficult to cope with circumstances that appear to be beyond their control look for someone to blame. These are years of "devil" theories: someone must have caused the crisis and must be identified and condemned, or perhaps these are portents of the Apocalypse. At its depths, the society as a whole is afflicted by psychological depression. But as with the inflationary spiral on the upswing, the deflationary vortex pulls the downswing too far. The weak and the old have been removed; opportunities emerge for the vigorous and the new, forming the basis of the next upwave.

What exactly is the evidence for the existence of such long-wave rhythms for the United States? I will briefly summarize the findings presented in *Long-Wave Rhythms* (Berry, 1991) in graphic form. Figure 5A shows the trough-peak-trough movements of the growth rates of U.S.

Figure 5. Long-Wave Rhythms: Peak-to-Trough Movements of the Growth Rate of Prices in the United States, 1789–Present. The upper graph (*A*) shows the annual growth rates of prices at peaks and troughs. The lower graph (*B*) averages the peak and trough growth rates to reveal the idealized long-wave rhythms of acceleration from Kondratiev trough to Kondratiev peak, collapse into a primary trough, and secondary recovery before decline into a Kondratiev trough. The long waves are (1) 1789–1815–1825–1837–1844; (2) 1844–1865–1873–1882–1893; (3) 1893–1920–1937–1948–1956; (4) 1956–1981–1987–.

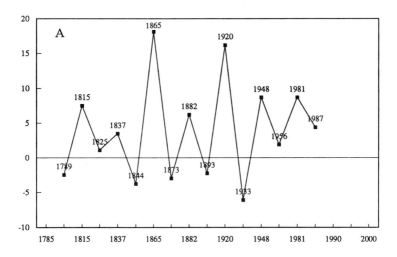

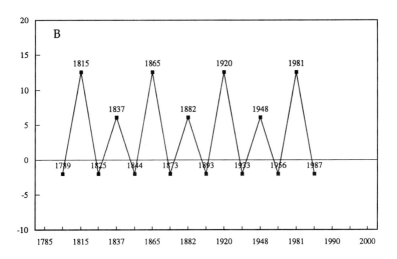

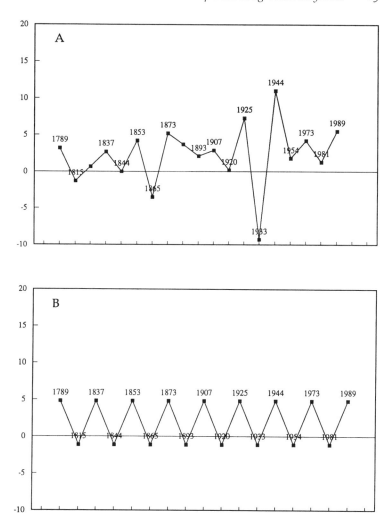

Figure 6. Rhythms of Economic Growth: Peak-to-Trough Movements of the Growth Rate of Per Capita GNP in the United States, 1789–Present. As in Figure 5, the upper graph (*A*) shows the actual annual growth rates of per capita GNP at peaks and troughs. The lower graph (*B*) averages the peak and the trough rates to reveal the idealized 25–30 year Kuznets cycles.

wholesale prices since independence. There is one discontinuity. Unwise federal intervention translated the primary trough of 1929 into the Great Depression. Subsequently, the New Deal introduced deficit spending as an integral component of Keynesian macroeconomic policies. As a result,

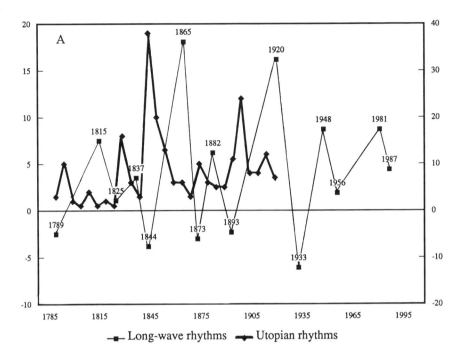

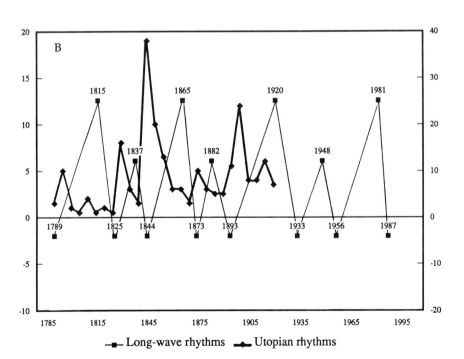

the underlying inflation rate about which the long waves fluctuate was increased from less than 1 percent to close to 5 percent per annum, and the repetition of inflationary and deflationary epochs was replaced by an inflationary/disinflationary regime. The federally induced disruptions were so great that the long wave beginning in the 1890s took almost a decade longer to complete than the two that preceded it.

Abstracting from this discontinuity, the essential long-wave rhythm of prices is revealed in Figure 5B, in which I have averaged the inflation rates at the primary and secondary peaks and in the troughs. From each Kondratiev trough (1789, 1844, 1893, 1956) prices are seen to accelerate to a Kondratiev peak (1815, 1865, 1920, 1981), descend into a primary trough (1825, 1873, 1933, 1987), and climb to a secondary peak (1837, 1882, 1948), before descending again to the Kondratiev trough. Each sequence normally lasts fifty to fifty-five years.

Figures 6A and 6B repeat the process for economic growth, measured as the growth rate of per capita gross national product. A succession of Kuznets growth cycles of twenty-five to thirty years duration is evident, summarized in Figure 6B. Economic growth troughs coincide with Kondratiev troughs in deflationary depressions (1844, 1893, . . .) as well as with Kondratiev peaks in stagflation crises (1815, 1865, 1920, 1981), thus separating "upwave" growth cycles (1844–1853–1865; 1893–1907–1920; 1954–1973–1981) from "downwave" growth cycles (1815–1837–1844; 1865–1873–1893; . . .) in a pattern of two Kuznets cycles per Kondratiev wave. Innovations cluster in downwave growth cycles, form the basis of the next upwave growth surge, achieve market saturation at the end of the following long wave, and are replaced by succeeding technology in the next (*Berry*, 1991, pp. 40–50).

Now compare Figures 4 and 5: Between 1787 and 1919 each domestic utopian surge coincided with a deflationary episode, either a primary trough or a Kondratiev trough. On the other hand, compare Figures 4 and 6: Only the growth troughs coinciding with price troughs experienced utopian surges; utopian surges occurred in deflationary depressions but did not accompany stagflation crises. This suggests that the triggering

Figure 7. Contrapuntal Long-Wave Rhythms of Prices and of Domestic Utopian Community Formation. The upper graph combines Figure 4(B) with Figure 5(A) to reveal the contrapuntal movements of utopianism and prices between 1789 and 1919. (The left-hand vertical axis plots the growth rates of prices, and the right-hand axis the numbers of communities formed.) The lower graph combines Figure 4(B) with the idealization of Kondratiev waves in Figure 5(B), to sharpen the image. Utopianism surges in deflationary environments; it is depressed prices and asset values that produce a "downwave psychology." After 1920, each of the additional price troughs saw another utopian surge, and one appears to be forming at this time.

mechanism for the utopian rhythms does not reside in slowdowns in economic growth but rather in the despair that accompanies depressed prices and collapsing asset values, although the greater utopian surges occurring in deflationary depressions also suggest that slowdowns in growth may compound the problem of depressed prices. Primary deflationary troughs are accompanied by briefer and less intense prognoses of doom than are depressions.

This long-wave rhythm/utopian counterrhythm is confirmed by Figure 7, which combines the information from Figures 4 and 5. There are exquisite contrapuntal dynamics. Following the charted utopian data, derived from Okugawa's (1980) 1787–1919 inventory, we also know that the two succeeding utopian surges occurred exactly where they should: in the primary trough of the 1930s and following the Kondratiev trough of the 1950s. And as Chapter 20 will show, there has been another upswing in the formation of "intentional communities" during the present downwave.

Clearly, utopian surges have been downwave phenomena, neatly antithetical to the long-wave rhythms of prices. Is it in fact downwave psychology that links the two, precipitating and precipitated by end-of-the-world excitement? It is necessary to turn to the individual utopian movements for evidence. Chapters 3, 5–8, and 13–18 analyze successive American responses to the nation's long-wave rhythms. The chapters are arrayed in an approximate time sequence, interspersed by Chapters 4 and 9–11 which complete the utopian community-building story, describing each of the immigrant utopias at the time of their entry to the United States, a time (as noted) responsive to *external* factors rather than to American long waves. For some of the immigrants, their later history became attuned to America's rhythms. Others, remaining isolated, have histories determined by their own internal dynamics. Chapter 19 pulls the argument together and offers a theorized interpretation. Chapter 20 concludes the book, looking at yet another utopian surge that now is forming.

CHAPTER THREE

Shakerdom

The first utopian community-building movement in the newly independent United States began amid the depression and millenarian excitement
that followed the Revolution. The United Society of Believers in Christ's
Second Appearing, the "Shakers," dominated community building in the
first two postindependence decades. There was a second Shaker upsurge
in the primary trough of the 1820s, and the final two Shaker villages, both
unsuccessful ventures into the South, were built during the depression
of the 1890s (Figure 8). Prior to the formation of the Harmony Society by
George Rapp and his followers in 1805, Okugawa (1980) records only three
other postindependence utopian experiments in America, all in the same
backwoods New England zone: Jemima Wilkinson's Society of Universal
Friends at Jerusalem, Yates County, New York;[1] the community of Dorrilites at Leydon, Franklin County, Massachusetts, and adjacent Guilford,
Windham County, Vermont;[2] and the Union, at Clark's Crossing in St.
Lawrence County, New York.[3] Discussion of these is placed in the Notes.

In all, twenty-four Shaker communities were built in two principal
phases, plus the last gasp of the 1890s (Table 1).

In the first wave of development, settlements were planted along the
Hudson River and northern New England frontiers, followed after 1800
by a group of "western" communities in trans-Appalachian Kentucky and
Ohio (Fig. 9). There was active growth of membership until midcentury
but steady decline thereafter (Fig. 10). In all, the twenty-four communities
are believed to have had some seventeen thousand members, although
historians continue to dispute the statistics. What is remarkable is the missionary effectiveness of the first two Shaker revivals, the extraordinary
longevity of many of the Shaker communities when compared with most
other utopian developments, and the influence they had on succeeding
communal experiments and the development of socialism.

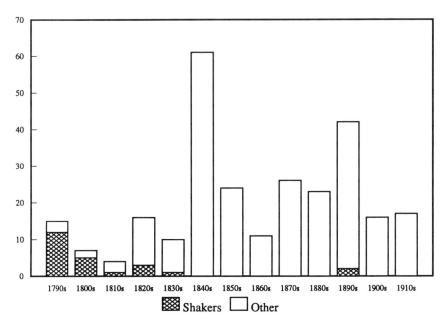

Figure 8. The Shaker Years. This frequency histogram plots the same data as in Figure 2 but in a manner designed to reveal the relative dominance of particular movements in each decade. The period in which utopian activity was dominated by the Shakers is clear. Note the slight resurgences in the 1820s (primary trough) and 1890s (deflationary depression).

Shaker accounts trace the movement's English roots to two sources (Foster, 1981, pp. 23ff.). One was in a sect of revivalist French Protestants, the Camisard Prophets, who took refuge in the Cevennes Mountains in southern France during the religious persecutions of the early eighteenth century. Their ideas were carried to England by survivors known as the French Prophets. There, joined by a group of English Prophets, they produced a movement that may have shared members with a group of English convulsionaries led by ex-Quakers Jane and James Wardley, who had formed their own small group because they felt the Quakers had lost their early fire. Joined by a Manchester factory girl, Ann Lee, during the early phase of confrontation between handicraft producers and early capitalist mechanization, the group developed a primitive social consciousness—a concern for the disillusioned, among whom they recruited their members. Coming at the end of the period of serious religious differences within Christianity but before the emergence of major doctrinal differences within socialism, the Shakers "thought they had introduced a new era, that of the "Millennial Church," which they envisioned as a dual

Table 1

Community	Started	Ended
PHASE I		
Mount Lebanon, N.Y.	1787	1947
Watervliet, N.Y. (also had a branch of black Sisters in Philadelphia)	1788	1938
Hancock, Mass.	1790	1960
Enfield, Conn.	1790	1960
Harvard, Mass.	1791	1918
Tyringham, Mass.	1792	1875
Canterbury, N.H.	1792	Present
Shirley, Mass.	1793	1908
Enfield, N.H.	1793	1923
Alfred, Maine	1793	1932
Poland Hill, Maine	1794	Present
Gorham, Maine	1794	1918
PHASE II		
Union Village, Ohio	1805	1912
Watervliet, Ohio	1806	1910
Pleasant Hill, Ky.	1806	1910
South Union, Ky.	1809	1922
West Union, Ind.	1810	1827
Savoy, Mass.	1817	1825
North Union, Ohio	1822	1889
Whitewater, Ohio	1825	1907
Sodus Bay, N.Y.	1826	1836
Groveland, N.Y.	1836	1895
PHASE III		
Narcoosee, Fla.	1894	1912
White Oak, Ga.	1898	1902

creation achieving pristine Christianity and a definitive form of socialism" (Desroche, 1971, p. 4; for other—and to many religious historians, less controversial and more reliable—sources on the Shakers, see Andrews, 1953; Foster, 1981; and Brewer, 1986).

The Camisards' millenarian message is summarized in the Shaker classic *A Summary View of the Millenial Church* (Green and Wells, 1848), which said that the prophets

testified that *the end of things drew nigh,* and admonished the people to *repent and amend their lives.* They gave warning of *the near approach of the kingdom of God, the acceptable year of the Lord:* and in many prophetic messages, declared to the world that those numerous scripture prophecies concerning *the new heavens and the new earth; the kingdom of the Messiah; the marriage of the Lamb; the first resurrection,* and *the new Jerusalem descending from above, were near at hand,* and would shortly be accomplished. (p. 8; italics in original)

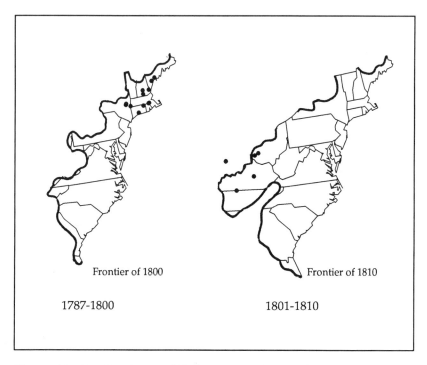

Frontier of 1800   Frontier of 1810

1787-1800   1801-1810

Figure 9. The First Two Surges of Shaker Activity: The Spatial Pattern. Early Shaker activity was in backwoods New England locations, followed quickly by the planting of western gatherings as the Second Great Awakening brought revivals to the Kentucky frontier.

It was this message that was carried to England by the French refugees in 1706. The Shaker histories say the Wardleys were "endowed with the spirit of [the French] witnesses." In 1747 they moved to Manchester, forming a small society of thirty members, the Wardley Society, that, by retaining the emotionalism of early Quakerism and Camisard revivalism, earned the epithet "Shakers"—the Shaking Quakers.

In 1758, Ann Lee joined the society. The Shaker narratives report that she had married blacksmith Abraham Stanley in 1752 and had four children, three of whom died in infancy. The fourth, a girl, died at age six. The Shaker *Testimonies* (Young, 1856) record that Ann had profound problems with the unremitting cycle of sexual relations, pregnancy, and infant death, and consulted with Jane Wardley: "Some time after I set out to live up to the light of God manifested to me through James and Jane Wardley, I fell under heavy trials and tribulation on account of lodging with my husband and I looked to them for help and counsel, I opened my trials to

Eastern Communities

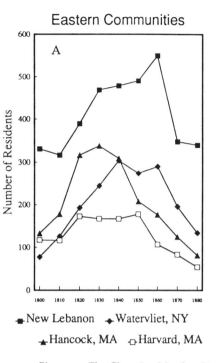

Western Communities

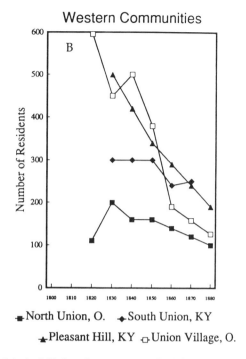

Figure 10. The Changing Membership of the Principal Shaker Communities. The left-hand illustration charts data tabulated in Appendix B of Priscilla J. Brewer, *Shaker Communities, Shaker Lives* (1986). The right-hand graph is adapted from Henri Desroche (1971), using data from Daryl Chase, *The Early Shakers* (Ph.D. dissertation, University of Chicago, 1938). With the exception of New Lebanon, Shakerdom had peaked by 1840.

Jane; she said: '*James and I lodge together but we do not touch each other more than two babes.*' You may return and do likewise" (quoted in Desroche, 1971, p. 47). Ann Lee was to make celibacy a central element of the Shaker creed, testifying to the Wardley group about carnal sin and becoming convinced that lust was the root of all evil and corruption in the world. Her ideas ultimately led to the development by Joseph Meacham of the Shaker Family, a social structure and set of living arrangements that marked a new relation between men and women, correcting the imbalance between the sexes (Foster, 1981, p. 25).

She was imprisoned in England in 1770 on charges of profaning the Sabbath. It was during this imprisonment that she had the first of her revelations, giving her "a full and clear view of the mystery of iniquity, and of the very act of transgression committed by the first man and woman in the Garden of Eden" (Green and Wells, 1848, p. 5). She testified that "no soul could follow Christ in the regeneration, while living in the works of natural regeneration, or in any of the gratifications of lust" (ibid., p. 16). After her release, she assumed leadership of the Shaker group as Mother Lee, the female prophet.

The second revelation came in 1774: that the group would have to seek refuge in America, and "at the same time she received a divine promise that the work of God would greatly increase, and the millenial church would be established in that country" (ibid., p. 19). Permission to accompany her was given to "all those of the society . . . who were able, and who felt any special impressions on their own minds so to do" (ibid.). Accompanied by eight men and women, she set sail 19 May 1774, disembarking in New York on 6 August.

The group dispersed. John Hocknell and William Lee left to explore the Hudson Valley and settled on a tract of land at Niskeyuna (later Watervliet). The rest of the group, including Ann Lee and James Whitaker, made their way to Albany, New York, but Abraham Stanley fell sick, left Ann Lee, and set up house in New York with another woman—"a prostitute" according to the Shaker chronicles.

Niskeyuna was in a remote area "in the wilderness" northwest of Albany, and there the group began to clear land to create a monastic retreat. The revolutionary war broke out, and because Hocknell, who had gone to England to raise capital, returned via Philadelphia, critics charged the Shakers with British sympathies. The Shakers retreated to solitude in the years 1776–79. Yet during these years, sporadic revivals were occurring along the New England frontier. A new sect appeared, the Freewill Baptists, who rejected predestination and embraced evangelical revival doctrines, insisting upon the personal union of the believer with God at the moment of regeneration, which required repentance as a precondition. Their exuberant gatherings earned them the nicknames "New Lights" and "Merry Dancers." "This cyclical revivalism, coupled with the revolutionary upheaval that seemed to many to presage the second coming, provided the arena in which the . . . Shakers arrived" (Brewer, 1986, p. 4). As New Light revivalism reached its height, Ann Lee informed her companions that "the time was just at hand when many would come and embrace the gospel, and directed them to make provisions for it, which they did according to their abilities" (Green and Wells, 1848, p. 23). This pronouncement followed her meetings with Joseph Meacham (whose father had been converted by Jonathan Edwards during the First Great Awakening).

In the 1770s, Joseph Meacham was a lay preacher in the Baptist church at New Lebanon, New York. He led a revival of the New Light Baptists in the Albany area in 1779. Fortuitously, he visited Niskeyuna, was impressed, and converted to Shakerism, bringing with him many of his followers. Ann Lee spoke of him as "the wisest man that has been born of a woman for six hundred years." He carried the Shaker message back to the great Baptist revivals at New Lebanon in 1780 and 1781, amid the stirrings of the Second Great Awakening, and began to make converts.

White and Taylor (1904/1971) write of Meacham:

Laboring for an increase of light and for redemption from the power of evil, he entered the dark days of the Revolution, that time of war, when passion and frenzy seemed to turn men to demons and let loose hordes of evil spirits to bear sway over mind and matter. At such times, men and women of religious nature turn in disgust from the emptiness and rottenness of society in church and state and exercise themselves toward God. Joseph Meacham became a leader among such spirits. (p. 98; quoted in Desroche, p. 90)

In the spring of 1780, Mother Lee and the other leading Shakers were imprisoned, accused of being British sympathizers. They were set free when they were judged harmless (Green and Wells, 1848, p. 26; Young, pp. 63–64). After their release, the first Shaker missionary expedition set out. Between May 1781 and September 1783, Mother Lee and other senior Shakers traveled up and down the Hudson Valley gathering in converts and encountering hostile mobs. On their return to Niskeyuna, however, the original Shaker leadership was decimated. William Lee died in July 1784, followed by Mother Ann Lee in September of the same year and by James Whitaker in 1787.

On Whitaker's death Joseph Meacham took command. It was he who, three months later, organized the Shakers' first "gathering," the process of organizing the converts into a community. Up to this point the Shakers had lived on their own farms, linked by religious practices, spiritual solidarity, and celibacy. But it was increasingly difficult to maintain group solidarity as the number of converts increased. Meacham's solution was to create a new kind of social structure: the Family. Desroche (1971) observes: "'True Believers' who had decided to erase from their lives all notions of a past or future marriage of the flesh were brought together and incorporated into Families; this is the precise meaning of a 'gathering'" (p. 93). To ensure that women were equal to men at all levels of the society, Meacham also appointed Lucy Wright as his co-equal to establish a women's order of the Shakers with that objective in mind (Foster, 1981, p. 37).

The first gathering was at Mount Lebanon (the "Holy Mount") in September 1787. This community replaced Niskeyuna as the center of Shakerism. It was there that Meacham and Lucy Wright began the codification of Mother Lee's Covenant. She had defined the doctrines of the faith and prescribed how a Believer should function within the living church, spelling out the doctrines in a contractual "covenant" that Believers signed when they joined the society. As the membership increased, the parent ministry tried to guide the behavior of Believers into perfect gospel union. As the communities increased in number, the ministry tried to shape them to share a sense of continuity with each other. In time the precepts of the founders were used as a basis for developing a more specific code, called "Orders and Rules of the Church," or as it is commonly known today, the Millennial Laws.

After the gathering at New Lebanon, other communities followed quickly, havens to which people moved to escape the disorder and disillusionment that gripped western Massachusetts and the Hudson Valley at the time. These were the years of Shays's Rebellion, an uprising, chiefly of farmers, in 1786–1787. The rebellion was the culmination of five years of restless dissatisfaction growing out of high taxes, heavy debts, and a decline in farm prices: 1789 was the Kondratiev trough. The legislature's repeal of the legal tender status of paper money and its refusal to permit the offering of goods to satisfy debts meant that obligations had to be met with hard-to-obtain specie. From excises the state paid 6 percent interest in specie on securities and promised redemption in full, although speculators had bought them at a fraction of their face value. Those who could not pay their debts faced trial by an expensive and inefficient court system. They could be jailed until they paid or have their possessions auctioned off to satisfy creditors.

People assembled in conventions in five counties during the summer of 1786 to list demands for relief, also calling for an amendment of the state constitution to reduce the costs of the government. A quickly summoned legislature passed a tender law but did little to settle the grievances. Ignoring its act of indemnity, insurgents in several counties took up arms and organized regiments, one of them captained by Daniel Shays. Shays failed in an attempt to seize the federal arsenal at Springfield, Massachusetts. Most of the fighting ended when the militia routed Shays's forces at Petersham, 4 February 1787. Shays took refuge in nearby Hudson Valley Vermont and New York.

A second wave of Shaker growth came after 1804, amid religious revivals in Kentucky, as the Second Great Awakening swept through the frontier (McNemar, 1807). McNemar describes the social malaise that preceded the revivals. The Shakers heard of ferment in this trans-Appalachian area and dispatched their ablest missionaries, who attempted to translate the revivalists' millenarian expectations into Shaker community growth. They attracted and converted many of the New Light Baptists and produced a number of additional gatherings.

The period 1837–44 also saw great religious fervor within Shakerdom, which Desroche (1971, pp. 104–5) ties to the same economic events that inspired the final frenzy of Millerite millenarianism and the new Fourierist and Mormon movements. The beginning was the Crisis of 1837, the most severe economic crisis experienced by the new republic. On 10 May 1837, New York banks had to suspend all payments in cash, a measure soon put into effect by all banks in the country. The Shaker revival started on 16 August 1837. The collapse of the economy led some to think that the end of the world was near. A group of ten- to twelve-year-old girls meeting for worship at Watervliet began to exhibit strange behavior. Some went into trances. A fourteen-year-old girl, Ann Maria Goff, began to have visions: In a dazzling white house she saw a large number of girls in golden dresses and decorated with stars on their shoulders and feet; on their heads there were crowns, and around their hands were halos of bright light; Jesus, who was placing his right hand on their heads and calling them his little children, seemed to feel a great tenderness for them. "Spiritual manifestations" continued to appear in Watervliet until January 1838, accompanied by highly emotional religious behavior. The ministry at New Lebanon quickly forwarded news of the visions to the other Shaker societies. The result was a chain reaction of similar spiritual manifestations that rapidly produced a full-fledged revival, lasting until 1844 amid the depths of a deflationary depression and the peak of Millerite millenarian fervor. Rituals developed to link the earthly utopia to the Kingdom of Heaven, with many new songs and dances. There were trances and spiritualist seances, attempting to make contact with the dead.

A final outburst of fervor came in 1847, followed by torpor as a new cycle of economic growth unfolded. The Shakers were no longer able to recruit, and because they did not reproduce, the communities ossified. The patterns of life were those developed in the innovative growing years, but even they were temporized. Attempts were made to advertise for new members. For example, in 1874 the following appeared in New York newspapers: "Men, Women, and children can find a comfortable home for life, where want never comes, with the Shakers, by embracing the true faith and living pure lives. Particulars can be learned by writing to the Shakers, Mt. Lebanon, NY" (quoted in Whitworth, 1975, p. 75). There was but little success. After a last gasp of growth, including the attempt to build two new communities in the South during the depression of the 1890s, Shaker communities aged and finally disappeared one by one. There now remain but a few members at Sabbathday Lake in Maine. Shakerism had expanded first in the depression following the revolutionary war and had benefited from the religious fervor that emerged in trans-Appalachian Kentucky after the turn of the century. Even as it experienced its last great revival, in the depression of the 1840s, its growth was cut short by emergence of the Fourierist and Mormon alternatives. To be sure, there was a lesser resurgence as Americans sought refuge from the depression of the 1890s; but from the Civil War on, Shakerism withered.

What were the dimensions of Shaker religion and society? There was a distinction made between *Earthly Space*— geometrically correct, neat, and orderly, with distancing to separate the sexes and to isolate members from the outside world—and *Heavenly Space*: Jerusalem. Achievement of perfection on earth would bring the millennium and establish Jerusalem. In the interim, song, dance, and ritual were to link the two spheres. Hayden (1976) notes:

The Shakers' plan for the gradual redemption of the world aimed at nothing less than transforming the earth into heaven. This allowed them to maintain two simultaneous visions of an ideal community. In what they called the earthly sphere, they envisioned rural settlements of millennial believers based on Mother Ann's precepts; in the heavenly sphere they projected a New Jerusalem as described by the evangelists. Daily work and religious rituals were designed to foster belief that both spheres were accessible to members. The believers experienced earthly millennial life and simulated the experience of heavenly life. (p. 71)

The Shaker settlements were, of course, first and foremost religious communities settled by progressive millenarians. According to Persons (1952, pp. 132ff.), they believed that

1. The advent is behind us. It was begun with Ann Lee.
2. It comes out of the earth, rather than down from the heavens.
3. Rather than being instantaneous and overwhelming, it can be achieved slowly, by evolution.
4. It requires perfection; achievement of perfection will signal the millennium.

Shakers believed that the Second Coming had been announced by Ann Lee. Her message stressed the ascendancy of women to a position of leadership: "As the order of nature requires a man and a woman to produce offspring, so where they both stand in their proper order, the man is the first, and the woman the second, in the government of the family . . . but when the man is gone, the right of government belongs to the woman; so is the family of Christ" (Young, 1856, p. 256). It was logical, therefore, to believe in a woman Messiah, Ann Lee, and in celibacy as the main axis of perfection. It was only by overcoming physical nature and conquering the desires of the flesh that men and women could achieve salvation.

As the millennium approached, Christ was expected to be seen "coming in the clouds of heaven" (*Matt.* 24:30, 26:64; *Rev.* 1:7). This is why other groups had withdrawn to the mountains or, like the Kelpian community in Philadelphia, organized their life around an observatory. To the Shakers, however, the clouds were spiritual and could be observed in the minds of witnesses who communicated from trances and via song and dance. The dances ranged from mildly exuberant to highly explosive. On the mild side were rhythmic exercises in which the participants would march with their hands held out in front of the body, elbows bent, moving the hands up and down with a sort of swinging motion as though gathering up something in their arms. This motion signified "gathering in the good." They also believed in "shaking out the evil" (Andrews, 1953; Holloway, 1966; Brewer, 1986).

The Shakers also were among the forerunners of modern spiritualists who believe that the living can communicate with the dead. Such communication with the spirit world varied from one Shaker community to the next and also seems to have varied over time, the 1840s being a particularly "vibrant" period. For a while, the religious services were so animated that the elders closed them to visitors.

Key to the structure of Shaker society were the families into which the new Church Order was organized after 1787. Each community was divided into two to six families of 30 to 150 members each. There were three types of families, essentially classed according to their degree of commitment:

1. The First, or Novitiate, Family, living in separation, were the converted, who still lived in their own households and managed their own affairs.

2. The Second, or Junior, Family, living in cooperation, still owned their own property but had joined the production-consumption cooperative that was the economic backbone of Shakerism. All exchange was symmetric and gratuitous.

3. The Third, or Senior, Family, living in communion in a form of lay monasticism, renounced property ownership and signed the Covenant to donate their worldly goods to the Society. Members had to be adult, and they lived within the community's residences.

Each family was governed by two elders and two eldresses appointed by church leaders in New Lebanon (Kephart, 1987, p. 201 ff.). Their rule was absolute. They heard confessions, conducted meetings, enforced rules of conduct, served as preachers and missionaries, and acted on new applications. They also were responsible for work assignments and relations with the outside world. That there was consistency in the way in which order was maintained was a consequence of the written Millennial Laws that regulated every aspect of life.

A key cultural theme was celibacy (for an extended discussion, see

Foster, 1981). Men and women ("brothers and sisters") slept in different rooms on different sides of the house. They ate at different tables in the common dining room. They were not permitted to pass one another on the stairs, and many of the dwellings included separate doorways. Even the halls were purposely made wide so that the sexes would not brush by one another. All physical contact was prohibited, including shaking hands, touching, and "sisters mending or setting buttons on the brethren's clothes while they have them on" (Kephart, 1987, pp. 203–4).

"Union meetings" between men and women were held three or four times a week in one of the brethren's rooms, a half-dozen or so of the sisters sitting in a row facing an equal number of brothers. The two rows were a few feet apart, permitting each sister to converse with her counterpart. The pairs were matched on the basis of age and interests. The principle of the union meeting was to encourage a positive relationship between the sexes rather than the strictly negative one that might arise from forced segregation (ibid.).

There was an expectation of hard work. Ann Lee had said that idle conversation was time lost from work. There also was an overriding sense of order—not simply the social and moral order of the families but also the *orderliness* that was required for perfection, made possible by economy and simplicity of design. The same inner commitment that prompted the Believers to work hard also was responsible for the exceptional quality of their labor. Innovative quality work constituted the Shaker trademark, and they made significant cultural contributions to Americana. Their innovations (not necessarily their inventions) included the circular saw, screw propeller, flat broom, clothes pin, and brimstone match. Of equal importance was their stylistic contribution to American furniture. In the musical sphere the Shakers contributed a substantial number of folk songs and spirituals that, Andrews (1933) concluded, no less than their furniture and artifacts, were a true folkart.

Most important, they were able to demonstrate to the world that their communal system (Gospel Order) could be made to work. Friedrich Engels, in particular, took note of this in 1845:

In America and, generally speaking, in the world the first to found a society organized according to the principle of common ownership of goods were the people called Shakers.

They constitute an unusual sect with special religious ideas; they do not marry, they forbid all intercourse between husband and wife, and have other, similar rules. But those rules are of no importance to us here. As a sect, the Shakers were founded about seventy years ago. The founders were poor folk who gathered together to live in brotherly love under a system of common ownership of property which permitted them to worship God as they saw fit. Although their religious views, particularly the interdiction of marriage, have alienated many people, the Shakers attracted many adherents and now have ten large communities, each of which has from 200 to 800 members. Each one of these communities is a lovely village with well constructed homes, factories, workshops, meeting halls and barns. They have gardens for flowers as well as vegetables, orchards and forests, vineyards, meadows and fields in abundance. They have cattle of the finest quality, horses, cows, sheep, hogs and chickens. In every case there is more than they need. Their barns are full of wheat; their storehouse shelves are stacked with so much cloth that an English traveler who visited them declared that he could not understand why a people who lived in such abundance would still work. According to him, the Shakers labor only to pass the time; otherwise they would have nothing to do. Among them no one is forced to work against his will and no one fusses uselessly in his job. They have no poorhouses, no homes for the aged, because they have no poor, no needy, no widows, no abandoned orphans. They know no poverty and have nothing to fear. In their ten villages there is not a single policeman; there are no judges, no lawyers, no soldiers, no prisons, and yet everything functions normally. As far as they are concerned, the laws of the country do not exist, and indeed they could be abolished without anyone in the community knowing the difference, since these peaceful people have never caused anyone to be sent to prison. They live, as we said, owning all their worldly goods in common, and neither business nor money plays any part in their lives. . . .

Thus we see that communal ownership is not absolutely impossible. The success of these people's efforts testifies to the contrary. We also see that people living communally live better and work less, that they have more leisure time in which to develop their minds, and that they become better and more moral men than their neighbors who stayed in the system of private property. This is what Americans, Frenchmen, Englishmen, Belgians and even a large number of Germans have already understood. Everywhere there are people who have made it their task to disseminate this information and who have thrown their lot in with the party of the community.

This is important news for all men but it is especially important for the poor workers who possess nothing, who are always spending their wages as soon as they are paid, and who run the inevitable risk of finding themselves without bread to eat. For them this opens the way to an independent life of security and serenity, by giving them equal rights with those who because of their wealth are in a position to bully the worker into becoming a slave. It is for these workers that communism is most important. In other countries the workers form the nucleus of the party calling for common ownership of goods; it is the duty of German workers to take their example to heart. (Pp. 351–66)

Not only was Shakerdom seen by Engels as providing an alternative to early industrial urbanism in microcosm; it also was viewed as signaling the possibility of radical alternatives to capitalism in macrocosm—

of the socialist reconstruction of a world plunged deep into capitalism's Armageddon.

Why did the Shakers succeed? Why, ultimately, did they fail? In her fine monograph *Shaker Communities, Shaker Lives* Priscilla Brewer (1986) says that the answer to both questions is deceptively simple: "the Shakers tried to be perfect" (p. 203).

CHAPTER FOUR

German Separatists Adjust: The Rappites, Zoarites, and Amana Colonists

The next utopian experiments were the transatlantic transplants of several groups of Wurttemberger Separatists, led by George Rapp, Joseph Bäumeler, and Christian Metz. Initially responding to forces outside the rhythms of the American economy, they came seeking religious freedom. The Rappites and Zoarites became communal societies in response to the problems they encountered in building a new life in America, and they and the Ebenezer/Amana settlers all ended as successful capitalist enterprises.

Desroche (1971) comments that the Rappites:

did not arrive in New Harmony with the express intention of practicing common ownership of goods and property; but when they gathered around their leaders in this unknown land, where everything seemed so hostile, they observed that a few of them had resources and that most of them were in dire need. Their religious orientation led them to compare themselves to the first Christians in Jerusalem surrounded by Gentiles, and it was the analogy between the two predicaments that gave birth to an analogous solution. In Judea, acting on the advice of the apostles, the rich had shared their worldly goods with the poor. The rich among the Rappites decided to do likewise, and this was not so difficult for them, since their belief in Christ's imminent return to earth had rendered them almost indifferent to personal property.

It was the same with the founders of Zoar, who were so poor that they had to hire themselves out to the surrounding farms as laborers. During the Atlantic crossing from Germany the rich had shared their fortunes with the needy, but all expected that once the voyage ended they would return to a regime of private property. However, some of the exiles had no money to pay for their share of the land, and others were too ill, old, or feeble to earn a living. Their leader and his advisors were made to understand that the only way of avoiding a catastrophe was to form a communistic society. The decision to do this was made in 1819. (Pp. 192–93)

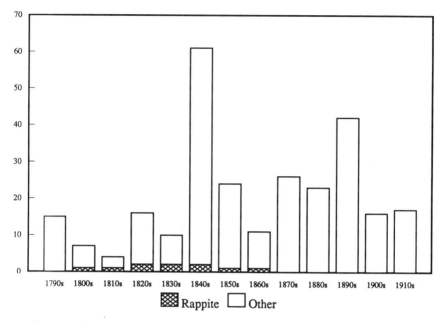

Figure 11. The Timing of Rappite Settlements. This immigrant group's communal activity spread over several decades after the initial settlements were planted, as the principal Rappite home was relocated and as schisms occurred. Typical of immigrant initiatives, no long-wave rhythms are evident.

The same thing happened, Desroche says, in a number of other communities in the 1840s. At Bishop Hill, the Swedish community started as a religious group and was led to communal arrangements by a combination of millenarianism and poverty. Olaf Janson, the founder, had intended to separate the "children of God" from the rest of the wicked world and take them to America, which would be their base for conquering the globe. When this had been achieved, the millennium would begin. But without money, food, or medicines, the Jansonites faced the hard winter of 1847–48 shivering in holes in the ground and huddled together in sheds built against the hillsides. That they were able to survive reflected the communal sharing that had been necessary for the sect to immigrate.

Desroche (1971) concludes that "in each of these cases it was the sense of brotherhood in the framework of a religious ideal brought from Europe that fomented on American soil some form of economic communism as a way around obstacles which threatened to undermine the religious ideal" (p. 194). In the Rappite and Zoarite cases he is correct, but his argument is overstated. The Ebenezer group already lived communally in Hessen

Frontier of 1820

Figure 12. Location of the Rappite Settlements. As they were established over a period of half a century, Rappite offshoots from the base in Economy, Pennsylvania, kept close to the frontier. This map shows the frontier of 1810 inside that of 1820.

before they migrated, and communal arrangements were necessary for the Jansonites to be able to move.

The Rappites

The first Rappite settlement was established in 1805, and ultimately more than a dozen direct-line, offshoot, and schismatic communities resulted. Eight were planted by 1836, and the last was started in 1862. Figure 11 shows that Rappite community building was not responsive to long-wave rhythms; Figure 12, that the communities were built both in frontier locations and around the original base at Harmony. Figure 13 charts the genealogy of the community-building sequence.

The leader of the migrant Separatists was George Rapp, born in 1757 in Wurttemberg. Rapp, the son of a peasant, became a weaver but one whose interest in religion was sparked early. Pietist and mystic teachings led him to question the dogma of the established Lutheran church. When he began to preach against that dogma, his charisma soon attracted a growing congregation of adherents.

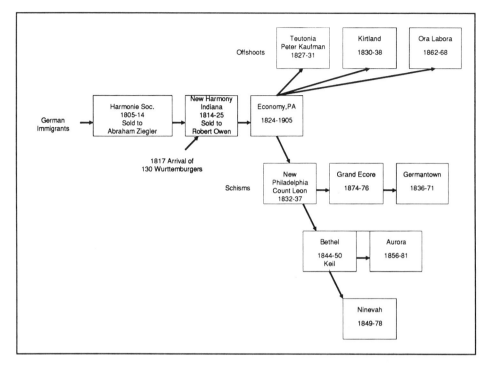

Figure 13. The Rappite Community-Building Sequence, Including Offshoots and Schismatic Groups. This genealogical diagram reveals the relationships among the twelve communities that emerged from the initial Rappite migration in 1805.

Responding, the government in Wurttemberg asked him to draw up his group's principles so that they could be acknowledged as a separate sect. They responded in 1787 with a list that included rejection of Lutheran ritual, adult baptism by choice and through conviction, agape (the love feast, or common meal of fellowship) as an expression of their spiritual wholeness, separate education for their children, refusal to swear oaths of allegiance to the government even while recognizing its legitimacy, and conscientious objection to military service. In 1791, Rapp announced: "I am a prophet and am called to be one."

At the end of the eighteenth century a number of forces directed the Rappites toward emigration. In addition to growing hostility of both the established church and the government in Wurttemberg, the Napoleonic Wars in Europe were seen as portending the millennium. While some of the German Separatists turned eastward to Hungary and Russia as places to establish communities that prepared them for the Second Coming,

George Rapp and his followers looked to the New World. In 1803 he led a small group to acquire land for the sect to follow. Five thousand acres were purchased in Butler County, Pennsylvania. In 1804 the first group of five hundred arrived to settle there. The Harmony Society was created 15 February 1805.

The contract that legalized the society laid out its principles. Members were committed to the Christian beliefs of the sect and were required to transfer their entire property to the society: Harmony was organized as a commune.

Such a communal life-style was not part of the original Rappite construct. But there were substantial variations in wealth and resources among the members of the group. The communal arrangement enabled Rapp to take care of the old, the sick, the orphaned, and the poor, individuals who otherwise would have been hard-pressed to survive on the western frontier (Holloway, 1951, p. 89). The land was cleared, vineyards were planted, and homes, workshops, flour mills, and sawmills were built. In 1806 the community started to weave woollen cloth. New settlers continued to arrive, and the settlement numbered eight hundred in 1810.

The Harmony Society also went through a religious revival in its early years, leading the members to focus on preparations for the Second Coming. To the communal economic system were added simple styles of dress, celibacy, and rejection of such things as tobacco. Although families continued to exist, sexual relations were forbidden, and the Rappites ceased to reproduce. This change was not received well back in Germany. The flow of new recruits slowed and then ended in 1819.

The industrial superintendent of the society was Frederick Reichert (who was adopted by Rapp). A man of business and executive ability, he organized and maintained a highly successful economy. He was entrusted with all of the external and financial affairs of the society. Later he held title to the total estate of the society in his own name (Duss, 1972, p. 19). He divided the internal organization into departments, each with an appointed superintendent who was charged for money and materials and credited with the products. This allowed Frederick to judge from the periodic reports whether the society was profiting or not.

George Rapp was the colony's spiritual elder, a stern and commanding leader. He introduced celibacy only in part as preparation for the millennium. Duss (1972) says that it also arose from economic and social necessity. Food was scarce, and so was labor. Pregnancy and suckling took women away from work. More children meant more mouths to feed. Celibacy meant more workers and more community product.

The focus on the economy was successful. The society prospered. But they wanted more—more land, a more diversified economy—and relations with others around Pittsburgh, already becoming densely settled, were strained. In 1814 a search produced a location with a tract of twenty-five thousand acres of government land on the Wabash River in what later became Indiana. Moving there, they established Harmonie (subsequently New Harmony). They sold the original Harmony Society's estates, comprising 9,000 acres of land with 130 buildings, to Abraham Ziegler for $100,000 (Williams, 1886, p. 14) and in 1814 transferred the group to the new location.

The land was fertile and cheap but also malaria-infested. In spite of this, hard work prevailed, and the community once again prospered, becoming the focal point of settlement in the new state. In 1817, 130 new settlers arrived from Wurttemberg. They were so satisfied with the community they found that in 1818 they destroyed the documents showing what each member had contributed.

The rapid development of Harmonie was a matter of great wonderment and repute. As the Rappites diversified from agriculture to manufactures, however, they discovered the problems of remoteness. Western pioneers wove their own cloth. There were not the ready markets of Pennsylvania.

The society was a positive force for change in Indiana, for example, opposing slavery. In 1820, Rapp's adopted son Frederick was on the committee that designed Indianapolis.

Yet relations with their neighbors deteriorated once again, despite the Rappites' offers of help. Success, they discovered, also breeds envy. Many were unhappy, too, because Indiana would not support viticulture, and there was a yearning for an area free of malaria and with a predominantly German background. In 1824, Frederick Rapp asked Richard Flower, an English colonizer, to help him sell Harmonie. Flower arranged a deal with Robert Owen, selling him the entire property for $150,000. It was here that Owen tried to transplant his own utopian dream to North America, as will be seen in Chapter 5.

The group returned to three thousand acres purchased in Beaver County, Pennsylvania, arriving on the *William Penn*, a steamboat built for them in Pittsburgh. Still expecting the millennium in their lifetime, they built their new settlement of Economy as "a city in which God would dwell among men, a city in which perfection in all things was to be obtained" (Arndt, 1965, p. 308).

The community specialized in the branches of industry in which they had developed skills, choosing their site with respect to easy waterborne transportation, east and west. They soon were a well-organized and highly profitable economic unit, adding silk weaving, hat making, production of wines and whisky, and flour milling to their enterprises. They had marketing agents in most big cities and dominated the Pittsburgh economy. Again they became a threat. In 1828 they were denounced because they voted as a bloc for Andrew Jackson. In 1829 local papers accused them of unfair competition and monopoly practices. Yet external assault and internal schisms strengthened the group's resolve. As their activities increased, they hired outside labor. At the peak, when they owned the Economy Oil Company near Titusville, ten outsiders were employed for each member.

Economy was built with a simple yet spacious plan, with two-story buildings of deep red brick that, together with backyard flower gardens, centered on the church and on George Rapp's forty-five-room Great House. They disavowed missionary activity, emphasizing instead the perfecting of the individual by self-denial, humility, and an attitude of "each in honor preferring the other." They separated from the world to create a perfect commune that would serve as an example to the rest of the world (Williams, 1886, p. 60). Music was central to religious life, and there were three annual feasts: 15 February, the Harvest House Festival in August, and the love feast in October. They believed they were carrying on the prophecies in the Book of Revelation concerning the gathering place of the elect 144,000. There were twelve hundred in the community when Rapp died in 1847.

After Rapp's death, membership began to decline (recall that the depression of the 1840s also marked a turning point in the Shakers' abilities to attract new settlers, as alternative utopian communities emerged). Several of the enterprises failed (the silk factories in 1852, the cotton factories in 1858, and the distillery in 1862). Sale of the properties brought capital that was invested in bonds and resource development, and Economy in fact became a capitalist enterprise in which the work of the commune was done by hired labor and the communards constituted the capitalist corporation. In the 1850s, Economy was one of the biggest investors in coal mining. By 1868 they produced one hundred thousand barrels of oil, and in the 1870s they were the most active and respected drillers in the Pennsylvania oil fields. But even as these enterprises flourished, the commune stagnated and shrank.

After the Civil War, management passed into the lands of Jacob Henrici, who controlled a financial empire of millions of dollars without any kind of bookkeeping (Oved, 1988, p. 77). He extended financial help to the other Separatist communities at Zoar and Amana and was particularly helpful to the Hutterites. To try to maintain membership the society adopted and educated German children. They became involved in philanthropic enterprises and in helping in recovery from fire and flood disasters. They aided immigrant families detained at ports, donated land for the establishment of Geneva College, and gave or loaned large sums of money to help individuals. But excessive generosity may be blamed for ultimate decrease in the society's fortunes (Williams, 1886, p. 47) By the 1890s, membership had declined to the point that Harmony was no longer a functioning commune. There was litigation over the final disposition of the inheritance. John Duss, who saved the society from bankruptcy in the financial disaster of 1892, won out in complex litigation and put the commune's resources into his and his wife's names. He used vast sums to support the Metropolitan Opera and to promote his own musical career. Finally, in 1905 half of the remaining capital was placed into a trust by the Commonwealth of Pennsylvania to maintain Economy as a historical site.

The Rappite Offshoots

Economy produced a number of offshoots, some established by members who left, others by those who were impressed by Rappite achievement, and some as a consequence of the worst crisis of the Harmony Society, the Count de Leon schism of 1831.

One offshoot was the Society of United Germans at Teutonia, Ohio (1827–31). This settlement was established by Peter Kaufman, a perfectionist born at Munster-Maifeld in Germany in 1800. A sometime student of the ministry, he first came to Philadelphia in 1820 and established a labor-for-labor store as a way of implementing Christian perfectionism. "Aiding the urban poor was necessary according to the principle of brotherly love" (Easton, 1966, p. 101). Moving on, he became Economy's language teacher, but left to found Teutonia in 1827.

The society's constitution called upon all Germans in the United States and North America to join. The aim was the "health and welfare of all mankind" (ibid., p. 102) The members were committed to a community of goods. They pledged their property to the communal store for ten years and shared in the community's labor. They promised to give the community's surplus to the education of homeless children regardless of their race or creed (ibid., p. 102). The society planned to publish a weekly paper, but apparently the publication never materialized. The commune lasted only for four years. In 1831, Kaufman left the society to settle in Canton, Ohio. He published several books, almanacs, and newspapers and served as the postmaster of Canton in 1837. He died in 1869.

A second community influenced by the Rappites was that at Kirtland, Ohio (1827–31), established by Sidney Rigdon, a Baptist preacher in Pittsburgh who was impressed by Economy's achievements and also was influenced by Alexander Campbell, founder of the Disciples of Christ Church. Moving to Ohio, Rigdon organized a group of Campbellites in the town of Kirtland into a commune. Preaching about the return to the

Scriptures, restoration of the ancient order, and the millennium, he was instrumental in converting a large number of Baptists to the doctrine of the Campbellites.

Rigdon and his group converted to Mormonism when Joseph Smith, Jr., moved to Kirtland from New York, however, and he came to play an important role in the development of Mormonism, completing the church hierarchy and serving as spokesman (*Dictionary of American Biography*, s.v. "Sidney Rigdon").

There was another side to his activities. "Rigdon like his colleagues became deeply involved financially in the craze of land speculation. The debacle of the 'Kirtland Safety Society Anti-Banking Company,' which had unloaded illegal bank notes on creditors and the general public, brought on such a storm of protest that many followers apostatized, and Smith and Rigdon fled to Missouri to escape mob violence and judicial action in 1838" (ibid., p. 601). The speculative activities provide a direct link between the Crisis of 1837 and the evolution of Mormonism.

Rigdon died in 1876. He is regarded as the one who carried furthest the Campbellite's ideas of "faith, repentance, baptism for the remission of sins, the gift of the Holy Ghost, and the belief in a restoration of the gospel of the millennium" (ibid.).

Other Rappite offshoots derived from the Count de Leon schism (Oved, 1988, p. 73). According to the sect's millennial doctrine, 1829 was to be the year of divine manifestation (later postponed to 1836). While they were under the spell of millennial expectation, a letter arrived from Germany proclaiming that the "Annointed of the Lord, the Lion of Judah" would reveal himself and prepare the community for the millennium. George Rapp accepted the letter and invited Count de Leon to Economy. The count was, in reality, Bernhardt Müller, a religious mystic and entrepreneur born in Germany in 1787 who had collected a group of followers determined to join Harmony. Müller had predicted the early downfall of Napoleon and in 1813 changed his name to Proli (Son of God) and set up a secret society in Ireland.

A group of fifty arrived at Economy with Müller in 1831, was greeted with great formality, and lodged in Rapp's Great House. Too late, Rapp realized that Müller was an imposter. The count advocated marriage, contrary to Rapp's rules, and quickly became the focus of discontent. Joined by 250 new members, a struggle developed for control of Economy that was not resolved until March 1832, when Count de Leon and 176 members left. They were paid $105,000 to go. Some 250 adults remained loyal to Rapp.

De Leon's disciples bought a spot on the Ohio River ten miles north of Economy that they called New Philadelphia (1832–33). They built their houses and laid out their streets in the manner of those of Economy, but they could not be compared in architectural quality to those in Economy. Müller was not an effective leader, however. The money they received was spent unwisely, and attempts to gain more by lawsuits against Economy failed. They even attempted to take things from Economy by force, but the raid was unsuccessful.

Müller left New Philadelphia with a few of his original German associates and established another community at Grand Ecore in Natchitoches Parish, Louisiana (1834–36), at the same latitude as Jerusalem. He died there, and his followers moved on to the more healthful location of Germantown, Webster Parish, Louisiana. Joined by new German migrants, they organized as a communal group that prospered through cotton production and real estate investments. Germantown was dissolved peacefully after the Civil War. The remaining New Philadelphia secessionists moved into the Bethel Community (1844–80), founded by William Keil in Shelby County, Missouri.[1]

A final Rappite settlement was the Christian German Agricultural and Benevolent Society of Ora Labora (1862–68), located in Huron County, Michigan. The community of thirty German Methodist families was modeled after the Harmony Society by its leader, Emil Gottlob Baur, and was partially funded by the Rappites. The settlement was decimated by Civil War conscriptions and the war's financial burden.

The Separatists of Zoar

A second group of three hundred German Separatists led by Joseph Bäumeler arrived in Philadelphia in August 1817 after suffering persecution in Wurttemberg. Too poor to afford their own fares, they were financed by the English Quakers (Holloway, 1951, p. 88). On arrival in America, they immediately bought fifty-six hundred acres in Tuscarawas County, Ohio, with a fifteen-year loan from the American Quakers (Nordhoff, 1965, p. 99). Bäumeler and a few members went to Ohio to built their first log house in December, while the rest remained at Philadelphia. In the spring of 1818 they joined Bäumeler, but were so poor that they had to work for the neighboring farmers to support their families and to repay their loans.

Initially, they had not contemplated a communal society. Their goals were religious, to establish a perfect society in anticipation of the millennium. But they realized that dispersion to find work would cause disintegration of the religious community. Bäumeler therefore suggested a commune. On 19 April 1819 the members signed a charter to abolish all private accounts and establish a community of goods. The name Zoar was given to the community (Gen. 19:22) because it expressed their millennial expectations, an oasis of purity amid a desert of sin and violence. During the first years the sect practiced celibacy, but it was never taken seriously and was dropped after a decade, when Bäumeler decided to marry a pretty young member of the commune who was in charge of his housekeeping. Thereafter, families took an active part in social life. Meals were cooked centrally but eaten in the family home. Supplies were allocated from the central store. Each family had a house and garden. Until 1845 children lived and were educated collectively in special houses but thereafter were raised by their families. Houses were plain, often shabby, except for their flower gardens and for Bäumeler's "palace." Bäumeler sought to provide spiritual leadership, but he avoided becoming a cult figure.

The Zoarites emphasized order in their lives, in their contractual obligations, and in the members' rights and standing. In 1832 they were formally constituted by the Ohio legislature as the Separatist Society of Zoar, run by three trustees elected to three-year terms. The trustees appointed the supervisors of the industries and directed each member's work. The trustees, though they had unlimited powers in the community, were to consult in difficult cases with the Standing Committee of Five, which was a high court and a general council for agent and trustees. The agent was the commercial intermediary with outside world. The cashier was the treasurer and accountant, who controlled all of the money in the community. All officials were elected by the majority vote of all adult members, including women. The constitution was subject to amendment by a two-thirds vote (Nordhoff, 1965, pp. 96–103).

The society was divided into two classes: one of probationers and children, the other of full members. The members of the probationary class did not give up their property, but they had to deposit all of their money—when they signed the covenant after a year's probation—to have the right to vote and hold office. If the probationers desired to leave the community, they could receive their money without interest. If they wanted to be received into full membership, they could apply to the trustee with all of their properties.

They concerned themselves not only with religious matters but also with the minor morals, manners, good order in housekeeping, cleanliness, and health. They had a very strict regular schedule. Most of the houses accommodated several families. The young girls were taught the work of the household, and the boys were taught trades or put on the farm when they finished their education. As with the Shakers and Rappites, singing and musical performances were important elements of the religious experience, a way of linking earth and heaven.

Their prosperity began with construction of the Ohio-Erie canal, which they contracted to help build as well as to provision the work camps. Not only did the canal provide access; the money they raised was used to increase their land holdings to twelve thousand acres. Their population reached 500 with 170 new arrivals from Germany. This enabled them to diversify their economy, adding sheep to their agriculture, plus sawmills, a wool-weaving factory, looms for weaving linen, a dye house and tannery, a foundry, a distillery, and a cider press. By 1838, when a cholera epidemic struck, their wealth had increased to $2 million.

The epidemic caused labor shortages, and like the Rappites, they then began to employ outside labor. Bäumeler died in 1853, and for the next decades Zoar survived because of its economic strength, not because of the power of charismatic leadership.

The community's factories ultimately were swept aside by technological innovation and industrial growth. The remaining members aged, and many of the young left, no longer sharing either the millenarian visions or the commitment to communal life of the earlier emigrants. In the 1890s, it was Bäumeler's grandson Levi who launched an attack on "communism," saying that only fools or religious bigots were so blind as to believe in the "hypocrisy of equality," the belief that there were no differences in rank or fortune. Communism, he said, enslaves man to work, and behavior is imposed by an elite (quoted in Oved, 1988, p. 85).

In the face of such assaults, the community disintegrated, and the property was divided. Each of the 220 members received $250 in cash, a piece of land, and a share in the rest of the property. The farm was divided into 135 units, and everyone received property worth $2,500. Most of the young sold out and left. A few true believers remained, including one who, in 1900, said, "Communism is the only true way of life. In heaven, everything is communal and the community is the way to prepare people for the next world" (ibid., p. 87).

The Ebenezer Communes and The Amana Inspirationists

In 1842, amid the turmoil of the Kondratiev trough, a third wave of German Separatists began to arrive in the United States from Wurttemberg: members of the Community of True Inspiration (Barthel, 1984; Oved, 1988, pp. 87–95). The sect, which originated in 1714 among the German Pietists who rejected the Lutheran state-polity and ritualism, believed in Biblical prophecy and came to establish independent communal settlements, led by God's "chosen instruments," Christian Metz and Barbara Heineman. In contrast to the Rappists and Zoarites they had first gathered into a communal settlement at Engenthal in Hessen. There they developed their cooperative organization of work in agriculture and industry and an educational system for their children. For a while they prospered, but then they were hard hit by drought and experienced deteriorating relations with their neighbors and growing intolerance in Hessen. They decided to move to America.

In 1842 a group of elders explored possible locations, followed by Metz in 1843. Some five thousand acres were purchased on what had been a Seneca Indian reservation near Buffalo, New York. Three hundred twenty emigrants arrived in 1844, and four thousand additional acres were purchased.

The first settlement was called (Middle) Ebenezer (1 Sam. 7:12). By 1845 the population had increased to eight hundred, most of them poor peasants and artisans, and Middle Ebenezer had spawned Upper, Lower, and New Ebenezer.

Members initially maintained individual property rights, and gaps in affluence quickly appeared, leading some to call for complete privatization. The community leaders realized that this would lead to disintegration of the religious community, however, and used the principle of mutual sharing to assure equity. The rift was avoided by the "chosen instruments" (prophets) who were "inspired by the Holy Spirits" to preach in favor of communal organization. A provisional charter was drafted in 1843, and the community was legalized as The Ebenezer Society in 1845. The legal framework provided protection for the communal organization and, when combined with the religious sanctions that could be marshaled by the theocratic government, constrained those who demanded private ownership. In 1854 the chosen instruments ordered the ejection of the doubters to strengthen the community.

What emerged was a confederation of economically successful Ebenezer communes until disputes about land titles emerged with the Senecas and the rising price of land along the Erie Canal introduced further temptations to privatize. In August 1854, Christian Metz "was ordered by the Holy Spirit to move the sect west." Emissaries bought twenty thousand acres of land twenty miles north of Iowa City. Some one thousand acres of this land had been owned in 1851–53 by a group of twenty German Swedenborgians from St. Louis who had left Germany after the 1844 revolution. They had intended to establish Jaspis Kolonie as a communal society but succumbed to privatism.

The first Amana town was planted in 1855. By 1859 twelve hundred members were settled in seven new settlements: Amana, East Amana, Middle Amana, West Amana, South Amana, High Amana, and Homestead. In 1859 they were recognized as a religious and benevolent society by the state of Iowa, establishing the communal idea as the central principle of their society. They supported abolition but were conscientious objectors in the Civil War, contributing, however, both cash and material.

Metz and Heineman died in 1861 and 1883, respectively, and along with them the "chosen instruments" as bases of religious authority. The Amana colonies prospered as a communally organized economic federation, efficiently managed by elected trustees, with communal kitchens and consumption, growing as a result of both natural increase and of migrants from the disintegrating Zoar and Harmony communities. But the deaths of the religious leaders made it difficult to use spiritual authority to combat secular and religious threats. The young became dissatisfied with communal life and the absence of private property. In 1918 Amana's young men were conscripted, and they learned about the wider world. English replaced German as the everyday language. When the Great Depression hit in 1929, it brought Amana near to bankruptcy. In 1932 the community was reorganized to survive (Barthel, 1984). Real estate and factories remained community property, operated collectively. Ownership was divided into stock. Members worked for pay. The factories were able to become successful corporations owned and operated jointly. The big change was in community life. The communal kitchens were abolished. What held the seven settlements together was their religion, the Amana Church Society, and pride in a distinct cultural tradition that still exists. The Amana Society continues today as a church with seven congregations, one in each of the seven settlements.

Bishop Hill Colony

A final note should be made of the Bishop Hill Colony (1846–62) in Henry County, Illinois, established by another persecuted European sect, Pietist farmers and artisans from Swedish Norrland driven out by the Lutherans because of their millenarian beliefs. Led by Eric Janson, they too sought religious freedom. Janson called for his followers to establish in America a New Jerusalem, the core of the Church of All Saints that would greet the Messiah on his Second Coming.

Within the sect were many who could not afford the journey to the New World. Communal sharing of wealth made it possible for the entire sect to migrate, and communal arrangements were established as the principal moral tenet of the Apostolic Church.

Within two years eight hundred Jansonists had arrived in Illinois, initially living in great hardship in caves dug out of hills. By 1849 they had constructed living quarters and have developed a solid economy, growing flax and weaving linen.

Janson was murdered in 1850, but his successor, Jonas Olsen, had a constitution legalized by the state of Illinois. Democratically elected trustees were to run the communal society, which they did well for a decade. Their agricultural enterprise flourished, and by 1856 they owned eighty-five hundred acres. Money flowed in from contracts to help build the Quincy Railroad, and the trustees set up an independent financial organization in Galfa under Olav Johansen. Material standards within the community were good. Families lived separately but consumed collectively. The fundamentalist religion prevented other than basic education, however, and ultimately led to other problems. Influenced by the Shakers, Olsen, who had absolute religious authority, declared Bishop Hill celibate in 1854. Those who objected were forced to leave. Then the Crisis of 1857 hit. Olaf Johansen's financial enterprise went bankrupt. The young and the disaffected rebelled, and in 1859 they demanded that the commune be dissolved. Finally, in 1862 the property was divided. Many sold and left. Few retained the religious desire to remain organized.

CHAPTER FIVE

The Owenite Experiments: Secular Socialism Arrives

Settlement pushed westward after the War of 1812. America experienced its first wave of urban-industrial development as new mill towns brought factory production to the continent. An ebullient upswing of growth brought new opportunity to many. But problems resulted from the downward plunge of agricultural prices and land values into the primary trough of the 1820s, which sharpened inequities between the urban elite and the backwoods farmers. Amid the resulting social ferment, the political system that had emerged after the Revolution began to unravel. Participation in the political process already had been broadened by the removal of property qualifications for voting. Although Andrew Jackson lost the election of 1824, his support for the poor versus the rich, the "plain people" versus "the interests," captured an increasing base of support that elevated him to the presidency in 1828 and led to the emergence of the two-party system: his new Democratic party versus the Republicans, exemplified by Henry Clay and John Quincy Adams.

Almost as a knee-jerk reaction to the primary trough that bottomed in 1824, ten short-lived Owenite experiments were started in 1825 and 1826. Nine more were built in a second wave (see Table 2), seven of them amid the deflationary depression of the 1840s. See Figures 14 and 15. They introduced a secular presocialism to the menu of utopian alternatives.

What was Owenism, and who was Owen? Robert Owen was born in Montgomeryshire, Wales, in 1771, the son of a blacksmith. At age ten he joined his brother in London and was apprenticed to a clothier. He bloomed early. By 1790 he was superintendent of a large Manchester cotton mill, rising to be manager and partner. In 1800 he persuaded his partners to buy the textile mills at New Lanark in Scotland.

He was appalled by factory working conditions and began to formulate a practical reform program that included better housing and sanitation, in-

Table 2

Community	Started	Ended
FIRST WAVE		
New Harmony, Ind.	1825	1827
Yellow Springs Community, Ohio	1825	1826
Coal Creek Community, Ind.	1825	1832
Goshen Community, Ind.	1825	1826
Franklin Community, N.Y.	1826	1826
Forestville (Coxsackie), N.Y.	1826	1827
Kendall Community, Ohio	1826	1829
Valley Forge Community, Pa.	1826	1826
Blue Spring Community, Ind.	1826	1827
Nashoba Community, Tenn.	1826	1829
SECOND WAVE		
Equity, Ohio	1833	1835
First Community of Man's Free Brotherhood, Ind.	1833	1835
Promisewell Community, Pa.	1843	1844
Goose Pond Community, Pa.	1843	1844
Equality, Wis.	1843	1846
Fruit Hills, Ohio	1845	1852
Grand Prairie Community, Ind.	1845	1847
Kristeen Community, Ind.	1845	1846
Utilitarian Association, Wis.	1845	1848

fant care, and limits on employment of children. The program became the basis for his *New View of Society*, first outlined in pamphlet form in 1813. He portrayed limited numbers of aristocracy resting on the broad base of the working class and argued that community of property would eliminate this inequality and create "abundance unlimited." A labor theory of value was asserted: "That which can create new wealth is worth the wealth it creates." Producers were to have a fair share of what they produced if there were to be a just and rational society.

By 1817 he was issuing calls for reform of the economic system and subordination of machinery to man. A public call in London's newspapers brought statesmen and social reformers to New Lanark to see his model factory and environmental improvements. He began to advocate construction of new cooperative communities in which work and its results would be shared. With growing working-class consciousness in England, his views were quickly accepted by the emergent labor unions as expressions of workers' aspirations. Despairing of his fellow capitalists, he thought that industry could benefit humankind if competition were eliminated and if bad education were countered by rational enlightenment. This could be achieved by cooperative control of industry and the creation of Villages of Unity and Cooperation, in which the settlers,

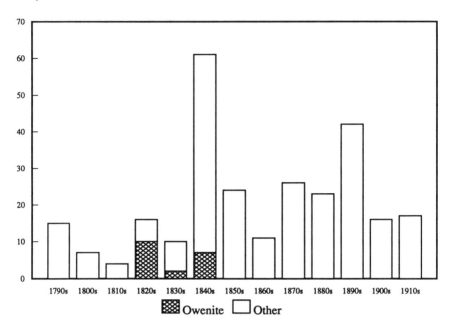

Figure 14. The Owenite Surges. The principal surge was in the primary trough of the 1820s, followed by another flush of interest in the deflationary depression of the 1840s.

in addition to raising wages, would improve their physiques and their minds. He thought that the cooperative and trades union movements should be joined in a "great trades union," and he left a series of important messages that helped inform the socialist movement: the indictment of capitalism, the stress on cooperation and education, the stress on environmental improvement.

Owen rejected all kinds of organized religion, arguing that if people were dedicated to the pursuit of happiness, the only appropriate religion would be that which naturally resides within them, determined by the laws of nature. Likewise, he felt that the family as it existed promoted disharmony. In order to promote a peaceful existence for all humankind, the single family should be replaced by the community of families. Only in such a community would there be satisfactory social relations. These ideas were both sources of inspiration to his followers and sources of problems once his ideas were brought to the United States.

Chapters of his *New View of Society* had been reprinted as "A New Outlook on Society" in the Jeffersonian periodical *Aurora* in Philadelphia in 1817 (Oved, 1988, pp. 109ff.). Roughly at the same time, Quaker Cornelius Blatchly, drawing on the Shaker and Rappite experiences, began to advo-

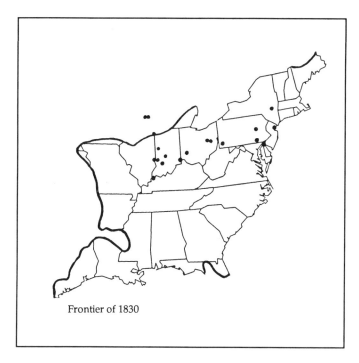

Frontier of 1830

Figure 15. Location of the Owenite Communities. The short-lived Owenite experiments highlight the contrast between North and South before the Civil War that was discussed in Chapter 1. When combined with the Fourierist phalanxes, with which they share a common reaction to early industrial development, they trace the outlines of the American manufacturing belt that came to dominate the economic landscape after the Civil War. Figure 21 maps the Fourierist locations.

cate similar ideas in America. In 1820, Blatchly founded the Society for Promoting Communities in New York, and in 1822 the Society published *Essay on Commonwealths*, in which they reproduced Blatchly's ideas, chapters from Owen, and articles on the Rappite Harmony Society. Through the New York Society, Owenite ideas reached Cincinnati, Ohio, which was experiencing a religious revival and beginning to organize communitarian groups. The first of these was James Dorsey's Rational Brethren of Oxford, in 1816. In Philadelphia another circle of Owenites crystallized, led by William Maclure, president of the Academy of Sciences.

The stage was set for Owen's arrival in the United States in 1824. Blatchly's followers introduced him to New York society. He visited the Shakers at Watervliet and presented them with his plans for a succession of communal settlements. He thought these communes should comprise, ideally, eight hundred to one thousand people (at the most, twenty-five hundred), organized cooperatively and eliminating the waste of the middleman, benefiting from the most advanced scientific improvements yet sufficiently isolated to be free from the influences of "corrupting society."

After passing through Philadelphia, Owen arrived at the Rappites' settlement of New Harmony. On 3 January 1825, he purchased the commune's 20,000 acres and 180 buildings. This was followed by a hundred-day propaganda tour, in which he invited people to join the community. Received by James Monroe and John Quincy Adams, he addressed Congress. The speech was published nationwide. When he returned to New Harmony, he found eight hundred people waiting for him. He never applied his own managerial skills to the enterprise, however, instead preferring to travel, preaching the advantages of his New Jerusalem. It was his son William and his friend Donald MacDonald who were left to attempt to mold the diverse gathering of Indiana farmers, urban intellectuals, and social activists into a community. Key issues that never were satisfactorily resolved were those of private property rights and criteria for acceptance to membership.

Initially, Owen proposed a "halfway house" in which the group lived in the existing buildings purchased from the Rappites, owned their own property and furniture, and drew goods from the community store. At year's end the community's profits would be shared and individuals' consumption deducted from their shares. But there was no way of assuring that everyone contributed to the community. Many of the newcomers lacked essential skills. Others were freeloaders.

Owen seemed oblivious to the problems. Soon he was on the road again on additional propaganda tours. But as his ideas became better known, he encountered growing resistance, especially because of his antireligious stance and his opinions of the family. The press became increasingly critical.

He returned to England briefly and, coming back through Philadelphia, persuaded Maclure's Philadelphia intellectuals to join New Harmony. But when he arrived in Indiana, the community was moribund. It was clear that the settlers lacked the requisite agricultural and industrial skills and that essential organizational and management abilities were lacking. At the end of the year New Harmony was in debt. Owen covered the deficit. This is not to say that there was not excitement. Many of the settlers praised the harmonious tolerance that existed for a while in a group with such diverse religions and ideologies. The community's schools were opened with great enthusiasm. More and more intellectuals arrived. Others left to found additional communes.

Owen called for immediate transformation of the halfway house into a complete Community of Equality, but adoption of the new constitution in 1826 quickly brought to the surface conflicts between the urban intellectuals and the backwoods farmers. A direct challenge came from the farmers—Methodists who rejected Owen's secularism. Owen turned over thirteen hundred acres of uncleared land to 150 of them to create a second community, Macluria, two miles from New Harmony; it disintegrated late in 1826. Soon thereafter, a second separatist group of English immigrant farmers hived off, taking seven hundred acres of New Harmony's best land to create a third commune, Feiba Peveli. Another secession threatened by young intellectuals was quickly stemmed by the offer of another tract of woodland, land that they would have to clear if they were to build log cabins. They decided not to accept the offer!

The debt owed George Rapp fell due in 1826. Maclure and others proposed reorganization to ensure that the communards were providing as much labor as they took out in product, thus eliminating freeloading. At the same time, however, Robert Owen delivered a radical Fourth of July speech, titled "A Declaration of Mental Independence," in which in which he called for the abolition of private property and of organized religion, as well as of the institutions of family and marriage. Widely circulated, the speech engendered open hostility among mainstream Americans. External opprobrium was joined by increasing internal opposition. Maclure objected to Owen's wasteful and inefficient paternalism and broke away to establish an independent and highly regarded school. More radical communards were unhappy that progress to the new society was so slow. Repeated attempts to develop new constitutions failed. Owen's financial situation deteriorated. He left in June 1827, and New Harmony ended as a social experiment.

The Owenite excitement had, meanwhile, spread from New Harmony. Nine other Owenite communities were established in the years 1825 and 1826, several established by believers who first had been at New Harmony. None lasted long. Many were wracked by internal strife, factionalism, and withdrawals. Some were established by urban intellectuals lacking farming skills. Others met hostility from neighbors because Owen's ideas threatened private property, the family, and religion. The most successful, the Kendall community in Ohio, disbanded when farmers found they were no better off living a communitarian life than if they farmed individually.

None of these Owenite experiments took root in American soil. Owenism and the American mainstream culture were basically incompatible. Americans believed in the power of individuals to dominate the environment; Owen believed that people were shaped by circumstances and could not control their own destinies. Americans believed in individual achievement as the driving force behind social mobility; Owen believed in sharing and redistribution. To achievement-oriented Americans, inequality was inevitable; to Owen, it was undesirable. Americans, too, had strong religious attachments; Owen's work was secular and rational. And Americans believed in their families; Owen believed that community should supersede family.

"One of the most dramatic confrontations of ideas in the first decades of the century" (Tuveson, 1968, p. 179) occurred in Cincinnati in April 1829. "For eight days . . . the English reformer Robert Owen and the American church leader Alexander Campbell debated the validity of Christianity" (ibid.). The debates highlighted the evolution that was to occur in utopian settlement, from religious communities preparing for the millennium to secular communities designing an alternative to capitalism.

Owen argued that there was a misapprehension of the primary laws of human nature because of the notion of original sin. He was, he said, "convinced that the real nature of man is adapted, when rightly directed, to attain high physical, intellectual, and moral excellence, and to derive from each of these faculties, a large share of happiness, or of varied enjoyment." The three "most formidable prejudices" he discovered, on further rumination, to be false ideas taught by religion, the principle that marriage is indissoluble, and excessive regard for the rights of private property. Together, they "form a chain of triple strength to retain the human mind in ignorance and vice, and to inflict every species of misery, from artificial causes, on the human race."

We should, he said, "no longer consider man to be the ignorant, vicious, and degraded being, that, heretofore, he has been compelled to appear, whether covered by the garb of savage or civilized life." It is society, then, not man that is fallen; and man is man, whether he live in the woods or in Cincinnati.

Scottish immigrant Alexander Campbell, who had broken with the Presbyterians and became a Baptist, then departed the Baptists in 1832 to establish the Disciples of Christ, responded by insisting that utopia can be attained only by radical changes in the human spirit. "It is called the Reign of Heaven, because down into the heart it draws the heavenly feelings, desires, and aims. From heaven it came, and to heaven it leads. I will shake the heavens and the earth, says the Lord. I will revolutionize the world; and how, my friends, but by introducing new principles of human actions?" But this is to be a change in the world as it is. Christianity "contemplates the reformation of the world upon a new principle." The nations of this world are to become the City of God, as "the religion of Jesus Christ melts the hearts of men into pure philanthropy." The purpose of God in his dealings with men is to bring about a peaceful and just democracy in which they may dwell: "the development and introduction of that political and religious order of society called THE MILLENNIUM, which will be the consummation of that ultimate amelioration of society proposed in the Christian Scriptures" (ibid., pp. 80–81).

Campbell prevailed. It was not yet time for Owen's ideas in America. Disillusioned, he returned to England later in 1829 and resumed his activities there. The wave of secular communitarianism that began in 1824 waned, and all of the extant Owenite communities were dissolved. His idea of secular communes as an alternative to life in the American mainstream remained, however. When the economy collapsed in the Crisis of 1837, plunging toward the depression of the 1840s, seven new (and equally short-lived) Owenite experiments were started. Simultaneously, Noyes pioneered perfectionism at Oneida, Transcendentalism bloomed in New England, utopian socialism appeared in the new wave of Fourierist communes, and Mormonism provided a millenarian alternative. Restorationism, the restoring of the apostolic church that had been lost, a major Disciples of Christ concept, was added to Joseph Smith, Jr.'s, Mormon theology by his confidant Sidney Rigdon, who had formerly been a Campbellite.

Yet it was the Owenites who had introduced the basic concept of a secular social system in the 1820s. And by 1840 socialism and Owenism were so closely associated that the two had become virtually synonymous. Owenites willingly adopted the socialist label because it stressed their emphasis on the social system for answers to societal problems as opposed to an individualistic, capitalist approach. "Owenite socialism was the true social or cooperative and communional system, a blend of communitarian theory, anticapitalist economics and a science of society. These three elements made up the main part of the doctrines of Owenism and together gave it distinctive characteristics as a philosophy of social reform" (Harrison, 1969, p. 46). To the Owenites, institutions that fostered the concept of man as an individual were detrimental to the formation of satisfactory human relationships. The only way to achieve harmony within a society was through a general concept of community using a labor theory of value, not the laws of a competitive system. The abolition of individual ownership and the holding of common property were an essential part of a "communional" system. The community itself was a method of social reform. Through the formation of experimental communities, Owenites believed society could be radically transformed without the violence of revolution.

CHAPTER SIX

Mormonism: From the Burned-Over District to the Deseret Kingdom

Even as the Owenite enthusiasm waned in the west, millenarianism had the Burned-Over District aflame. The completion of the Erie Canal in 1825 promoted rapid economic and social change in the district, and a particularly extreme variety of millennial revivalism, "Ultraism" surged, rising to a peak in the 1830s. Among those caught up in the excitement was Joseph Smith, Jr., born in Vermont in 1805 but living in Palmyra, New York, in the 1820s. His visions occurred amid the excitement of the mid-1820s. His move to Illinois was a direct outcome of the Crisis of 1837. He was murdered in 1844, and Brigham Young began the relocation of Mormons to the Great Basin in 1847.

Passions ran high in Palmyra and its environs, where there were frequent revivals—Methodist, Baptist, and Presbyterian. Within the Smith family, there was awareness of religious alternatives. Joseph Smith, Jr.'s, uncle, Jason Mack, established a communal religious community in New Brunswick. In 1820, at age fourteen, Smith claimed that angels had appeared to him and warned him against joining any existing religion. In 1823 he said that the messenger Moroni had revealed to him the location of ancient records, and in 1827, at age twenty-one, he said he had been entrusted with the golden plates on which the records were written. Three associates claimed that they too had seen the plates and the angel Moroni, and as a result Smith's family and friends recognized him as a prophet. During the next three years, using the magic stones Urim and Thummim, he deciphered the writing, producing the Book of Mormon.

The book related the history of a group of Hebrews who had migrated from Jerusalem to America in 600 B.C., led by a prophet, Lehi. They split into two groups. One, the Lamanites, forgot their beliefs and became savages, the American Indians. The other, the Nephites, were taught by Jesus; they flourished and built great cities but then were destroyed in

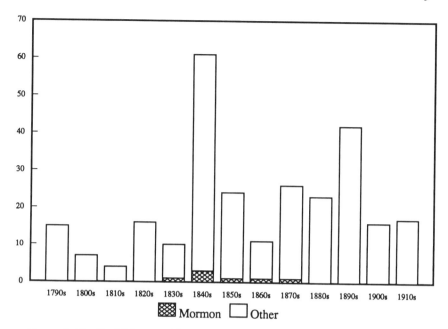

Figure 16. The Establishment of Communal Settlements by Schismatic Mormon Groups. The focus in this chart is on communities planted by offshoots from mainstream Mormonism.

400 A.D. Jesus' teachings, Smith said, were recorded on the golden plates by the prophet Mormon. Mormon's son Moroni buried the plates, returning as an angel fourteen hundred years later to reveal their hiding place to him. (For a discussion and presentation of his autobiographical account, see Harrison, 1979, pp. 176ff. Allen and Leonard [1976] provide an accessible history of the Latter-day Saints.)

Smith preached about the need for salvation in the latter days before the Second Coming of Christ; hence, the Church of Jesus Christ of the Latter-day Saints. According to the faith, the Latter-day Saints were a modern Israel, and they were to gather to await the Second Coming in Zion, a city that it was their destiny to build in America in preparation for the New Jerusalem, led by a prophet to whom was revealed both theological truth and day-to-day guidance.

From these beginnings there emerged the most successful of all of the millenarian movements. Although the number of communal settlements was small, largely planted by schismatic groups outside the Mormon ecumene (Figs. 16, 17), the Mormons twice experimented with cooperative systems, first under the terms of Joseph Smith, Jr.'s, Law of Consecration and Stewardship and then under Brigham Young's United Order of

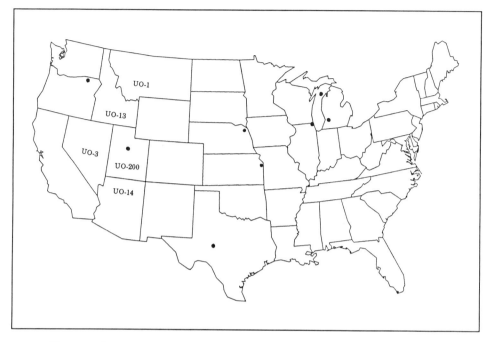

Figure 17. Locations of the Communal Mormon Settlements. What many do not realize is that the groups that separated from mainstream Mormonism, indicated by dots, relocated throughout the United States. Also shown are the numbers of United Order organizations formed in 1874–75.

Enoch. By 1880 the Mormon Deseret Kingdom stretched across a region one thousand miles long by eight hundred miles wide. In this region more than 140,000 members were housed in four hundred new communities, following a master plan that fixed the sizes and spatial patterns of cities, towns, and villages (Figs. 18, 19). When statehood was negotiated for the core of this region, Utah, there was not only this "mainline" Mormon settlement system but also a number of communities planted by schismatic groups according to somewhat different principles. Today the Mormon church is the fifth-largest religious organization in the United States, with more than 7.3 million members and with numerous offshoots (Shields, 1975/1982).

Smith began by organizing the Church of Christ at Fayette, New York, on 6 April 1830. He preached a new version of Christianity (Leone, 1979, p. 203), attempting to provide "a spiritual bridge between the old world and the new" (Kephart, 1987, p. 224). Membership grew rapidly. Within a year there were more than one thousand members. Members believed

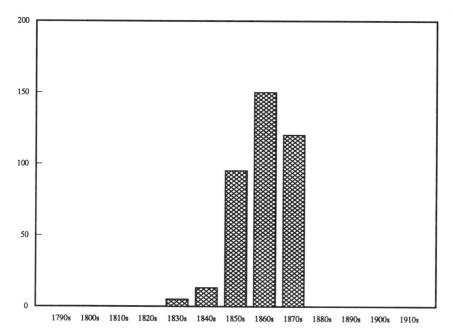

Figure 18. Settlements Planted by the Mainline Mormon Church. These settlements were not included in Figures 2–4 or in Figure 16 because they were not communal in their organization. The scale of mainline Mormonism dwarfs that of the progressive millenarians.

they were God's Chosen People. There was an aggressive style of witnessing, and Mormons believed that nonbelievers were destined for hell. Because they challenged the established religion, local opposition soon developed, and Smith was arrested several times for disturbing the peace. He determined to move west to escape harassment, and missionaries were sent out to explore alternatives.

On their way west to meet the Indians, Smith's missionaries stopped at Sidney Rigdon's Kirtland Community. Rigdon had first been associated with the Rappites at Economy, but in 1830 he organized a group of Campbellite Baptists (Disciples of Christ) into a communal settlement known as "The Family" (Chapter 4). Rigdon and one hundred members of his congregation were converted to Mormonism, an infusion of support that was critical to the movement. Smith determined to take refuge at Kirtland until a permanent site could be found to build Zion.

At Kirtland, Smith worked out his designs for a Mormon society, announcing his "inspired" plans in revelations. In February 1831 he promulgated the Law of Consecration and Stewardship. "The beginning of

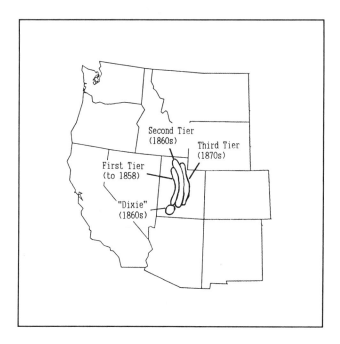

Figure 19. The Successive Tiers of Mormon Colonization. This map is adapted from Donald W. Meinig, "The Mormon Culture Region," *Annals of the Association of American Geographers,* vol. 55 (1965), pp. 202, 205. Meinig describes Mormon expansion from Salt Lake as a pattern of movement into successive tiers of valleys, each tier composed of a segmented series of lowlands along the front of or within the Wasatch ranges and high plateaus.

Mormon communitarianism . . . , the law was a prescription for transforming the highly individualistic economic order of Jacksonian America into a system characterized by economic equality, socialization of surplus incomes, freedom of enterprise and group economic self-sufficiency" (Arrington, Fox, and May, 1976, p. 15). It called for the consolidation of Mormon property in communal storehouses administered by bishops who would redistribute the goods according to members' needs, saying that "if ye are not equal in earthly things, ye cannot be equal in obtaining heavenly things." Bishops were to bestow an "inheritance" or "stewardship" on members (a house with a store, some farmland, or some tools) so that members could be economically self-supporting. Each "steward" had license to engage in competition, but surplus profits were to be dedicated to the community. These new economic arrangements, which sought to redistribute wealth to put all family heads on an equal economic standing, were designed to bridge the gap between the communism of Rigdon's original "Family" and the individualist orientation of Smith's followers from New York. Communal living was discouraged, perhaps because of conflicts in the Family, but the appeal to individual initiative was made within the framework of income redistribution and accountability (Hayden, 1976, p. 107).

After the promulgation, a number of groups attempted to comply with the Law—at Thompson, Ohio, and in Jackson County, Missouri. But through experimentation, the church leaders found that the system did not work as they wanted it to. They soon learned that if the individual was free to keep part of the surplus created, there was more of an incentive to produce a profit, thus guaranteeing the church its income. The Law of Consecration and Stewardship was set aside after three years, and the practice of tithing began to take shape, officially becoming adopted as a substitute in 1841.

By 1835 there were fifteen hundred to two thousand Mormons in and around Kirtland (Hill, Rooker, and Wimmer, 1977, p. 1). Short of capital, Rigdon and Smith became involved in land speculation as the boom of the 1830s accelerated. Their speculative activities were financed by paper issued by the Kirtland Safety Society, a financial experiment launched by Smith and the church hierarchy in the fall of 1836. In the economic crisis that began in May 1837 the bank failed, however; investors discovered that the bank notes they had been issued were not only worthless, they were illegal. Smith and Rigdon fled to Missouri to avoid mob violence and judicial action as the economy plunged toward depression (Allen and Leonard, 1976, pp. 110–14).

The intentions had been sound. "Without a sufficient national currency, and in need of capital, the Mormons launched their bank to transfer landed wealth into a more liquid form" (Hill et al., p. 42). The state legislature had refused all requests for banking charters at this time. The Mormons, seeking legal counsel, were advised to set up an unchartered bank. When the panic hit Kirtland, heavy demand forced the Safety Society to suspend payments. Had they been able to secure a charter, it is thought likely that the demand on their bank would not have been as heavy. However, this was not the case, and the hostility produced an explosive environment. Faced with an angry mob of creditors, church members, and civil authorities, Smith escaped. He and one thousand followers fled Kirtland "in the middle of the night" during January 1838, to take refuge in an already established community of Saints in Missouri (ibid., p. 69).

In 1830, before he moved to Kirtland, Smith had traveled west with his missionaries to Jackson County, Missouri, to a spot revelation identified as the "Center Place"—the city of Independence—where New Jerusalem could be built according to Smith's "Plat of the City of Zion," around a complex of temples. This spot, he thought, could serve as a gathering place where the latter-day kingdom could be established in anticipation of the millennial reign of Jesus Christ. Within two years the settlement had grown to almost twelve hundred, with life structured according to the Law of Consecration and Stewardship (Arrington, 1966, p. 7; Harrison, 1979, p. 179). Hostility soon built up, though, because neighbors were threatened by the economic success of the cooperative community and by the millennial visions predicting the establishment of a kingdom that, from its Missouri capital, would be ruled by the Latter-day Saints. Violence broke out. Businesses and homes were burned, people threatened, and the presiding bishop tarred and feathered (Arrington, 1966, p. 11). In 1833 the Mormons took refuge across the Missouri River in Clay, Caldwell, and Daviess Counties.

Several new communities were established, the largest of which was Far West (Allen and Leonard, 1976, pp. 104ff.). The persecutions that occurred had not dampened the ability of the Mormons to attract converts: between 1837 and 1838, eight thousand to ten thousand Saints gathered in the area. The church leaders bought land, dedicated a site for a temple, and planned for growth. They adhered to the practice of communal holding of property, but instead of contributing their surplus incomes each year they followed the new requirement of giving 10 percent of their income to the church. The revenue from tithing was used to buy land, pay the church officials, and provide an operating budget for the church. Agricultural cooperatives called United Farms were set up and were highly successful. There were plans to organize other types of industries, but again conflict intervened.

After leaving Kirtland, Smith and his close associates joined the settlers in Missouri, where new converts also were beginning to arrive in large numbers as a result of the success of the Mormons' missionary activities, including overseas in Britain. There still were fears about the Mormons' millennial kingdom, and in 1838 the so-called Mormon War broke out in Daviess County and quickly spread. There was mob action, confrontation between state and Mormon militias, and the massacre of Mormons at Shoal Creek by the state militia. Gov. Lilburn Boggs issued an order to exterminate the Mormons or drive them from the state. At Far West, Smith and the other church leaders were arrested. Gen. Samuel Lucas ordered Brig. Gen. Alexander Doniphan to have them shot, but Doniphan refused: "It is cold-blooded murder. I will not obey your order . . . if you execute these men, I will hold you responsible before an earthly tribunal" (Allen and Leonard, 1976, p. 128). The Latter-day Saints were, however, expelled from Missouri. Twelve to fifteen thousand Saints were forced to leave their homes and businesses at great personal loss. "According to one report, more than $300,000 worth of property was abandoned" (Arrington, 1966, p. 16). Another source puts the figure closer to $2 million (Carter, 1960, p. 2).

In the winter of 1838–9, five thousand Mormons crossed the Mississippi River into Illinois, and with a charter for an "independent principality," they founded Nauvoo. Nauvoo grew very quickly into the center of a growing region with great economic power. By 1844 twenty-five thousand Mormons lived in and around the new settlement (Flanders, 1965). It was here that they conceived two simultaneous visions of millennial architecture and attempted to build them side by side (Hayden, 1976, p. 105). "Eden" was a model of earthly paradise, a garden city of single-family dwellings. "Jerusalem" was a model of heaven, a cult center dominated by twin monuments, the temple and the prophet's residence. Conflict between these two ideals, which were never fully articulated, was expressed in the ambiguities of Mormon town plans and architectural styles, as well as in explosive debates about city scale and the role of central buildings.

In practice, many Mormon settlements, including Nauvoo, were laid out according to Smith's Plat of the City of Zion, which seems to have been inspired by the plan for Harmony. The village plot was to be one mile square, with each block or square containing ten acres. With twenty lots to the block, each lot would be a half acre in size. The lots were laid off alternately in such a way that no house would be exactly opposite another house. Uniform regulations would assure that there would be only one house to a lot and that each house would be located at least twenty-five feet from the street. A large block in the center was set aside for such public buildings as the bishop's storeroom, meetinghouses, temples, and schools. Streets would run north–south and east–west and would be wide. The city would contain about one thousand family units, each with a respectable garden space and grove, lawn, or orchard. Outside the city would be the farms. And when this city was filled up, wrote Joseph Smith, Jr., "lay off another in the same way, and so fill up the world in these last days" (Arrington, 1966, p. 10). The problem with Nauvoo was that it grew so quickly that it could never be determined whether there should be a repetition of Zion or a single great city with Jerusalem at its center.

At Nauvoo the Mormons established large agricultural corporations, began to turn to manufacturing, replaced the stewardship principle with joint-stock ownership, and established the Tithing Office to systematize church revenues. Tithing enabled the church to counteract the one aspect of a capitalist economy that Smith found objectionable, inequality. The community flourished. By 1845 it was the largest city in Illinois, with a population approaching twenty thousand.

Beginning in January 1841 all Mormon converts were commanded to move to Nauvoo immediately to build up the kingdom, a policy that brought the community far more members than most communitarian groups were able to recruit but did not allow for careful screening or for intensive socialization. Converts included many New Englanders eager to identify themselves as a chosen people, perhaps because of their upbringing in Puritan communities (the Mormon church has sometimes been called the Church of the Latter-day Puritans). English immigrants to Nauvoo numbered almost five thousand. A steady stream of newcomers arrived, and Mormon leaders simply tried to orient them to broad community-building goals couched in religious terms. Since all expected an imminent Second Coming of Christ and the destruction of the rest of the world outside the holy city, the atmosphere was charged with eagerness to do God's will (Hayden, 1976, pp. 113, 117). Private land sales were encouraged, to pay for Nauvoo's principal public works, including the Temple and Nauvoo House.

"Joseph Smith understood he had been appointed to build a society, not just a church, that it would inevitably conflict with the society from which it sprang, and that at some point the task must pass from his hands if it were to come to fruition" (Leone, 1979, p. 15). He thus molded Mormonism into what he thought would be its final design. But Smith was unwilling to compromise on questions of theology, resulting in internal schisms that opened the community to external harassment. Mormonism was "no longer just another revival movement or socialist utopia, it was a profoundly different version of Christianity" (ibid.).

One of the most controversial inspirations came when Smith set down the principle of plural marriage in written form on 12 July 1843, to reinstitute the polygamous marriage practices of the biblical patriarchs within the framework of a broader conception of marriage lasting through eternity (for an excellent discussion of Mormon marriage practices, see Foster, 1981). This radical reorganization of traditional family life became the most contentious of the Mormons' social experiments and was not revealed to the outside world until 1852, after Brigham Young had led the successful trip west to Salt Lake to escape prosecution, although there had been rumors of polygamy as early as 1836 at Kirtland. Making his announcement, Smith actually supported the patriarchal family as an institution, glorifying stereotypical sex-role differentiation. The family home was sanctified in articles and sermons that defined homemaking as women's proper sphere. For men the isolation of the family was countered by participation in the two orders of the Mormon priesthood, Melchizedek and Aaronic. The hierarchy of the priesthood provided both spiritual and temporal authority for all adult males. The Temple offices and the Seventies Hall provided communal territory for the men. Women were to share the reflected glory of their husbands' offices. When polygamy was introduced, the bonds of brotherhood became even closer. Mormon women, caretakers of the men's private homes, were isolated from collective decision making (Hayden, 1976, p. 110).

The first internal conflicts arose from the financing of Nauvoo House, leading to the development of an anti-Smith faction within the church. Led by William Law and Robert Foster, church leaders who worked as building contractors developing commercial and residential properties, the dissident group challenged Smith's allocations of funds to the Nauvoo House. He in turn accused them of making it impossible for the church to sell its land. They muttered of his profiteering. Doctrinal as well as financial issues divided the factions, and quarrels led to the excommunication of Law and Foster after they published the Nauvoo *Expositor*, which contained an offer to reform the Mormon church from the "vicious principles of Joseph Smith." Smith ordered the destruction of the *Expositor*'s press, an act that led to his confinement in the county jail. Encouraged by this schism at Nauvoo, anti-Mormon groups from neighboring towns seized the opportunity to halt the growth of the city and with it Smith's political ambitions. He had announced for the U.S. presidency in February 1844, with Sidney Rigdon as his vice-presidential candidate. Amid the depths of a deflationary depression that highlighted the contrasts between the Mormons' success and the rest of society's problems, he and his brother, Hyrum Smith, were murdered by a hostile posse in Carthage, Illinois, on 29 June 1844. This violence was followed by an order from the state government, which feared bloody reprisals, commanding the Mormons to evacuate their garden city and leave Illinois (Hayden, 1976, p. 124).

Brigham Young succeeded Smith to the presidency of the Mormon church after overcoming challenges by a number of other aspirants, including Sidney Rigdon and James Jesse Strang. He was able to lead the Saints on a westward journey that allowed them the freedom to establish and develop the dream that Joseph Smith, Jr., had begun. "Before Smith's assassination, he had considered plans to move his people into some part of the unsettled west outside the federal Union" (Meinig, 1965, p. 197). An extensive survey already had been made of the Great Basin. Smith had felt the time would come to move his followers across the Rockies in order for the religion to survive. After Smith's death, the hostility toward Mormonism was so intense that Young had no choice.

Immediately after Smith's murder, confusion overwhelmed the citizens of Nauvoo. Brigham Young, after fighting off leadership challenges, succeeded in uniting them with a strong plea that the Temple be completed as quickly as possible, both as a monument to Joseph Smith, Jr., and as the fulfillment of a sacred pledge to build a New Jerusalem. The Temple became the unchallenged center of Nauvoo. Baptisms for the dead were conducted as its walls rose. In this ritual all Mormons were called upon to undergo vicarious baptism for long-dead relatives and friends to promote salvation through the Mormon faith.

This practice of remembrance of the dead, which first was initiated by Joseph Smith, Jr., served to dramatize the crises of bereavement and reorganization that the members experienced after Smith's own death in Nauvoo. While baptisms took place in the basement, wagons for the journey west were under construction in the second floor assembly room, so the Temple housed both rituals and activities linking past, present, and future (Hayden, 1976, p. 141).

In April 1847 an advance company called the Camp of Israel departed for the new frontier. Heading west, Brigham Young ignored the attractiveness of California and Oregon and led the Mormons to the arid Great Basin, the largest unsettled region on the continent. Here the regional environment demanded cooperative endeavor in irrigation and farming for survival; dissidents could not afford to lose access to land and, more important, water. The Temple, which had been the focal point of communal life in Nauvoo, now shared priority with irrigation ditches, fences, and town centers.

A highly developed level of organization combined with experienced and dedicated leaders provided Brigham Young with the support for the long, hard trip to the Great Salt Lake. He personally led the crossing of more than ten thousand people into the Great Basin. It was this experience that solidified the organizational techniques that were used to help colonize the rest of the Great Basin at a later time. In the end, the journey was made by sixty thousand people who were willing to do so mainly for the sake of their faith. "The trip across the plains was more important as a unifier . . . than as a trial by hardship" (Meinig, 1965, p. 197).

The company led by Brigham Young was made up of 148 people. Young implemented the same organization plan used by Smith when he led an unsuccessful Zion Camp expedition in 1834. The mission of the Camp of Israel was to find the promised land and to explore the country while doing so. They made detailed maps, built ferries, and prepared the route for others to follow. The first group reached the Salt Lake Valley in July 1847, and the next expedition arrived in September of that same year.

The companies were tightly organized. Families were grouped into clusters of hundreds; these were subdivided into groups of fifty and further subdivided into groups of ten. Each of the smaller groups of ten had a captain appointed by the church who was responsible for each family and wagon under his authority. The captain had the duty of enforcing the rules of when to rise, pray, eat, sleep, and the like. It is no accident that Mormon movement west has been called "the best organized movement of people in American history" (Arrington, 1966, p. 101).

Scouting parties were always sent ahead, not only to find suitable campsites but to plow and plant plots of ground. These were harvested by the others coming later. Camps were established in Iowa at intervals along the trail. The main ones were Garden Grove, Mount Pisgah, Kanesville, and Winter Quarters (ibid., p. 19).

The settlement in the Salt Lake Valley was set up by using the same system of organization that was enforced on the journey. Resources were allocated equitably to assure group welfare, the Plat of the City of Zion was used to lay the groundwork of each city, and irrigation projects were undertaken immediately. Once the foundation for their new home was under way, the Mormons began a systematic exploration of the surrounding areas (Arrington et al., 1976, chap. 3).

Brigham Young's dream was to build an empire, for which he chose the name "Deseret." The name is used in the Book of Mormon to mean honeybee and to signify the industriousness of the Mormon clan. The search for new settlement sites was methodical. The church held the reins tightly, selecting the time, place, and specific people for the new colonies. In 1849 the Mormons petitioned the U.S. Congress to recognize Deseret as an independent state. Congress refused; instead it declared Utah a territory and appointed Young as its governor.

Salt Lake City was designated the capital of the territory. The Mormons wasted little time in settling the valleys to the north and south, forming a core area with the capital at its center. In the 1840s, settlements were planted in the Salt Lake, Weber, Utah, Tooele, Sanpete, and Carson valleys. Principal settlement zones in the 1850s were the Box Elder, Pahvant, Juab, Parowan, and Cache valleys, Las Vegas, Moab, Forts Supply and Bridger, and San Bernardino.

Ninety-six colonies were established in the 1850s; 150 towns were planted in the 1860s and 120 in the 1870s, including 100 outside Utah. In little more than a half a century the settlements grew to nearly five hundred. Around the periphery, forts and small settlements were established in keeping with Young's grand plan to dominate the whole area. His intention was to gain a foothold on the Pacific coast, to provide access to the "promised land" to those Europeans making their way across the ocean to join their fellow Saints (Allen and Leonard, 1976).

As the railroads came west, the boundaries of the Mormon kingdom of Deseret had to be negotiated with the U.S. government. The geographic

compromise was the state of Utah. The social concession was renounce-
ment of polygamy. Mormonism became a highly organized religion, concentrated in a particular region, supported by a successful economy that
ultimately was set firmly within the American mainstream, and using
the institution of tithing and the church organization to meet the social
objectives that capitalism could not deliver.

The United Order of Enoch

"Brigham Young believed strongly in social equality. Ideologically opposed to gradations of wealth and status among his people, he sought
instinctively for a scheme that would prevent aggrandizement of a few at
the expense of the many" (Arrington et al., 1976, p. 89). As settlement
stabilized in the 1850s, he first sought to revive the Law of Consecration
and Stewardship via the "consecration movement," an attempt to secure
a general consecration to the church of all property of all members. This
turned out to be a symbolic gesture, however, for few Saints were willing
to give up their property rights.

Committed to Mormon economic independence and self-sufficiency,
Young then turned to promoting cooperative mercantile and manufacturing associations, the most successful of which was the Brigham City
cooperative, established by Lorenzo Snow in 1864 (ibid., p. 79ff.). "The
Mormon enthusiasm for cooperation became so widespread . . . that
the name was given to virtually every new enterprise. . . . The small
settlements comprised intimate communities that entered collectively into
a larger community of communities, embracing the entire body of the
church. Cooperation for them meant the willing pursuit of any enterprise,
in whatever form that promised to benefit the whole body" (ibid., p. 109).

The success of cooperation, plus Brigham Young's continuing commitment to the Law of Consecration and Stewardship, came together "in
the wake of the Panic of 1873, which . . . suggested that the time was
right for a more radical reconstruction of the economic institutions of the
Latter Day Saint commonwealth. The depression hit first the mining industry. . . . Bank deposits dropped by one-third during the twelve months
following the panic. . . . Unemployment and economic stagnation were
the result" (ibid., pp. 136–37).

Young used the depression as an opportunity to make changes within
the economic institutions of the Mormon territory. His idea was to in-
sulate the community by concentrating all efforts on local industry. The
community would then provide its members with the opportunity to eat,
pray, and work together. At this point the Church asked for the cooperation of each member to participate in the "cooperative principle" and to
sever all economic ties to the outside world.

Beginning at St. George in southern Utah in 1874, Mormon villages were assigned the task of establishing a cooperative store that handled all commodities sold. These were placed under the auspices of the bishop. The profits derived from the cooperatives were used to support industries such as mills, herds, and shops. The manufacturing and merchandising industries were formed into a larger cooperative called a United Order. The United Order, unlike the co-ops, envisaged the pooling of labor as well as capital, to achieve the economies of both joint use of capital and specialization of labor. United Order communities were envisioned by Young to provide people with all of their needs and in addition provide a surplus that could be sold to the outside world.

Organized and proclaimed in mid-1874, the United Order spread rapidly. More than 230 United Order organizations were created, 200 in Utah, 13 in Idaho, 14 in Arizona, and the rest scattered, the majority founded in 1874 (Arrington et al., 1976, Appendix 9, provide a list of names and locations).

There were several different types. One type had common dining halls, the members wore identical clothes and shared equitably, and all work was assigned. Another type ran its farms, shops, and factories by a central cooperative, proceeds were divided according to one's contribution, and each family ate separately. Yet another type was a community that operated cooperative industries, dividends were paid to investors, and a small amount of private economic activity continued. Some of the settlements lasted for many years, but the majority survived only a few months. It is thought that most failed because the group members were taxed too highly in both material and emotional terms.

Brigham Young's vision of the United Order was of a " 'well-regulated family' . . . characterized by sharing of resources according to need, contributions of labor according to ability, and a concern for the welfare of others in the group that transcended selfishness and promoted harmony and unity" (Arrington et al., p. 203). The United Order community of Orderville, established in southern Utah, was considered to be a perfect example of such a family.

Orderville was started in 1875, with 150 people who had been part of a colony on the Muddy River established to provide a stopping place for immigrants. Orderville settlers were a select group of people who had been trained and had the necessary skills for the cooperation needed in starting an order. All property was deeded to a community corporation. Apartment-type houses were built in a fort arrangement, with a common dining hall in the center. The members operated farms, factories, shops, and dairies. Families worked without wages for the first two years and were provided with food and clothing from the corporation. The Orderville settlement remained viable until 1884. It grew to about seven hundred persons within the first five years. The church recommended it be disbanded when the settlement was weakened because many of its leaders had gone into hiding to avoid prosecution by the federal government for polygamy.

For the most part the United Order movement was soon over. "The Saints . . . seemed wary of efforts to alter dramatically their accustomed economic and social problems. The accomplishments of their cooperatives greatly complemented but did not supplement traditional economic forms" (ibid., p. 224). Brigham Young died in 1877, and within five years "the church had changed significantly its position in regard to the United Order and other forms of cooperative enterprise. Except for the institution of Zion's Board of Trade in 1879, the church increasingly gave its sanction to economic individualism restrained only by a proper respect for the rights and the welfare of others" (ibid., p. 311). Only under the stresses of the Great Depression did the church move aggressively once again to develop a new Church Security Program. In 1936 it established a chain of storehouses, redistributing surpluses through a church-organized Welfare Plan, and in 1938 created work through the establishment of Deseret Industries, reflecting the tendency, at critical junctures, to return to "grand designs for building greater economic cooperation among the Saints" (ibid., p. 360).

Mainstream Mormonism thus has experienced the same tensions between individual and collective values as has society as a whole. Joseph Smith, Jr.'s, initial expression of the Puritan ethic in the 1831 Law of Consecration and Stewardship, Brigham Young's reaction to the Crisis of 1873, the United Order, and the Welfare Plan formulated in response to the Great Depression, each has reflected the tendency of the church to adopt cooperative arrangements when the Mormon way of life is threatened by adverse economic conditions. "[S]o long as millennialism remains a part of official doctrine, the potential for sudden renewal of Mormon communitarianism remains. . . . The most devout Mormons still promise in solemn ceremonies to consecrate all they have to the church if called on to do so . . . it is possible to imagine that Mormon prophets, as in the past, might issue a call for the Saints to pool their reserves and cooperate to insure group survival" (ibid., p. 362).

Secessionist Groups

From the beginning there were schisms within Mormonism, and there were many secessionist groups (Shields, 1975/1982), but only one apostate organization achieved any size and importance: the Josephites, now known as the Reorganized Church of Jesus Christ of the Latter Day Saints.

In the Nauvoo era, Oliver Olney left and set up his headquarters at Squaw Grove, Illinois, and Gladden Bishop did likewise at Little Sioux, Iowa. The first schismatic group to organize after Brigham Young took over was led by Sidney Rigdon, excommunicated in September 1844 after attempting to take over the Mormon church following Joseph Smith, Jr.'s, assassination (Van Noord, 1989, p. 11). In 1845, Rigdon returned to Pittsburgh with a small number of followers. The group denounced polygamy and claimed that Joseph Smith, Jr., was a fallen prophet. By 1847 the group had dissolved, but Rigdon continued to try to rally support for thirty years. Later, the Bickertonites were formed out of Rigdon's Pittsburgh group. Neither group ever reached a size of any consequence. In 1849, Alpheus Cutler left Nauvoo and established the True Church of Jesus Christ at Manti, Iowa. After his death, his successors established the town of Clitherall, Minnesota, where they were unsuccessful in implementing the communal United Order.

The Strangites, led by James Jesse Strang, were one of the most important of the splinter communities. "Only the prophet-pretender . . . Strang possessed both the intellectual brilliance and organizational talent to mount a serious and sustained challenge to Brigham Young" (Foster, 1981, p. 190). Like Sidney Rigdon, Strang attempted to assume leadership of the Mormon hierarchy after Joseph Smith, Jr.'s, assassination; like Rigdon, he was excommunicated as Brigham Young took control (Van Noord, 1988, p. 10). Soon afterward Strang claimed that he had been visited by an angel who had directed him to the Wisconsin backwoods, where he discovered the "Rajah Manchou" plates. He had, he said, been designated the next prophet, and Voree, Wisconsin, was to be the next gathering place. Five hundred families joined the Voree community, including several apostles who had lost their standing in the Nauvoo church. As the Mormon trek west was organized and begun, Strang worked to divert support from their enterprise. After having himself designated "imperial primate" at Voree, he headed east, doing battle with the Brighamites at each stop (Van Noord, 1988, pp. 51ff.), claiming that he had a letter from the Smith family designating Strang as Smith's successor.

He returned to internal dissension and schism at Voree and shortly thereafter relocated his group to Beaver Island, the largest island in Lake Michigan. There he founded the "Kingdom of St. James" according to the principles of the Law of Consecration and Stewardship. By the end of 1848 the Kingdom had some 150 citizens, half from Voree (Van Noord, pp. 76ff.). As more residents were attracted from Voree, however, the idea of communal association quietly vanished, and a social organization centering on plural marriage emerged. Strang claimed new revelations and that he had translated the Plates of Laban on which his new Book of Law was based. On 8 July 1850 he had himself crowned king of Beaver Island (ibid., pp. 105ff.). Mormon–Gentile problems soon erupted into violence on the island, however, and in 1851, President Millard Fillmore moved against the Mormons; but after a tumultuous trial in Detroit, Strang and his associates were acquitted. The Gentile families on Beaver Island left, as did a number of apostates. By 1852 the Strangite community numbered some five hundred. But turmoil continued, and Strang was shot by rebellious followers in June 1856. Gentile posses roamed Beaver Island, robbing and expelling the Strangites. The Strangite church did survive at Voree, and one Strangite group subsequently made its way to New Mexico.

Before the Mormons left Nauvoo, Strang and Rigdon were the only ones to offer an organized alternative to those Mormons who did not want to follow Brigham Young. Subsequently, several other groups emerged. In 1847 a group of 150 Mormons settled in Burnett County, Texas, in a community named Zodiac. Their leader, Lyman Wight, had been a member of the community at Independence. He left the main settlement because he refused to acknowledge the leadership of Brigham Young. Only Lyman Wright and his son practiced polygamy. The group set up a gristmill, a school, and a small temple on the Pedernales River. In 1853 the mill was destroyed by flood, causing the gathering to look for other sites. They moved through several counties in Texas, of which Mountain Valley on the Medina River was the last. After Wright's death the community disbanded, most of his followers joining the Reorganized Mormons in Missouri by 1858.

In 1853 the community of Preparation was founded in southern Iowa by Charles B. Thompson and a group of fifty to sixty families who had broken away from the westward movement. Thompson held complete ownership of property, and in addition he imposed tithing on the members. When the settlers obtained a court order against Thompson to divide the property, he left. The community disbanded in 1858.

Another small Mormon sect was formed by Boston actor George Adams. Adams had attempted to introduce polygamy to Boston in 1844 and had been one of the principal followers of Strang. His Church of the Messiah, as it was called, was formed in 1861. Adams became a laughing-stock when he attempted to move the group to Palestine in 1865.

In 1867, William W. Davis, a Welsh mystic, took forty schismatic Mormons to Washington state to found a Kingdom of Heaven. New members were recruited from San Francisco, and the community grew to seventy. When Davis's sons (the elder known as the "Walla Walla Jones") died of diphtheria, the community ended.

The Reorganized Movement is the most significant of the schismatic Mormon groups. This movement began in Wisconsin with a small band of families that opposed the practice of polygamy. The band, led by Jason Briggs, denounced the authority of Brigham Young as president. At first, Briggs and his followers joined Strang at Voree. However, they soon rejected Strang's doctrines and moved to a community led by William Smith (brother of Joseph). Smith and his group, like the Voree members, also practiced polygamy, and once again Briggs and his band moved on.

The Briggs group became convinced that the prophet's oldest son, Joseph Smith III, was the true heir to his father's seat. Their movement became known as the Josephites. They were joined by several other groups seeking an alternative to the leadership of Brigham Young. The Josephites held their first conference on 12 June 1852. Jason Briggs was elected interim president until the nineteen-year-old son of Smith was ready to take over; he did so in 1860.

The Reorganized Church of Jesus Christ of the Latter Day Saints, as it was officially named, professes to reject the entire Nauvoo experience. They define their theology within the conservative limits of Joseph Smith, Jr.'s, earlier days. It is said to be a stance between standard Protestantism and Utah Mormonism. They do not believe in polygamy, the plurality of gods, baptism of the dead, secret rituals, sealings, and celestial marriages. Unlike the main Mormon Church their temples are open to the public. The Reorganized group does, however, have several things in common with Utah. They both have a president and twelve apostles, they rely on the nonsalaried services of elders and priests, and they accept the Book of Mormon as divinely inspired through the prophet Joseph Smith.

Today the Reorganized Mormons claim 250,000 members, principally in the Midwest. Their headquarters are in Independence, Missouri. The relationship between this group and the Salt Lake City church is described as "polite but not warm." They base their identity on early Mormon and modern ecumenical Christian principles. They did not build utopian communities, although there were active efforts to introduce the United Order of Enoch into the Reorganized Church, as well as into a number of the other splinter groups.

The Fundamentalists

After the Civil War was over, the federal government put much of its energy into trying to gain control of the Mormon territory. Legislation was passed against plural marriage. Twelve hundred Mormon leaders were jailed on polygamy charges. Attempts were made to disincorporate the church in 1886. After a long struggle, the Mormon church renounced plural marriage in its Manifesto of 1890, one of the concessions made in order to attain the statehood they so wanted.

Just as the acceptance of polygamy had caused schisms within the Mormon community, the move to dissolve plural marriages created a split. The Fundamentalists believed that in 1886, four years before the Manifesto, then Mormon president John Taylor had dictated from his deathbed that the practice of polygamy be continued at all cost.

Reliable information is difficult to obtain concerning the Fundamentalists today because they are spread out over a large area and because they choose to remain hidden. There are at least five groups, the largest of which, the United Effort Order, is headquartered at Short Creek, Arizona. Many have migrated to isolated areas of Mexico, Arizona, and California. It is estimated that there may be some thirty thousand polygamists, one-third in the United Effort Order. Local governments are slow to prosecute them because of the welfare burden the families would present to their neighbors, as the state of Arizona discovered in 1953 when they raided Short Creek and arrested the men.

Whereas other schismatic groups were not a problem to the main congregation of Mormons, the Fundamentalists are, because they prolong the association in the public's mind between polygamy and Mormonism and because of the continuing violence within and among the groups. They are denounced vehemently by Salt Lake City as an embarrassment to the modern church, which has made itself acceptable to national and international society, its members among the most successful of Americans.

The Fourierist Outbreak

The Crisis of 1837, the worst depression experienced by the new republic to that date, produced widespread unemployment and led the country into the deep deflationary depression of the 1840s. The crash followed hard on the heels of speculative fervor that "after devouring its rations, is made to prey upon itself." (John Humphrey Noyes, *The Perfectionist*, 31 Aug. 1835, cited in Barkun, 1986, p. 121). Economic hardship and social frustration fed an upsurge of millenarian fears and expectations that appealed especially to the rural and the remote. Predictions of the Second Coming were widely voiced by a broad range of Americans. Among the intelligentsia, already exposed to Robert Owen's secular presocialism, there was widespread interest in social reform, and a limited attempt was made to develop new Owenite communities (Chapter 5). More attention was paid to the ideas of Charles Fourier, however, largely as a consequence of the missionary work of Albert Brisbane who, responding to the Crisis of 1837, "began his propaganda campaign in 1837 and by 1839 had managed to acquire a strong following, mainly in the populated areas of New York and Pennsylvania. When Brisbane's version of Fourier's ideas was published in 1840 as a book, *The Social Destiny of Man*, it soon became evident that this book fell on fertile ground and had enormous impact on the period" (Oved, 1988, p. 130). "[H]is energetic and persistent propagandizing—boosted immeasurably by Horace Greeley of the *New York Tribune*—created a burst of Fourierist activity in the northern states almost overnight" (Guarneri, 1991, p. 2; Guarneri's book is the definitive study of Fourierism in America).

Thirty Fourierist communities were established in the years 1841–47 (Fig. 20) across a broad belt of the northeast (Fig. 21), following the configurations of what became the American manufacturing belt. "Fourierist ideologues insisted that they were motivated by fears that 'industrial

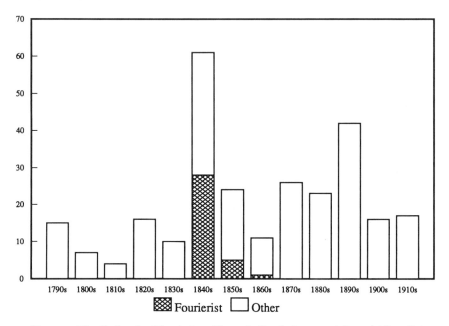

Figure 20. The Outbreak of Fourierism. The main Fourierist surge followed Albert Brisbane's popularization of Fourier's ideas in the aftermath of the Crisis of 1837, as the economy slid into the depression of the 1840s.

feudalism' was arising in existing cities and towns, not by any anxiety concerning the future of the unsettled West" (Guarneri, 1991, p. 4). "Fourierism envisaged a centuries-long reign of love in humanity's future; the social utopia created by phalanxes became identical in Fourierist minds to the millenial kingdom. . . . Lectures and tracts cast the Fourierists as prophets heralding a New Jerusalem where human instincts would be guided by cooperative harmony and become truly divine" (ibid., p. 74). Yet just as quickly as they were created, the Fourierist communes vanished (Guarneri talks of the "utopian boom and bust"), as did a subsequent cluster of five communities established athwart the Crisis of 1857 (see Table 3).

Who was Fourier? What was Fourierism? Charles Fourier was born in Besançon, France, in 1777, son of a prosperous cloth merchant who, in his will, specified that Charles was to enter the world of commerce by age twenty or forfeit 80,000 livres. Charles grew up in the turmoil of the French Revolution, brought up by a mother who punished him daily for minor misdemeanors. Self-educated and anti-intellectual, he lost his property by confiscation in the siege of Lyon, and at age twenty-seven he became a traveling salesman.

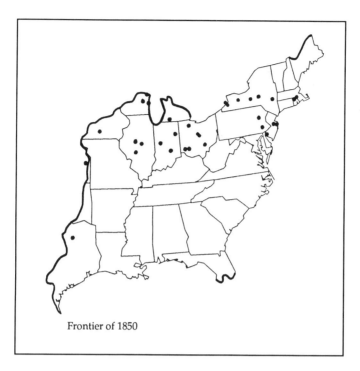

Frontier of 1850

Figure 21. Locations of the Fourierist Communes. Again, the sharp North–South regional difference seen in earlier maps is evident. As with the Owenite communities, the phalanxes were not built in frontier locations but were reactions to early capitalism in crisis.

Already, at age nineteen, he had shown a lively interest in architecture, writing to the Bordeaux city government about how the city should be planned. He was concerned less with physical planning than with the social consequences of planned activity: reductions in crowding and in the risks of fire and disease. These notions later were embodied into his concept of the Phalanx.

He gradually came to believe that a natural social order exists corresponding to Newton's ordering of the physical universe, that both types of order have evolved in eight ascending periods, and that in Harmony, the highest stage, man's emotions could be freely expressed. He set alongside this a belief that competition in commerce was generally dishonest, placing greater misery on the poor, who had to pay for the inefficiencies of industry. He suggested that individuals' associations with commerce could be placed on a foundation of honesty and truth by the use of "algebraic" methods and that trade associations could be developed to weed

Table 3

Community	Started	Ended
Brook Farm, Mass.	1841	1847
Marlborough Association, Ohio	1841	1845
Social Reform Unity, Ohio	1842	1843
Hopedale Community, Mass.	1842	1867
Northampton Association, Mass.	1842	1846
Jefferson County Industrial Association, N.Y.	1843	1844
Sylvania Association, Pa.	1843	1845
Morehouse Union, N.Y.	1843	1844
Bureau County Phalanx, Ill.	1843	1844
North American Phalanx, N.J.	1843	1856
Fruitlands, N.Y.	1843	1844
Lagrange Phalanx, Ind.	1844	1846
Sodus Bay Phalanx, N.Y.	1844	1846
Bloomfield Union Association, N.Y.	1844	1846
Leroysville Phalanx, Pa.	1844	1844
Ohio Phalanx, Ohio	1844	1845
Alphadelphia Phalanx, Mich.	1844	1845
Clarkson Association, N.Y.	1844	1845
Mixville Association, N.Y.	1844	1845
Ontario Union, N.Y.	1844	1845
Clermont Phalanx, Ohio	1844	1846
Trumball Phalanx, Ohio	1844	1848
Wisconsin Phalanx, Wis.	1844	1850
Iowa Pioneer Phalanx, Iowa	1844	1845
Philadelphia Industrial Association, Ind.	1845	1847
Integral Phalanx, Ill.	1845	1846
Canton Phalanx, Ill.	1845	1845
Columbian Phalanx, Ohio	1845	1845
Spring Farm Phalanx, Wis.	1846	1848
Pigeon River Colony, Wis.	1846	1847
Utopia (Trialville), Ohio	1847	1858
Raritan Bay Union, N.J.	1853	1858
La Réunion, Tex.	1853	1859
Memnonia Institute, Ohio	1856	1857
Union Grove, Minn.	1856	1858
Fourier Phalanx, Ind.	1858	1858
Kansas Cooperative Farm, Kans.	1870	1884

out the inefficient and corrupt. He expressed views on sexual repression that anticipated Freud and criticisms of capitalism that preceded Marx and Engels, who said his theories had "a vein of true poetry" (quoted in Sowell, 1985, p. 25). His views on the role of women are surprisingly modern: "social progress occur[s] in accordance with the progress women make towards freedom, and the social order becomes decadent in accordance with the reduction of women's privileges is the general principle of all social progress" (cited in Spencer, 1981, p. 57).

Throughout his life, he evidenced a pseudoscientific attachment to numerology: there were seven different scourges of civilization, thirty-six different types of bankruptcy, and so on. Fourier believed that it was not the duty of mankind to work for the sake of existence. Rather, work should be a pleasant experience, appeal to the senses, and become an integral part of the many pleasures that mankind would labor for. Politics, he wrote, should "find a new social order that insures the poorest members of the working class sufficient well-being to make them constantly and passionately prefer their work to idleness and brigandage to which they now aspire" (cited in Beecher and Bienvenu, 1971, p. 31).

He published his *Théorie des quatre mouvements et des destinées générales* in 1808, elaborated in 1819 by *Le nouveau monde amoureux* and in 1827 by *Le nouveau monde industriel et sociétaire*. In these works he spelled out his view that human society is motivated by twelve basic passions: five sensuous (sight, sound, smell, touch, and taste), four affective (friendship, love, family, and ambition), and three distributive ("cabalist," seeking intrigue; "butterfly," seeking variety; and "composite," seeking synthesis). He envisioned a world where love and work are the occupations of communities called Phalanxes.

He argued that there were eight stages of history. His own, the stage of "civilization," was dominated by individualism and capitalism. It was to be followed by the stages of Guarantism, Simple Association, and Compound Association, or Harmony, the stage reminiscent of Maslowian self-actualization in which humans could freely indulge in the twelve passions. Harmony's Phalanxes, cooperative agricultural communities, would guarantee all citizens minimum incomes and satisfying sexual lives. Life in the Phalanx involved continual shifting of the members' social roles, eliminating conflicts between rich and poor and resulting in more equitable distribution of wealth than exists under capitalism. Such Phalanxes, he thought, could be introduced into any political system, even a monarchy.

A Phalanx was a six-thousand-acre, sixteen-hundred-person agricultural community centering on a principal building, the phalanstery: a structure with wings of dwellings linked by interior "galleries of association," destined to encourage spontaneous meetings and sexual relations or "passional attractions." Children and elderly people were to be housed away from the promiscuity of the galleries. There was to be communal dining and the best of heating, ventilation, and sanitation. In the surrounding landscape, fields, orchards, and gardens were to be laid out to permit a natural alternation of work and passional attraction

Fourier was not only a philosopher. He sought funding to put his ideas into practice, publishing a journal, *Le Phalanstère*, and attracting a number of disciples, including Victor Considérant and Clarsie Vigoreau. Considérant, a young graduate of the École Polytechnique, developed the first plans for a phalanstery, massive and Versailles-like. Finally, an experimental Phalanx was established near Condé-sur-Vesgre in 1832 but soon failed. Fourier was infuriated, saying that "the whole scheme was ill-conceived is not in doubt; the architect was clearly either incompetent or a lunatic: the most luxurious part of the buildings was the pigsty, except that no provision for an entrance had been made" (quoted in Spencer, 1981, p. 17). This was the closest he came to putting his plans in action. He died 10 October 1837, soon after the panic that induced formation of a multiplicity of experimental Phalanxes in the United States.

The Panic of 1837 brought the era of Jacksonian prosperity to an end. As specie became unavailable in exchange for bank notes, nine-tenths of all of the factories in the eastern states were said to be closed. A secondary collapse drove the nation into depression. Between 1837 and 1843 prices fell by 42 percent (by comparison, between 1929 and 1933 they only fell 31 percent). In the resulting distress, some turned to William Miller and his predictions of the Second Coming in 1844. Others tried to reestablish utopian havens along Owenite principles. That many were attracted by Fourier's notions was largely due to the efforts of Albert Brisbane.

Brisbane was the son of a wealthy Burned-Over District land speculator who studied with Fourier during an extended European tour in 1833–34. He arrived back in the United States in 1834 and is believed to have spent time speculating in land, hoping to make money for the Fourierist cause. But "the Panic of 1837 burst Brisbane's bubble" (Guarneri, 1991, p. 31). As the panic occurred, he began to spread Fourier's message in an aggressive propaganda campaign. By 1839 he had acquired a strong East Coast urban following, so his version of Fourier's ideas, published in 1840 as *The Social Destiny of Man, or Association and Reorganization of Industry*, had a ready audience and a major impact.

He did not simply translate Fourier but "adapted Fourierism to the American mentality" (Oved, 1988, p. 130). The principal proposals were laid out as a simple plan of action, free of Fourier's fantasies and purged of his unacceptable ideas about women, marriage, and morals. A key idea was that work leads to riches; the Fourierist addition was the right to work for an equitable share. He emphasized the notion of "attractive work" that eliminated concentration of wealth in the hands of the capitalists and impoverishment of the majority. Association of work and capital could eliminate this inequality.

The right to work and to receive an equitable share of the product of that work was broadly appealing and was the basis of Fourierist associations. Brisbane established the Agricultural-Industrial Association to advance the cause. "His ideas were absorbed by the many who had lost their social standing and sense of security and by intellectuals who were searching for solutions for the social ills" (Oved, 1988, p. 131). Horace Greeley, editor of the *New York Tribune*, gave Brisbane the opportunity to lay out the principles of Association before the public in a subsidized front-page column in the newspaper, beginning in March 1842. His ideas quickly took hold across the Northeast. He intrigued New England Transcendentalists such as George Ripley and William Henry Channing, already involved in building an idealistic community at Brook Farm. He reached urban businessmen and artisans, as well as rural farmers who read the *Tribune*'s lengthy agricultural columns. In 1843 and 1844 the Boston and Philadelphia Unions of Associationists were meeting; by 1846 they had formed a national organization. He was opposed by conservative politicians and churchmen. Hayden (1976) cites Horace Greenough's denouncements of the "Furyites" and of the regularity of life in a planned community: "I hate thy straight lines, and thy arrangements for the elbows, and thy lid that fits over all, with the screws ready in thy hand. . . . The measure which thou hast scientifically taken of me is my measure now, perhaps . . . but I feel that I am destined to outgrow thy feet and inches hereafter" (pp. 155–56).

In October 1842, Brisbane announced in the *Tribune* that he wanted contributions to finance the establishment of an experimental community. In 1843 he published *A Concise Exposition of the Doctrine of Association, or Plan for the Re-organization of Society*, in which he defined his tactics: "The whole question of effecting a Social Reform may be reduced to the establishment of one Association, which will serve as a model for, and induce the rapid establishment of others" (pp. 72–74).

He realized that capital and labor had to be sufficient to establish a community and proposed that the community have no fewer than four hundred participants, as well as agreeing that shareholders could be from outside the community. The initial funding for the community would require $400,000 to $500,000, shares being valued at $1,000 each. By 1843 the *Tribune* reported "that no less than a dozen associations were in various stages of settling" (Oved, 1988, p. 132). The earliest associations were organized near major urban centers. A new independent journal, the *Phalanx*, appeared in 1843 to carry the message forward. Brisbane returned to France to study with Fourier's disciples there.

Several communal settlements that already existed in Massachusetts (Brook Farm, the Hopedale Community, and the Northampton Association) became early Fourierist ventures when they adopted Fourierist theories. Brisbane reported on them in the *Phalanx* in 1843. Hopedale had been organized as a community of "Practical Christians" by ex-Universalist minister Adin Ballou and later formed itself into a Fourierist joint-stock association. It had an offshoot at Union Grove, Minnesota. Northampton originated in a silk company and by 1835 was a communal secular industrial enterprise noted for the participation of freed black slaves. But the community that attracted the most attention was Brook Farm, largely because its Transcendentalist founders were adept at public relations. Both Hopedale and Brook Farm are discussed in Chapter 8.

The most successful of the Fourierist communities was the North American Phalanx (1843–56) in Monmouth County, New Jersey. Hayden (1976) notes that the sixty founders, mainly businessmen and professionals, came from Albany, New York. Most of them were feeling the economic squeeze following the Panic of 1837, for their collective resources amounted only to about $7,000, which they used as the down payment and working capital for a 673-acre farm in Colt's Neck, New Jersey. They adopted Brisbane's hypothetical name, North American Phalanx, before Brisbane realized the limits of their finances; and although he protested, they would not relinquish it. Reluctantly, he and the Fourierists centered in New York gave the group from Albany their provisional support, although at some future date they hoped to establish a larger and more "scientific" experimental community. Because of the publicity surrounding the name, and eventually because the Phalanx existed for thirteen years, John Humphrey Noyes (1870), in his *History of American Socialisms*, judged that "this was the test experiment on which Fourierism practically staked its all in this country" (p. 449).

The North American Phalanx had only 125 to 150 members during its thirteen-year existence yet could have supported over one thousand. It was more secular in outlook than other Fourierist communities, such as Hopedale. With the disintegration of Brook Farm, the North American Phalanx became the center for the Fourierist movement.

The community built a phalanstery that was nearly 150 feet in length, had separate apartments of three rooms each, and bachelors' quarters. The large dining hall could seat as many as two hundred people. There were ongoing visits by nonmembers and individuals of other organizations, both secular and religious, including Robert Owen, Frederika Bremer, and George Ripley. Bestor argues that an intricate web of personal relationships existed among the phalanxes. Members would transfer from one community to another, and cross-fertilization of ideas and experiences provided a bridge across the United States (Bestor, 1950, p. 57; Guarneri, 1991, p. 416).

Fourier's view on equality of the sexes was very much a part of the North American Phalanx. Bremer "found [women] to be intensely involved in community affairs, work, and social activities" (Oved, 1988,

p. 155). In 1849 the fashion of "bloomers" was adopted beneath "daringly short" skirts.

The Phalanx wrote a new constitution in 1848 under guidelines that more closely followed Fourierist principles. They changed and improved the work system of "series" and shared considerable success. The products of agriculture were sent to nearby cities, principally New York, and were considered to be of high quality. There were active educational and cultural programs. At their apex in 1852 they were contented and prosperous.

The troubles began in 1853 with the arrival of religious missionaries. One group of intellectuals left to establish the Raritan Bay Union, centered on an educational institution for surrounding areas. They were joined by a group that had been at the bottom of the Phalanx's pay scale, creating a gap in the system of production. In 1854 the flour mills burned, and the insurance company went bankrupt, leaving them with a debt of $30,000. Rather than borrow, the members decided to sell.

Many other Phalanxes were started in New York, Ohio, Illinois, Indiana, and Wisconsin in the years 1843–46. Of these, only the Wisconsin Phalanx was in existence in 1850. It had lasted six years and actually returned a profit to its members when it was dissolved. Many of the Phalanxes were too small and lacked tight organization. Most were barely able to raise the capital needed to acquire the land, and they were settled by urban idealists lacking the experience necessary to make the farms, workshops, and mills work. It is characteristic of such idealists that they also lacked the focused commitment to goals that made the more disciplined religious experiments work. The spiritual authority of a charismatic leader was inconsistent with the values of utopian socialism. The heterogeneity of the Fourierist settlements, combined with a lack of planning and preparation, led to dissolution of most within a couple of years.

The proponents of phalansterian association comprised the cast of a stock political melodrama: an eccentric genius; sycophantic, ambitious lieutenants; sympathetic, well-to-do intellectual supporters; idealistic, committed recruits. Fourier provided detailed instructions for the design of an ideal community, but his architect created fantastical illustrations in a rather different spirit. Failing to perceive this difference, the patrons of Fourierism in America accepted the architect's grandiose blueprint, while the members of experimental communities took a more practical view. At the North American Phalanx, members built a viable communal dwelling but were criticized because it fell short of their patrons' conception of what a phalanstery should look like. Conflicts over authoritative and participatory processes of design ranged the patrons against the members; struggles over communal and private territory contributed to the schism. When the patrons shifted their support to other experiments favoring authority, privacy, and uniqueness, the members gave in to bitter recriminations about the economic interests which no amount of "passional attraction" could eradicate. (Hayden, 1976, p. 149)

The Fourierist outbreak, a reaction to the Crisis of 1837 and the deflationary depression of the early 1840s, lasted no longer than the depression itself. In contrast to other communal experiments the Fourierists' critique of American social problems had been sociological rather than moralistic. Rather than retreating from modernization, they sought to exploit the techniques of the industrial revolution for group rather than individual benefit. And they committed themselves to the notion of universal reform rather than communal withdrawal (Guarneri, 1991, p. 8). Yet as a new era of growth asserted itself, enthusiasm for the security and equality of the communes gave way once more to the pursuit of individual gain. "As the depression of the early 1840s lifted and the business cycle began its climb, opportunities for employment increased, and workers who had flocked to phalanxes found new options for mobility and security" (ibid., p. 274). Disenchantment was reinforced by the defeat of utopian socialism in France following the revolution of 1848 that America's Fourierists had hailed and some had rushed to join. Brisbane returned to America chastened, switching his interests from revolutionary reform to cooperation. Others made their peace with capitalism.

By 1850 the nation's recovery from the depression of the 1840s was complete, and the economy was in high gear. . . .These developments belied the Associationists' gloomy predictions of an "industrial feudalism." . . . Especially when compared with an Old World that had sunk back into despotism and social stratification after its revolutions failed, the United States seemed a political and economic miracle, even to those who had been its severest critics five years earlier . . . the Fourierist accommodation with capitalism in the 1850s was especially easy because . . . [of] its acceptance of the pursuit of wealth, and its openness to gradualism. (ibid., pp. 342–44)

Oneida's Perfectionists and the New England Transcendentalists

The Fourierist utopias were not the only products of the deflationary depression that afflicted the 1840s. In the Burned-Over District yet another concept of utopian life emerged at John Humphrey Noyes's perfectionist community at Oneida, New York, after germinating in Putney, Vermont. Meanwhile, the intellectualizers of evangelical Unitarianism, the New England Transcendentalists, attempted to give material expression to their interest in social reform by establishing communal settlements at Brook Farm and Fruitlands in Massachusetts, and former Universalist preacher Adin Ballou founded the Hopedale community as an experiment in "Practical Christianity." Perfectionism and Transcendentalism offer contrasting glimpses into ideology, organization, and success. Oneida was the more successful communal experiment, but it ended in 1880 when the members formed a joint-stock company and rejoined the economic mainstream on the mainstream's own terms. Brook Farm and Fruitlands quickly failed, their ideas of the preeminence of the individual inconsistent with the needs of communal organization, but Transcendentalism had a lasting effect via influential thinkers from Emerson and Thoreau to Pragmatists such as William James and John Dewey, via the movement of the church into social reform, and via Eastern religions and Theosophy, forerunners of the New Age philosophies that emerged after 1960.

The Perfectionists at Oneida

The Oneida concept was uniquely a product of founder John Humphrey Noyes's personality and experiences (Parker, 1935/1973; Carden, 1969; Foster, 1981), a characteristic that reappears in the multiplicity of other communities, both secular and religious, that were developed in impulses from 1850 to 1910 that coincided with periods of economic crisis.

John Humphrey Noyes was born in Brattleboro, Vermont, in 1811, of respectable Yankee heritage. Both of his parents' families were politically active. His father sat in Congress for Vermont. His cousin, Rutherford B. Hayes, was elected nineteenth president of the United States in 1876. His mother was religious, and as the result of an intense spiritual experience during her fourth pregnancy, she believed the child she would soon bear had been chosen by God to carry out a predetermined purpose.

John was a moody, sensitive child who struggled to gain self-esteem and could not tolerate self-confidence and self-sufficiency in others. Ironically, he despised in others the very characteristics he so longed for himself. Journal entries indicate continual struggles with shame and self-consciousness as he wrestled with society's expectations for proper behavior.

Upon graduation from college, Noyes decided to study law. He experienced difficulty as a result of the intense competitiveness, and his first day in court brought severe criticisms from his instructor. Soon he moved back home to Putney, where he had plans to continue his study of law at the prestigious firm of one of his uncles. It was 1831. His mother urged him to attend a revival meeting being held in Putney by Charles Grandison Finney, a prominent evangelist. He experienced a very emotional conversion a few days later and believed he had finally found the key to solving the inner conflicts that troubled him. His plans to study law were abandoned, and in 1832 he moved to Yale Theological Seminary.

He soon discovered that the inner conflicts he suffered before his conversion now were translated to the spiritual realm. During his first year in seminary there were many confrontations with a faculty whose traditional theology clashed with Noyes's recently acquired version of truth. In his view the Second Advent of Christ took place with the destruction of the Temple in 70 A.D., and the millennium was imminent. He rejected the notions of original sin and man's inability to save himself but struggled to find the path to salvation. On the advice of a sympathetic professor, Nathaniel W. Taylor, he joined a church with liberal interpretations of the Bible. Combining heresy with convention, he developed a notion of "perfection" in which, if most attitudes and motivations were right, one's actions would follow a path acceptable to God—the path to salvation (Foster, 1981, p. 77). He announced his intellectual breakthrough in 1834, declaring that he was "perfect." The declaration was misconstrued and he was promptly dismissed from the seminary for preaching the necessity of "perfect holiness."

Even greater controversy arose with the unintended publication in 1837 of a letter detailing his thoughts on sex and marriage (the key paragraph appears in Foster, 1981, p. 81). He explained that there would be no marriage in heaven; therefore, sexual relations should not be restrained in a society of sanctified believers: "When the will of God is done on earth, as it is in heaven, there will be no marriage. The marriage supper of the Lamb is a feast at which every dish is free to every guest." The resulting furor caused Noyes to write and preach with increased intensity, for he saw a responsibility to educate the public. His new ideas were condemned even by the liberals, and he found himself ostracized from the very group responsible for his spiritual awakening. If Noyes's perfectionism was to survive, it required severance from the parent denomination. Noyes's efforts shifted from society as a whole—the macrocosm—to a small, close-knit group of followers, including his wife, Harriet Holton, whom he married in 1838, one of his two brothers, and his sisters and their husbands—a perfectionist community in microcosm.

This small community came together in Putney after 1838, complementing the nucleus of the Putney Bible School that he had founded in 1836. The group sought a communal life-style appropriate to their theology of perfectionism. Noyes led Bible studies each day, and the group read *The Harbinger*, a Fourierist journal published at Brook Farm, and any other communitarian publications they could secure. Noyes published a succession of periodicals to spread the word: the *Witness*, the *Perfectionist* (later the *Perfectionist and Theocratic Watchman*), and the *Spiritual Magazine*.

The Perfectionists gave the name "Bible Communism" to their new philosophy. They asserted belief in common ownership of property and developed the ideas that led to two communal practices when they later moved to Oneida: "mutual criticism" and "complex marriage." Mutual criticism required a member to appear before a committee of older members, who evaluated his or her personal strengths and weaknesses. Occasionally, a person was called before the whole membership for criticism. It was thought that collective insight could eliminate problematic attitudes and behavior; mutual criticism assured conformity to the community's goals through consistency of belief and practice.

Complex marriage derived from Noyes's prediction that in heaven there would be no marriage but a divine "feast" at which every "dish" is free to every guest. While he admired the Shakers, complex marriage would, he thought, solve the problems that abstinence and celibacy created. All members believed themselves united in a group marriage. Men and women could seek each other's company to engage in *coitus reservatus* (intercourse without ejaculation), but individuals were encouraged to "keep in circulation" and avoid exclusive personal attachments that might overshadow group feeling. There should, Noyes thought, be controlled spiritual sharing of sexual partners.

When the members of the Perfectionist community began to test their radical ideas by living communally and practicing complex marriage, their neighbors ran them out of Putney. Groups of citizens banded together to "cleanse" their community of the "immoral and unacceptable behavior." In 1847, Noyes was arrested for adultery and was advised to leave Putney along with his followers. The community disbanded.

By the end of 1848 members of the group gathered at Oneida, in the Burned-Over District of central New York State, where a few converts to Perfectionism owned farms. One donated twenty-three acres to the displaced community. The new arrivals purchased 160 acres of additional land to launch a model community. A branch commune was opened in Brooklyn, New York, in 1849 for publishing and business purposes, and in the next few years small branches were established in Wallingford, Connecticut; Newark, New Jersey; Putney and Cambridge, Vermont; and Manlius, New York, where some converts owned property. Eventually, all of these communities were disbanded, except for Wallingford, which lasted as long as Oneida itself. Oneida was always the center of the Perfectionists' activities, flourishing for almost forty years, the model estate they hoped would enshrine communism and complex marriage.

Like Putney, the social experiment at Oneida had three central principles: complex marriage, male continence, and mutual criticism. Members were required to gain permission from a third party before participating in sexual relations and were forbidden from forming long-term attachments. Only the most spiritual male members were allowed to father children. As a result, men were required to assume the responsibility for birth control by learning the discipline of *coitus reservatus*. These behavioral requirements were achieved through the process of mutual criticism and training. Members were individually reviewed before Noyes and other group members, who publicly criticized the member's recent actions. Suggestions were made for improvement without creating an attitude of resentment. It was by this method that Noyes was able to maintain absolute control over the community. The success of the system can be gauged by the fact that from 1848 to 1869 there were only thirty-one births in a community of two hundred adults; of these only twelve were reported by the community to be unplanned. Under conditions of natural fertility with breast feeding, an adult woman would have borne a child every two years. If Oneida had been Hutterite (Chapter 10), at least five hundred children would have been born.

Within a few months of its founding, Oneida grew to fifty members who were dedicated to the communal life-style. Those who joined were required to pay off all debts and donate their private property to Oneida upon acceptance of the community's doctrine and beliefs. For a while, membership was open to anyone who wanted to join. Total membership soon reached 250 but then was restricted due to limited resources.

Although the members considered Oneida their new Promised Land, external resentment and pressures soon threatened to break up the community. Charges were brought, with Oneida's unorthodox sexual practices the central issue. A grueling trial resulted, and after numerous testimonies the court finally concluded that Oneida was a closed society whose sexual practices were privately conducted among consenting members. The decision helped establish Oneida as a viable entity within a land of extreme diversity.

All members lived under one roof at the common structure called Mansion House. Older members had separate bedrooms. Younger members slept two to a room. Babies were cared for by their mothers until they were weaned. They were then placed during the day in the infants' department of the Children's Wing of Mansion House. Between three and five years of age, they were separated from their mothers, even at night, and were cared for by elected members of the community. Thus, even the mother/child relationship soon gave way to communalism.

The work ethic was strong. With few class distinctions, positions of honor theoretically were suppressed, although according to a law of "ascending fellowship" younger members were bound to follow the guidance of older ones in political as well as sexual matters. At the top of the pyramid was John Humphrey Noyes, who exercised unchallenged authority, personally introducing many girls and women to complex marriage and refusing to submit to mutual criticism. The New England custom of social enthusiasm was carried on as members worked in bees, such as quilting bees or strawberry-picking bees. After visitors from the outside society had left, there were even cleaning bees to rid the community of detrimental influences.

Women's roles were ambiguous. Men and women were allowed to assume roles normally associated with the other sex in theory. But despite rhetorical support for women's rights to equal jobs and education, as well as women's adoption of short hair and of bloomers under short dresses, they continued to dominate traditional women's work, light manufacturing, and community support. Men dominated in industry and in heavy farm work. And Noyes himself, with a few chosen aides, controlled ideological administration (Foster, 1981, p. 104, citing Marlyn H. Dalsimer's 1979 Ph.D. dissertation, New York University). Women did, however, participate in group criticism sessions and daily religious and business meetings.

Oneida began by aiming for self-sufficiency, as had the original settlement at Putney. However, the land could not meet the needs of the community. John Miller, one of the original Putney members and a gifted economist, saw that manufacturing could provide the necessary economic base. Oneida began to produce chairs, brooms, shoes, and bags. The economy was integrated with the outside world. Oneida's manufacturing became both innovative and highly profitable. Emphasis on inventions derived from two sources: pressure to find novel or technically ingenious products and the psychological need to believe that they were not only superior to the rest of the world but unique. The means that were developed to foster inventiveness among the members were a high level of education, group support for unusual ideas, and rotation of jobs to encourage recognition of analogous design problems.

Eventually, the Perfectionists built the community of their dreams with the profits from their business enterprises, only to find that the world could not be converted to Perfectionism by the establishment of a single working model of a Perfectionist utopia. Thousands of visitors came to Oneida to view the community, but most could not accept economic communism and group marriage. In 1867, Noyes began to publish *American Socialist*, calling to all of the nation's communes to unite in a new national movement. He then retired as leader at Oneida, and the younger members introduced "stirpiculture"—planned procreation—and the birthrate increased. Many women chose Noyes to father their children, and of the fifty-eight born during the experiment, nine were his. In 1870 he wrote his *History of American Socialisms*, designed "to help the study of Socialism by the inductive method." Later in the 1870s sanctimonious preachers launched crusades against the community, which was already threatened by internal struggles over Noyes's succession. In 1879 legal action under an immorality law was threatened, and Noyes fled to Canada. At his urging the Perfectionists then decided to abandon communism and group marriage. In 1880 they formed a joint-stock corporation to manage their business enterprises and officially rejoined the larger society on that society's terms. They also stopped investing in the *American Socialist*. Many of the early factories closed, replaced by Oneida Silverware. The changes were none too soon. In 1881, Charles Guiteau, who had grown up in Oneida but had left fifteen years earlier, assassinated President Garfield.

The New England Transcendentalists

"Between 1841 and 1844—the depths of the depression generated by the Panic of 1837—Brook Farm emerged out of New England Unitarianism, Hopedale grew out of New England Universalism, and some thirty or more lesser-known and shortlived 'secular' Associations were formed"

(Foster, 1981, p. 86). In fact, even as Noyes was making his move from Putney to Oneida, different groups of New England Transcendentalists, philosophers of evangelical Unitarianism, attempted to implement their social reform goals, not simply at Brook Farm (1841–47) but also at Fruitlands, Massachusetts (1843–44). The "secular Associations" cited by Foster were the Fourierist Phalanxes. Both Brook Farm and Hopedale (1841–67) became among the earliest Fourierist ventures when their members embraced Fourier's principles.

The roots of these communal experiments are to be found in the rejection by the Congregational church of eastern Massachusetts of Jonathan Edwards's revivalism during the First Great Awakening. Boston's more liberal theologians, reaching out to the eighteenth-century Enlightenment for stimuli to reinvigorate religious feeling, discovered Unitarianism, which stressed the importance of reason, intellectual freedom, and moral duty (Rose, 1981, pp. 3–4), as well as the idea of a unitary God rather than a Trinity (Melton, 1989). These qualities appealed especially to an urban society in which life no longer centered on the instituted church, although at the same time Universalism, which also stressed reason in religion and affirmed that all will be saved, developed a following after it was introduced to rural areas by the French mystic George de Benneville after 1741. Both Unitarians and Universalists also began to show signs of "infidelism," the move toward a human-centered rather than a God-centered philosophy (Melton, 1989).

To the Unitarians, "character" was essential to peaceful social relations among freethinking people. Character formation was the gradual process of understanding, accepting, and acting upon moral truths (Rose, 1981, p. 22). The first Unitarian congregations were established between 1792 and 1803 and scandalized New England with success in appointing a professor of religion at Harvard in 1805.

Yet even as Unitarianism was organizing and developing, it was confronted by the stresses of the Second Great Awakening. Many Unitarians found the new revivalism problematic, doubting the efficacy of emotional conversion without rational understanding. A split developed between the moderates, who came to be numbered among the orthodox in Boston, and a new group of Evangelical Unitarians who wanted to reform Boston society by religious means. Major differences emerged between those committed to Unitarian rationalism and those who believed that religious faith could not thrive amid problems created by slavery, poverty, ignorance, and alcoholism. The evangelicals became social reformers.

In 1825, William Ellery Channing led in the founding of the American Unitarian Association, a liberal missionary group. Then, quarterbacked by Joseph Tuckerman, nine Unitarian churches united in 1834 as the Benevolent Fraternity of Christian Churches, committed to a missionary effort to the poor. Tuckerman became a leading advocate for free public education, penal reform, temperance, and efficient organization of charity. Voluntary associations were sponsored, as instruments of both self-improvement and reformation of the poor (Rose, 1981, pp. 29–30). Increasingly, there was a willingness to take political stands. But this led to strains between Boston's mainline Unitarians, who believed in the sufficiency of reason and moral improvement, and the liberals willing to step outside the bounds of Unitarian institutions to evangelize the working class and pursue an agenda of social reform. The differences came to a head in 1836 in the Transcendentalist controversy.

Transcendentalism is a system of belief that postulates the essential unity of all creation, the innate goodness of man, and the supremacy of insight over logic and experience for the revelation of the deepest truths. Central beliefs include the truth of intuitive perception and the rejection of any outside authority in favor of the individual, who can sense the forces emerging from his own soul (Dean, 1987, p. 23).

The Transcendentalists became the

philosophers of evangelical Unitarianism who stopped to consider the intellectual issues raised by the movement itself. For example, if feeling was as important as reason in religion, was the heart qualified to judge the Bible by the same logic of "higher criticism" as the head? . . . The Transcendentalists' answers made the Liberal awakening as much an intellectual movement as it was an emotional and practical one. For when they said that there was an intuitive source of truth independent of the Bible, they authorized men and women to change the forms of religious expression to suit their needs unhindered by the Christian tradition. (Rose, 1981, p. 38).

In so doing, they "rationalized the innovations of evangelical Unitarianism—and subverted its doctrine. . . . Transcendentalism was not Christianity . . . but some subjective usurper, with no more than an analogous connection with the religion of Christ" (ibid.). By developing a system of belief incorporating the European Romantics' notions of intuitive perceptions and intuitive reason—that individuals' own consciousness can reveal the great spiritual truths—Transcendentalists legitimized the evangelical Unitarians' move beyond the confines of the instituted church into the arena of social reform.

Transcendentalism attracted figures from Ralph Waldo Emerson and David Henry Thoreau to Orestes Brownson, Elizabeth Peabody, and Margaret Fuller and to George Ripley and Bronson Alcott. Brownson, a Universalist minister, placed man at the center of the scheme of redemption:

the problem is to create an outward religion that satisfies the twin demands of human nature, spiritual and material fulfillment. Ripley emphasized the importance of an individual's intuition and consciousness. Peabody built on Alcott's notion that the child is born with pure intuition of truth that can be drawn out by Socratic instruction, claiming in the case of religion that children's characters should not be formed into conformity with theology but that the truth of religious systems should be tested against the nature of children. Fuller explored the role of women, arguing that they have an identity beyond their sex because, via intuitive revelation, they have an individual relation to God. Emerson made the links to Eastern religions that fully emerged a century later in the New Age Paradigm (Chapter 18).

In the years 1836–40, conservative theologians launched a major onslaught on the Transcendentalists in Boston. These years of the "Transcendentalist controversy roughly coincided with the first depression in American history caused by unregulated economic growth. Between 1837 and 1843, widespread bankruptcies and high unemployment raised unanswered questions about the free market economy. . . . Some Bostonians reacted to the prospect of social disorder by exposing dangerous doctrines" (Rose, 1981, pp. 72–73). A battle was joined between these Bostonians and the evangelical Unitarians concerned with intellectual freedom and social justice. During the battle, Transcendentalism was recognized as a school of philosophy that stood in opposition to the conservative clergy's belief in revelation by God of the truths of religion, grafting social reform by collective means onto radical religion. "Writing to Emerson in 1840, George Ripley did not need to explain what he meant by 'the City of God which we shall try to build.' It would be the antithesis of the city of Boston. Alienated by a culture built on fear, the Transcendentalists took steps to establish social relations allowing freedom, growth, justice and love" (ibid., p. 93). It was in such an environment, with Transcendentalism now well established as a social movement, that the experiments at Brook Farm, Fruitlands, and Hopedale were started. To reach their ends, the Transcendentalists had to become social reformers, and these communal experiments were their expression.

Brook Farm, organized by George and Sophia Ripley, began as an experiment in practical Christianity (Swift, 1961; Sams, 1958). Organized antithetically to Bostonian Puritanism, "there was almost insatiable desire for pleasure: music, dancing, card playing, charades, tableau vivants, dramatic readings, plays, costume parties, picnics, sledding, and skating" (Rose, 1981, p. 131). These activities were used to promote the goodwill among members necessary for the commune to function as an economic unit. Themes were individual growth and freedom to live according to conscience. "Freedom to live according to conscience was the most important condition of reform."

The two-hundred-acre farm was located in West Roxbury, nine miles from Boston, and thirty-two people became members between 1841 and 1844, the majority concerned with intellectual and moral development. Purchase of the land was funded by $500 shares sold to the members. On the farm, supposedly to be worked communally and voluntarily, without hired labor, work was rotated among members via a daily roster. All members enjoyed equal social rights: Brook Farm was "a family of laborers, teachers, and students" (Oved, 1988, p. 145).

Soon Brook Farm was in trouble, however. Founding members began to discriminate against possible newcomers, and they were ambivalent about whether the commune should be a self-sufficient retreat or a viable economic enterprise. They moved to expand production of specialties for the market, such as shoes, displaying increasing interest in practical economics as a means to social justice. But by 1843 the community was in debt. Intellectuals such as Nathaniel Hawthorne at first glorified the manual labor but soon left the hard work. Most members were inexperienced in farming. Fourierism looked like a solution, and the constitution was changed in 1844 with the attempt to make the community a more effective alternative in an industrializing society. In so doing the members backed away from a religion that gave preeminence to the individual: "Some thought that the solitary individual had been glorified at the expense of man in society. . . . For the Brook Farmers their acceptance of Fourierism was a moral choice in favor of social involvement, not only with each other, but in society at large" (Rose, 1981, pp. 144–45). The introduction of Fourierist groups and series brought a more democratic system of labor, and the industrial expansion after 1844 helped remedy the farm's intellectual exclusivity. In 1844 the farm made a small profit, a year when sixty-seven new members joined the community. Many of the older groups, committed to moral progress, had left by then. The new group was more committed to social reform. Residents played an active role in the Fourierist movement—Charles Dana, for example, was active in the national society's attempts to coordinate the emerging network of Fourierist communities. Others were active abolitionists.

Brook Farm's strongest institution was its school, and this became its centerpiece: a prep school for Harvard. Early in 1844 the community's membership of seventy included thirty students in school. But with the transition to Fourierism there was internal tension between the remaining members, committed to intellectual growth, and the newer communards, who sought to correct the ills of wage labor. With these tensions the community was too fragile to survive a series of deadly blows. A chicken pox epidemic in 1844–46 caused the school, Brook Farm's principal source of income, to be quarantined. In 1846, as it was nearing completion, the new phalanstery burned. It had not been insured. Brook Farm did not survive the loss. The last members left in 1847, and the property was auctioned off in 1849.

The second Transcendentalist experiment, Fruitlands, was the brainchild of A. Bronson Alcott. Alcott was committed to educational reform, believing that the child is born with a pure intuition of truth that can be drawn out by Socratic instruction. This first attempt to implement his ideas in Connecticut ended in failure when children were withdrawn from his school. He then attempted to establish a school in Philadelphia in 1833, but there were not enough interested students. In 1834 he opened the Temple School where, for a time, he was able to implement his advanced teaching techniques. At first the school was successful and attracted children of influential families. Two years later he published his first book, titled *Conversations with Children on the Gospels*. Although Alcott believed his work properly belonged to the field of education, he met with severe reaction from critics, who claimed his unorthodox views were religious, not educational. Enrollment at the school began declining and disappeared entirely when a black child was admitted.

The early 1800s had brought the formation in London and its periphery of a group of mystic philosophers and reformers whose interests lay in the early education and training of children. They were "communists in property, anarchists in government, free lovers in marriage, vegetarians in diet, and, going beyond education to biological means to redeem the race, early eugenicists" (Rose, 1981, p. 121). In 1842, upon hearing of Alcott's efforts toward educational reform in America and aided by funding from Ralph Waldo Emerson, the group sent for Alcott, after whom they had named the newly established school Alcott House, a boarding school for about thirty children. During his visit to England, Alcott conceived the idea of creating a New Eden, a community where idealistic individuals could break from the narrow views and norms of tradition. Lacking funds, he formed a network of contacts with the English mystics, who remained interested in his efforts. Eventually, it was the generosity of Charles Lane that brought the establishment of the idealistic community to fruition.

In the summer of 1843 a scenic ninety-acre farm bordering the Nashua River was purchased near Harvard, Massachusetts. Aside from a Shaker settlement directly across the river, Fruitlands would be remotely located, separated from the rest of society. The intent was to attract members who had risen above conventionality and who possessed special acumen into human nature. In short, Fruitlands was to be for the strong, not a haven for the weak or ailing. It was believed that exclusion of personal imperfections would lead to social and political improvements for the whole of society. Property and economic enterprises beyond agricultural self-sufficiency were considered evil; self-denial alone would bring eternal life, and animal food of any type was not only forbidden but detestable. Just as abominable was the use of manure for increasing crop yields.

Central to Fruitlands was the Transcendentalist premise that the spirit abiding within each person would bond the group together and would reveal a method of organization and operation. Therefore, preconceived rules and plans were unnecessary for those truly committed to spiritual idealism. Anticipating the anarchist "self-realization" communities of the 1960s, any organizational structure was considered a hindrance to achieving the philosophical state of spirituality.

The fourteen-member community was, however, influenced by the reputation and practices of the Shakers. Celibacy and the purpose of the family unit were issues within the group. The unmarried members were quick to endorse the idea of spirituality through celibacy. Alcott, however, was married with children and experienced difficulty resolving the conflict between spirituality and sexual relations.

Alcott and Charles Lane were absent from the community much of the time, traveling to seek recruits. Money they received in donations or from speaking engagements allowed them to continue recruiting. Meanwhile, back at Fruitlands, cold weather destroyed crops, and the community was deserted by all but the most dedicated members. Life with the affluent Shakers was more appealing; the community was disbanded in 1844, less than a year after its inception, and the property sold.

The third Unitarian/Universalist offshoot community was Hopedale, established in Milford, Massachusetts, by Adin Ballou. Ballou had been a Universalist clergyman in Milford but left the church in a doctrinal dispute over the concept of punishment after death. He became increasingly interested in "practical" Christianity, forming the Massachusetts Association of Universal Restoration in 1831 to promote his views. He originally contemplated a joint experiment with George Ripley, but his reformist inclinations were too radical for Transcendentalist Ripley.

Hopedale was conceived as an experiment in Practical Christianity. Established in 1841, it was organized as a Fourierist-like joint-stock company with 31 original members, growing to 110 by 1852. The members were active in many social reform movements, especially peace, antislavery, and temperance. Ballou, a pacifist, also defended spiritualism. Close contracts were maintained with Brook Farm. The community was strong enough to launch a western movement of Practical Christians. Obtaining eight hundred acres of land, they established an offshoot at Union Grove, Minnesota, in 1856. The offshoot failed in 1858, however, a victim of the uncertainties accompanying the Great Sioux Uprising.

Success in manufacturing led Ballou's successor as community leader, Ebenezer Draper, to transform Hopedale from a joint-stock association to the business-oriented Hopedale Manufacturing Company. In 1862, Ballou withdrew, believing the community to have lost its moral purpose. In 1867, Hopedale was dissolved, merging with Hopedale Parish.

Practical Christianity survived longer at Hopedale than did Transcendentalism at Brook Farm and Fruitlands. Transcendentalism waned as quickly as it had taken shape as a philosophy of evangelical Unitarianism, echoing the collapse of the Fourierist experiments. "No event in America as dramatic as the European Revolution of 1848 divides . . . the 'age of revolution' from the 'age of capital' " but "by the early 1850s, the Transcendentalists spoke of their movement as history." It "ended in deflated hopes and cheerful acquiescence." "The most striking aspect of the transformation was the speed with which it occurred." "The financial and social success of the Transcendentalists after mid-century made their marginal existence as radical reformers seem, by contrast, almost unreal" (Rose, 1981, pp. 207–9).

The Transcendentalists who stayed in Boston became part of a new cultural elite of poets, historians, scientists, lawyers, and ministers. The first Transcendentalists had been radical intellectuals. They became social reformers when they realized that structural change was needed to achieve ethical ends, aiming "to reconstruct all aspects of life according to principle, as individuals, in families, and in cooperative groups. When Transcendentalism ended at midcentury, the reason was a failure of this vision. Capitalism came of age in America when it became clear that the Transcendentalists and other radical reformers had not been able to communicate to their contemporaries the belief in a social alternative, and had lost faith themselves" (ibid., p. 225).

Yet that being said, there were many who followed who were heavily indebted to the Transcendentalists' organic philosophies, including such Pragmatists as William James and John Dewey, environmental planners like Benton MacKaye and Lewis Mumford, and architects such as Louis Sullivan and Frank Lloyd Wright. Although the Transcendentalists failed to produce reforms in microcosm, they did plant ideas that took root in the "new light" of the Social Gospel and Liberal Protestantism that surged during the Third Great Awakening, from 1890 to 1920 (McLoughlin, 1978, pp. 145ff.), to which we turn in Chapter 12. And their interests in spiritualism and in Eastern religions ultimately came to undergird the New Age and Intentional Communities paradigms that will be discussed in Chapters 18 and 20.

CHAPTER NINE

Etienne Cabet's French Communard Icarians

As Oneida was being built in 1848, a group of French socialists arrived in Texas expecting to build a model communal society. Their adventure ended in 1898 in Iowa without ever having achieved their utopian goals (Figs. 22, 23). Theirs were settlements of immigrants, and they sought to build self-sustaining socialist communities walled off from the American mainstream. Their arrival was dictated by the disillusionment of their leader, Etienne Cabet, with France in the difficult depression years of the early 1840s. Their history followed their own internal dynamic (Fig. 24)— until, that is, younger members, adopting Marxist tenets, tried to take leadership in America's early flirtation with socialism.

The story begins with Etienne Cabet, born at Dijon in 1788, the year before the French Revolution. He was educated for the bar but became a politician and writer. He served successfully as a member of the Insurrection Committee of 1830 and then was appointed attorney-general for Corsica by Louis Philippe to remove a dangerous democrat from further revolutionary activity. Cabet was soon dismissed from this office because he continued to play an active role in the radical movement, writing several books and publishing *Le populaire*, one of the most popular radical weeklies. After his dismissal, he was elected as *député* in Dijon, but he was condemned to two years' imprisonment or five years' exile because of his revolutionary attitudes.

He chose to be exiled for five years. He went to Brussels at first, but he was expelled. He then went to England, where he became a disciple of Robert Owen and studied political history and sociology. During his stay he read Sir Thomas More's *Utopia*, from which he devised the idea for his own utopia, outlined in *Un voyage en Icarie*. Returning to France in 1840, he published the book, which became a best-seller.

Cabet outlined a history of communist theory, criticized the exist-

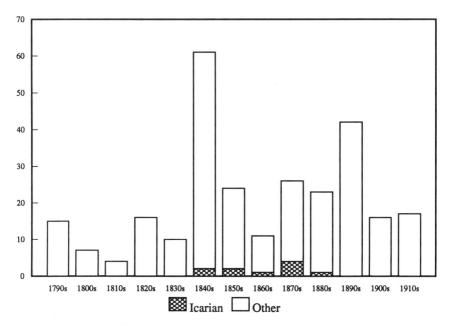

Figure 22. Timing of Icarian Community Building. The genealogy of these Icarian settlements, built by and for immigrant French communards, is charted in Figure 24. As
with other immigrant movements, there is no long-wave rhythmicity until the younger
Icarians responded to socialism in the 1870s.

ing social order, and made recommendations for translating communist
theory into fact. In the utopian Icaria there would be no rich, and everyone
would be required to work. Taxes would be fair, and there would be old-
age pensions. The products of industry would be equally divided among
the producers. Everyone would be required to marry, and sexual relations
would be orthodox. Education would be extensive. Rule would be by the
majority, with women allowed to state their opinions in assembly, though
not to vote.

Between 1840 and 1847 he devoted *Le populaire* and *L'almanche Icarienne*
to the propagation of his views. It is estimated that in 1844–45 there were
a hundred thousand radicals reading Cabet's material.

In 1845–46 sectarianism emerged among the Icarians. Their utopian
ideology, which required radical social change, conflicted with Cabet's
nonviolent convictions. The split was reinforced by millenarian intrusions.
In 1846, a time of profound social and economic crisis in France, many
Icarians became convinced that their message would bring salvation and
that Cabet was the Messiah. The political radicals wanted revolution in
France. The nonviolent millenarians opted for the New World, and in

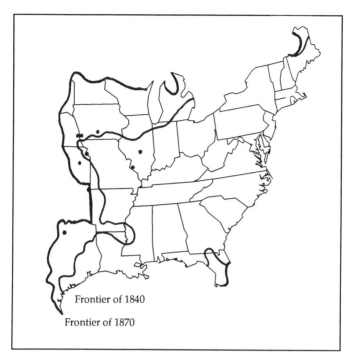

Figure 23. Locations of the Icarian Settlements. Like most other immigrant groups, the Icarians planted their communities on the frontier, beginning with the ill-fated move of the first settlers to Texas and later as they moved west from Nauvoo, which they had purchased from the Mormons.

May 1847, Cabet issued a manifesto proclaiming "Allons en Icarie!" He declared that it was useless to hope for an Icaria in France. New land was needed, where whole cities and villages could be built according to socialist principles. He expected that ten thousand or twenty thousand people would want to take part in establishing such a community, and a million more would join them within a short time. He suggested in *Le populaire* that America was the ideal place for such an enterprise.

There would be freedom of assembly and a perfect democracy with universal suffrage. Governmental positions would be elective, therefore temporary and recoverable. All citizens would be electors and eligible for all of the positions. There would be neither aristocracy nor inequality, only the purest democracy and equality based on the principles of fraternity.

The community would supply all of its members with lodging, food, clothing, sanitation, and medical care. Citizens would be co-proprietors of an undivided collective property. Instead of wages there would be equal

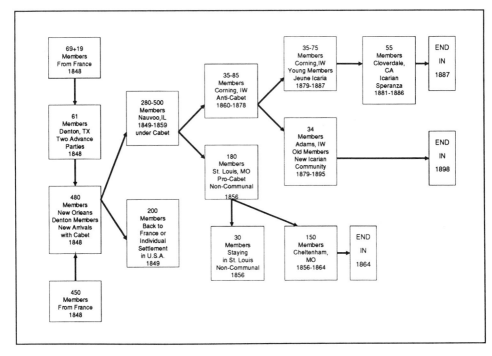

Figure 24. Genealogy of the Icarian Initiatives. With small self-contained immigrant groups, a chart such as this is useful to keep track of movements, schisms, and successive plantation of communes because their histories are impelled by an internal dynamic.

enjoyment of the product of labor. The workers would be the people, nation, society: they would govern themselves for the interest of each and all. The children would be educated by teachers with intelligence. All marriage would be in purity, and there would not be marriage portions nor any forced celibacy. Therefore, all would be equally happy.

Many people responded favorably to the office of *Le populaire* with enthusiastic letters and offers of gifts and money. In September 1847, Cabet went to London to ask Owen's advice on the community plan. Owen, who had already attempted to found a colony in Texas, convinced Cabet that Texas was the ideal location. In January 1848, Cabet contracted for 1 million acres in Texas, agreeing to a condition that the site should be occupied by 1 July 1848, barely six months away.

Cabet announced in *Le populaire*—under a headline that proclaimed with graphic simplicity, "C'est au Texas!"—that he had secured a land flowing with milk and honey. He needed to prepare his advance guard to go immediately to Texas. The sixty-nine-member party signed a social contract binding themselves to communism and sailed from Le Havre on 3 February 1848. Cabet wrote in *Le populaire* that he could not doubt the regeneration of the human race: "The third of February 1848 will be an epochmaking date, for on the day one of the grandest acts in the history of the human race was accomplished—the advance guard, departing on the ship Rome, has left for Icaria. . . . May the winds and waves be propitious to you, soldiers of humanity! And we Icarians who remain, let us prepare without loss of time to rejoin our friends and brothers!"

The Icarians expected to occupy a fertile million acres adjoining the Red River in Texas and believed that as many as 1 million French emigrants would join their community. They planned for their society to be governed by a fully democratic socialism that would offer them fraternity, equality, and mutuality.

When the initial group of sixty-nine Icarians arrived at New Orleans on 27 March 1848, their first expectation was dashed. They were informed at New Orleans that only one hundred thousand acres were provided in the contract. Moreover, their land had been allocated in checkerboard fashion, and they could lay claim only to alternate squares. The intervening spaces belonged to the state. In order to take rightful possession of these scattered sections, they would have to build a log house on each one before July. This was clearly impossible. The most they could claim in this fashion was ten thousand acres.

Before reaching their destination from New Orleans, the Icarians already had confronted many difficulties. Their only wagon broke down. They had limited supplies. Many of them were sick and exhausted. On arriving at Denton County, Texas, they built a log house and some wooden sheds and began to break the sod. In July 1848 four died of malaria, seven died of fatigue, and one was killed by lightning. Every Icarian at the site was ill, and their only doctor went mad. The remainder's only hope was the second advance party, due in September 1848. They expected fifteen hundred Icarians to arrive.

The second expectation was dashed by events in France while the first group was struggling in Texas. A revolution had taken place on 24 February 1848, only three weeks after the departure of the first Icarians. The Second Republic raised hopes among the working class. Few now wanted to risk their future in an unpredictable adventure. Cabet was urged to build his Icaria in France, and he was nominated as candidate for the presidency, but he refused to be diverted from the American experiment. The home party withdrew from the ranks of his Icarians.

Under these circumstances, it was difficult to find the volunteers for the second advance party, and only nineteen joined. A weary ten of the nineteen survived to arrive in Texas in September. The Texan experiment failed. After deciding to split up into several groups and to divide their money and supplies, the Icarians left for New Orleans. On the way, in the winter of 1848, six more of them died.

When Cabet heard of the advance party's hardships, he decided to leave for America. Already sixty years old, he left his wife and daughter in Paris, sailed on 15 December, and arrived at New Orleans in January 1849 with 450 followers. They decided to stay in New Orleans until they could find a new site for their experiment because they had only $17,000 available. Two hundred withdrew from the company, wanting to return to France or to seek their individual fortunes in America. They took $5,000. Cabet tried to find a new location through land agents while his remaining followers languished in New Orleans.

Cabet found one agent trying to sell the town of Nauvoo, Illinois, which the Brighamite Mormons had recently abandoned to trek west. He bought the temple, mills, shops, a communal dwelling house, several individual houses, and fifteen hundred acres of land and returned to New Orleans. A few more Icarians withdrew from the company. Finally, in March 1849 the remainder (about 280) began to establish a community at Nauvoo.

Cabet first had to establish an administration. A General Assembly was elected, but their affairs were administered by a Comité de Gérance—a board of six chairmen. Committees were arranged to manage education, health and amusement, finance and provisions, clothing and lodging, and publicity. The work of committees was subject to the approval of the General Assembly.

Most of the Icarians were French artisans with a native intelligence, eager for new knowledge and cultural amenities. They published publicity materials in English and German as well as French, acquired a library of five thousand volumes, and provided frequent musical and theatrical entertainments. Their schools were liberal, their sexual relations were orthodox, and their daily lives were conventional.

On the surface the arrangement seemed to safeguard all democratic rights, but in practice it led to the creation of two opposed parties. The committee, appointing foremen and other officers, built up an administration that was prepared to endorse every decree by Cabet, who was elected president annually. They had problems with agricultural skills because most of them were not farmers. Instead of training Icarians or hiring Americans, Cabet fell into the practice of buying food, producing a dangerous deficit.

As Cabet grew older, he became more intolerant. He decreed that the entire output of the distillery was to be sold because the evils of drink were to be banished from his paradise. He later prohibited tobacco. To enforce the rules, Cabet used spies who pried into the private lives of members.

An oppositional group of young members arose and dominated the General Assembly in 1856. The anti-Cabet party elected three directors, but Cabet refused to seat them. After confrontations between the anti-Cabet and pro-Cabet parties in the streets of Nauvoo, the majority anti-Cabetists announced in August 1856 that Cabet was expelled and should leave. This event was the beginning of the end of their expectation that they would be able to build a democratic socialist society with fraternity.

At the beginning of November, Cabet left for St. Louis with 180 supporters. On 8 November 1856, he died of apoplexy. The Cabet party decided to stay and obtain work at St. Louis. It was not difficult for them to get jobs because most of them were skilled artisans. They lived comfortably in the city, publishing *La revue icarienne,* which reported on their daily lives. Their children attended the public schools; their adults organized evening classes for English language training and met on Sunday for Christian instruction. Even though they did not live communally, they owned a large meeting hall, where they provided musical and theatrical entertainments.

After staying in St. Louis for eighteen months, the majority, about 150 Icarians, decided to move to Cheltenham, six miles to the west, while about thirty members remained in St. Louis. They bought a twenty-eight-acre estate. After they received financial aid from France, the Icarians at Cheltenham, recognized as the only true Icarian community, prospered. But ideological conflict emerged once more. The older members believed in a dictatorial leader; the younger members, in democracy. Forty younger members withdrew when the older members gained power. The younger members were the most skilled craftsmen. With such a loss, in 1864, with only fifteen men and women left, without funds and with the mortgage on the estate falling due, the Cheltenham community was terminated.

The Icarians of the anti-Cabet party who had stayed at Nauvoo also had severe debt problems; their industrial system was out of gear due to the withdrawal of 180 members to St. Louis. Without Cabet they were badgered by the agents of the Mormons for payment on account and by Illinois for taxes. They determined to move as soon as possible in order to avoid further disintegration. In 1852 they bought three thousand acres of land in Corning County, Iowa, hoping to set up a real communistic society. They began to move from Nauvoo to Corning in 1857, completing the relocation in 1860.[1]

In 1863 many members withdrew from the new site because of legal problems concerning property ownership. Only thirty-five were left, with a debt of $15,000. The Civil War made it possible for them to remain, however. Although supplies were short and prices rose, the Icarians made enough money to pay off their mortgage. They bought more land and bred cattle, hogs, sheep, and horses, which were sold to the neighborhood.

Since they were now out of debt, they could turn to building a communal society. They built a two-story building containing a common dining room with a kitchen, a provision cellar, and a room for a library. They also build apartments for families. In the spring of 1874 they built twelve frame houses, a dining hall, a wash-house, a dairy, and a schoolhouse. They had shops for carpentry, blacksmithing, wagonmaking, and shoemaking. The number of members doubled.

With prosperity the pattern of ideological confrontation between the older and the younger members was repeated, however. The older members thought that they deserved some private property because they were the members who had expanded their community. The younger members demanded that all private possessions should be surrendered to the community. Many of the young were deeply influenced by the writings of Karl Marx. More radical than their parents, they suggested equal political rights for women and admission of more young radicals.

In September 1877 the youth party demanded formal separation when the older members resisted their suggestions. The conflict went to the civil courts. The Adams County Court dissolved the community in August 1878.

In 1879 thirty-five youthful members agreed to stay on at Corning, reincorporating themselves as "the Icarian Community." Their new constitution abolished the presidency to secure more democratic participation and offered the right of suffrage to women. Even though membership peaked at seventy-five in 1883, the community was unstable because of frequent withdrawals. In 1881 several members moved to Bluxume Ranch near Cloverdale, California. When more members moved there in 1883, Corning began to decline. Another fifty-five members moved to Cloverdale in 1885, and Corning closed in 1887. The last members refused to transfer the property to Cloverdale, dividing what was left.

In 1881 the members of the Icarian Community who had moved to California organized Icaria Speranza with several French socialists who resided in the San Francisco area. They purchased nine hundred acres near Cloverdale and followed most of the Icarian traditions, except that there was some private ownership. In 1886 there were financial troubles. The community was dissolved by a court decree after the prosperous members divided the land in 1887.

The thirty-nine older members who lost power to the younger members at Corning reorganized themselves under the title "The New Icarian Community" in 1879. They moved to the eastern portion of the old village in Adams County, occupying about one thousand acres and eight frame houses. Under the presidency of M. Marchand, who had been one of the advance guard in Texas, the members of the New Icarian Community tried neither to build nor to acquire new members, however. Of the thirty-four members, eight were over sixty years of age, and twelve were children under the age of thirteen. The younger men drifted away, and the oldest members died. By 1898 only twenty-one members were left. The community was dissolved. E. F. Bettannier, the last president, was appointed receiver of the property, and each surviving member received a share.

CHAPTER TEN

The Hutterites

The last group of German-speaking Separatists to come to the United States intent on building communities in which they could follow their religious dictates free of outside interference began arriving during the 1874 trough (Fig. 25). Like the Icarians, they moved to the periphery—immigrants intent on building self-sustaining communes walled off from the American mainstream. By 1917 twenty-four settlements had been planted in the United States (Fig. 26), but they then relocated to Canada after a dispute about military service (see Table 4). There was a hiatus in the United States until the late 1930s, when changing American attitudes led to a reversal of that decision. In the three decades that followed, sixty-one settlements were established in the Dakotas. In addition, 170 Hutterite communities were started in Canada (Hostetler, 1974, pp. 359–66):

The *Directory of Intentional Communities* (Fellowship for Intentional Community, 1991) reports that there are now 391 Hutterite colonies in the United States and Canada: Alberta, 139; Manitoba, 93; Saskatchewan, 52; South Dakota, 51; Manitoba, 40; North Dakota, 6; Washington, 5; Minnesota, 4; British Columbia, 1.

Who are the Hutterites? The founding leader (c. 1520) was Jakob Hutter, who emphasized absolute obedience to God while stressing self-denial and community ownership of property within the body of believers. He was a militant reformer described as a pacifist, a millenarian, and a communitarian. There was no vision of utopia on earth but rather a life of continual trial and tribulation until death or the Second Coming of Christ, whichever came first.

Because the Hutterites withdrew from established society, they were continually oppressed by government officials, who wished to impose order and obedience on their citizens for political as well as economic

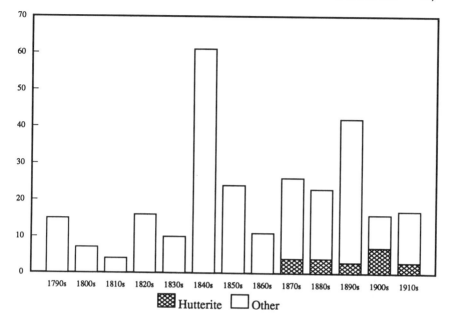

Figure 25. Establishment of Hutterite Settlements before 1920. After initial relocation from the Eastern European Pale, Hutterite expansion has been dictated by population growth in existing settlements and the ability to accumulate sufficient capital to acquire land for new spinoffs, close to the mother settlement.

reasons. Until the Reformation, church and state were unified, and the Hutterites' reconstruction separated church from state.

As a result, they were persecuted. Jakob Hutter and his wife were imprisoned while officials attempted to extract from them the names of other brethren committed to the movement. Hutter repeatedly refused to cooperate and was publicly tortured, then burned.

Until Hutter emerged as the leader, several internal crises threatened to divide and scatter the members. Among these crises were disputes over pacifism and the handling of community goods. However, the execution of Hutter served to move the group from fragmentation toward an integrated ideology and social structure. With the intensity and consistency of efforts to eliminate the Hutterites, only the true believers remained, and a homogeneous character emerged.

The next three hundred years brought continued political and religious pressures within Europe, with repeated efforts by Catholic rulers to pressure Protestants into submission and obedience. In 1622 the Hutterites were expelled from Moravia, their original home. Officials informed them

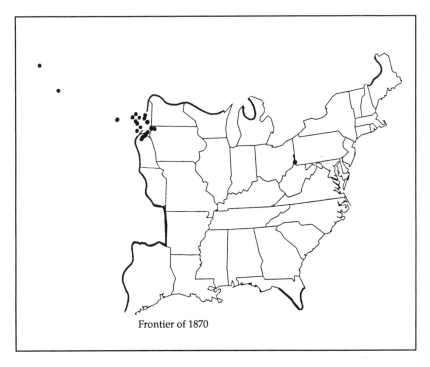

Frontier of 1870

Figure 26. Locations of the Hutterite Communities before 1920. Like the Rappites and Icarians before them, the Hutterites preferred the isolation of the frontier for their communes.

they could return if they would consent to instruction by Catholic priests. Those wearied by suffering accepted the offer. Twenty-four households did not and fled to Hungary, where officials welcomed the exiled group.

Relief was short-lived, however, as Catholics gained greater political influence in Hungary. In an attempt to undermine the Hutterian belief system, a decree was issued requiring all infants to be baptized. The Hutterites realized they could not ignore this requirement without risk of further exile and persecution. They allowed the priests to baptize their children, with the intent of rebaptizing them as adults.

Finally, stronger measures to exterminate the Hutterian brethren occurred during Maria Theresa's reign, from 1740 to 1780. The Jesuits were given free reign to convert everyone to Roman Catholicism. Attacks were made on Hutterian congregations, children were seized, and books were confiscated. Those who refused to attend mandatory Catholic services were tortured until they capitulated, swearing obedience to the pope and consenting to indoctrination by the Catholic clergy.

Table 4

	Schmiedeleut		Dariusleut		Lehrerleut	
	U.S.	Canada	U.S.	Canada	U.S.	Canada
1871–80	2	—	2	—	1	—
1881–90	2	—	2	—	1	—
1891–1900	1	—	1	—	1	—
1901–10	3	—	3	—	1	—
1911–20	1	8	3	7	—	5
1921–30	—	2	—	8	—	2
1931–40	3	6	1	5	—	7
1941–50	11	7	2	7	8	2
1951–60	5	12	3	16	2	7
1961–70	11	14	1	14	6	15
1971–73	7	6	1	12	—	7
In existence in 1973	91		77		61	
Extinct by 1973	11		11		4	
Total created by 1973	102		88		65	

Why continual persecution spanning centuries? How have the Hutterites managed to survive? The Hutterites turned inward, establishing close-knit, self-supporting communities. They consider their time on earth a transition into eternal life. Anything obstructing the millenarian vision is rejected for the benefit of the group. The Hutterites have functioned as a culture within a culture, internally governed and bonded by the Spirit of God in the midst of an evil world.

A remnant of brethren was allowed to settle in Russia, where they existed with virtually no persecution or outside pressure for almost one hundred years. It was, ironically, internal turmoil that threatened to destroy the Hutterites during this time of peace. The members who had experienced severe persecution began dying off, while the Hutterite population grew to the point that the economy could no longer support full employment. Tensions were compounded by a division among the brethren regarding whom to support in the role of leadership.

The European experience had been one of continual selection of the most faithful—those most committed to the Hutterian belief and social system—with constant defection by the weaker members. Commitment and zeal had brought the remnant group to Russia where they were almost completely isolated from society. Because there was no possibility for defection, there began an internal strife that resulted in abandonment of the communal life-style and threatened to eradicate the Hutterian way of life.

A group of demoralized members unsuccessfully petitioned the Russian government for assistance in moving to land better fit for agricultural use. A trustee of the government, who was also a member of a Mennonite colony, was successful in helping the Hutterites relocate to a Mennonite settlement. Although both groups were branches of the same Anabaptist movement, there were specific dress and speech differences. Regardless, the Hutterite settlement flourished alongside the Mennonites. The task of maintaining separate identities presented significant complications, however, as did friction regarding the reestablishment of communal living within the Hutterite settlement.

When George Waldner, a Hutterite preacher for thirty-three years, attempted to revive communal living in 1857, the resulting disagreement divided the Hutterites. Many Hutterites remained opposed to communal living, and those believing it to be God's will formed two groups. The first to reinstate communal living were called Dariusleut, after their leader Darius Walter. Michael Waldner, George's son, a powerful charismatic presence who frequently experienced supernatural visions and trances, was instrumental in establishing the second group, the Schmiedeleut. Both groups lived communally for some fifteen years before emigrating to the United States in 1874.

The desire for the groups to relocate at a greater distance from each other was aided by the Russian government's nationalist moves in 1864. Russian was made the national language taught in schools with passage of the Primary Schools Bill of 1864. When compulsory military service was introduced in 1871, Mennonite and Hutterite representatives sought exemption. When their offer of colonizing undeveloped territory in exchange for exemption was denied, the Hutterites made the decision to send delegates to other countries in search of a new home. The Russian government realized it was going to lose many of its most productive farmers and began making concessions to discourage emigration. Many Hutterites decided to stay. A remnant did not. Their destination would soon be America, where they believed they would experience the total religious freedom they so desired.

America was just completing the painful process of reconstructing a war-ravaged nation. Unemployment, high tariffs, and financial panic caused by overconstruction of railroads and the collapse of critical eastern banks dominated the political and economic scene. Racial tensions remained high in the aftermath of slavery. Reconstruction efforts had shifted from idealistic principles of moral reform to the more practical material interests of making money and establishing jobs and a stable environment.

Perhaps the economic chaos of the haven to which the Hutterites were drawn further encouraged their isolation and self-reliance. In 1874 they settled in the virtually undeveloped Dakota Territory. Although the Hutterites were at first uncertain of their final destination, mass migration led many settlers to the American West, where large amounts of land could be acquired. The Hutterites, Schmiedeleut, and Dariusleut colonies alike finally settled close to settlements of Mennonites, Rappites, Harmonists, and the Amana Society. Within three years, a third group of Hutterites, the Lehrerleut, would migrate from Russia to experiment with the communal life-style. Although virtually all Hutterites (approximately 1,265) eventually left Russia by 1879, all did not settle communally upon arrival in the United States. Those who established individual homesteads comprised almost half of the Hutterian population and eventually integrated with the Mennonite congregations.

Just as contact with the Mennonites in Russia had served to revitalize the Hutterian brethren before their migration from Russia, so did contacts and negotiations with similar utopian groups in the new communal establishments in America. During the initial period of economic hardship, money was borrowed from both the Amana Society and the Rappites, and favorable interchange was conducted among the neighboring colonies. In fact, the wealthy Rappites, who were concerned with their own obsolescence due to an aging celibate society, agreed to let a group of Hutterites settle on land they owned in Pennsylvania. Aside from the practice of celibacy and the use of musical instruments, the Rappites shared many Hutterian beliefs and were impressed with the dedication and simplicity of their life-style. However, the Pennsylvania land was unfit for agricultural use, and the Hutterites returned to South Dakota within three years.

The Hutterites experienced growth and prosperity in America. By 1915 there were over seventeen hundred members in seventeen communal settlements. The numbers grew mainly because of natural increase: the number of children per family averaged around ten. (Hutterite marriages are monogamous, and since couples do not practice continence of any form, a "natural fertility" regimen of a child every two years from marriage to menopause obtains.) As the numbers grew, more colonies branched out to maintain individual communities at a manageable level of approximately one hundred members each.

Although the Hutterites experienced economic hardships, crop failures, and leadership schisms, they were able to escape external pressures until 1917, when the United States entered World War I. Laws were enacted requiring military service with no provision for conscientious objection. Although no guarantees had been given upon immigration, the Hutterites had hoped for the continued religious freedom they had enjoyed for almost fifty years. The society that had virtually ignored these German immigrants suddenly became hostile.

From the time of their arrival in the United States the Hutterites apparently experienced no serious conflict with the mainstream of society. In fact, for all but economic activity involving the sale of feathers and brooms to outside markets, the Hutterites ignored society, and society reciprocated by ignoring the German-speaking immigrants. Hutterian colonies were located in peripheral locations, with main buildings typically hidden from view, and colonies intentionally established far from main roads and thoroughfares.

Remoteness did not give way to ignorance, however, as the Hutterites remained sensitive to the U.S. role in foreign relations and war. As a precautionary measure, the Dariusleut established a colony in Manitoba, Canada, during the Spanish-American War to ensure a safe haven in the event compulsory military service was required of the members. Canadian authorities welcomed the Hutterites and readily extended to them the immunities and privileges already given to Mennonite groups in an effort to attract more wholesome, hardworking immigrants. When it became evident that the United States would not require military conscription, however, in 1905 the Dariusleut were glad to leave the poor soil of Canada for the richer soil of South Dakota.

The different Hutterite groups had successfully kept separate their religious identities and institutions. Realizing the need for protection from external influences, the Hutterite Bruder Gemeinde (Hutterite Society of Brethren) was established in 1905. The purpose of this corporation was twofold: protection of communal property rights and protection from potential claims to property by former members. The significance of this organization lay in its contribution to the legal position of the Hutterite settlements within society as a whole. A committee representing the Hutterites to state and local authorities was elected for a three-year term by majority vote of all male members. This organizational structure provided both safety for the individuality of the separate communities and a means for integrating economic functions with the outside world.

Problems surfaced with passage of the Selective Service Act of 1917, which required all men between the ages of twenty-one and thirty-one to serve in the military, with no provision for conscientious objectors. The Hutterite leaders agreed among themselves that their young men, when drafted, should register and report for the required examination but should not cooperate further. They would not wear military uniforms, nor would they cooperate with work orders. As a result, young Hutterite men were considered stubborn and were ridiculed and treated cruelly at military training camps. On the other hand, Mennonite objectors were willing to compromise by accepting the degrading tasks assigned them as a result of their objections.

Persecution strengthened faith, but the Hutterites sent representatives to petition U.S. officials to recognize their conscientious objector status.

Compromise eluded them, however, as the secretary of war advised the group to allow their young men to be assigned to military training camps and to cooperate to the extent their consciences would allow. Disappointed, the Hutterites continued in their refusal to cooperate or serve in the military.

Conviction gave way to retreat after two young Hutterite men died after repeated beatings, solitary confinement, exposure, and starvation. After four months the men had become so ill they were hospitalized, but by the time their wives were informed, they had died. One of the wives had to beg officials for permission to see her husband's body, which had been dressed in the uniform he had so adamantly refused to wear.

These events, coupled with increasing hostility toward German-speaking immigrants generally, were the force behind the Hutterites' decision to relocate to Canada. Citizen groups considered them cowards and sought to ban the speaking of German in school, churches, or any public place. Livestock was driven away from a Hutterite colony after its members refused to buy war bonds or make donations to the Red Cross. Wine confiscated under the Prohibition Act was distributed during a county celebration for Armistice Day.

By 1918 fifteen colonies had been established in Canada. Most settlers had relocated from South Dakota, where their land was sold at extremely low prices. When the South Dakota State Council for Defense demanded that 5 percent of the proceeds be invested in war bonds and 5 percent be given to the Red Cross, the Hutterites lowered the land prices even further, leaving the responsibility for distributing the required funds to the buyers. Some colonies simply remained vacant, with Bon Homme the only one in South Dakota to remain populated for the twenty years following the exodus.

In 1935, South Dakota passed a tax act granting communal farms the same privileges as those granted to corporations. Communards were to pay local taxes but were not required to pay state and federal taxes. These inducements, coupled with the fact that colonies remained protected from claims to property by individual members, resulted in renewed expansion of Hutterite communities. In 1955 policy was again modified, however. Although no restrictions were placed on the formation of new colonies, existing colonies were prohibited from acquiring new lands, and corporate tax exemption was no longer granted.

In Alberta fear of land monopoly and unfair competition also surfaced in response to the Hutterites' ability and willingness to pay above-market prices for farmland. As a result, Alberta passed the Land Sales Prohibition Act in 1942 in an effort to prevent land sales to enemy aliens, including the Hutterites. Ironically, the Hon. Solon Low, who proposed the legislation, was a representative of the Mormons, whose land hold-ings exceeded those of the Hutterites. Five years later, the Land Sales Prohibition Act was amended to exclude the Hutterites from enemy alien status, and individual colonies were allowed to purchase up to 6,400 acres of land provided it was at least forty miles from an existing colony. As Hutterite colonies continued branching into Manitoba and Saskatchewan, local opposition and fear of monopoly continued to increase, however. Although attempts to implement restrictive legislation regarding a funda-mental right such as the purchase of land were unsuccessful, the threat of restrictive legislation drove many of the Canadian colonists back to South Dakota. This produced compromise, and Hutterite settlement since has spread rapidly on both sides of the international boundary.

What is life like inside the community of Hutterian brethren? All prop-erty is owned jointly by the community, with Hutterian colonies depen-dent upon agricultural lands for their basic resources. Communal sharing was made the norm in 1528, when the first community was established. Each person voluntarily surrendered his worldly possessions as cloaks were spread on the ground and stewards were appointed to oversee the goods. This tradition of sharing is carried on today in joint ownership of land, houses, and other means of production overseen by the spiri-tual council of baptized male members, through whom it is believed God reveals his perfect will.

The entire community is organized around work, and each member is expected to contribute as he or she is able. The Hutterites are committed to passing values from one generation to another, and the attitude toward work is no exception. Both men and women guide the younger children in the Christian life while demonstrating that hard physical work contrib-utes to the financial well-being of the colony. There is rotation of tasks. Competition and creativity are encouraged yet carefully monitored.

In contrast to the Amish, modern equipment and machinery are not shunned, but implementation is weighed against the need for full em-ployment. The Hutterite colonies are designed to be self-supporting. Their agricultural endeavors provide for the consumptive needs of the colony, as well as year-round employment for the members. Basic needs are met and distributed first according to need, with the remainder sold for a profit. It is more important that the Hutterite community support sev-eral projects that provide employment with small profits than to support only those efforts that realize large profits. Yearly meetings ensure careful deliberations concerning changes in production. Whatever the outcome, members of the Hutterite community understand that consensus has a higher priority than the desire of the individual.

The cohesion of the community is governed by custom rather than by law. Each member is expected to assume responsibility for the welfare of the community. Although the community is integrated around an absolute value system, its governance remains elastic enough to deal with emergencies, thus providing a high degree of security to the group as a whole.

Many common threads bind the different Leut ("our people") together, yet differentiations exist between the Lehrerleut, Dariusleut, and Schmiedeleut colonies. The Schmiedeleut are considered the most liberal since their clothing has been allowed to become more contemporary. Typically, austere Hutterite fashion requires distinctive dress. Men, who must wear beards after marriage, in biblical style, are expected to wear black denim trousers with suspenders, a black jacket or coat, and a black felt hat. White shirts are worn exclusively on Sunday, but other colors are acceptable on weekdays. Ankle-length gathered skirts of plaid or flower-print fabric, long-sleeved blouses, long aprons, and a vest or jacket make up the customary dress for Hutterite women. A black-and-white polka-dotted kerchief must be worn on the head at all times, covering long hair worn combed and pulled away from the face. Schmiedeleut women wear elbow-length sleeves; men's trousers have pockets, coats have lapels, and shirts have collars. These styles more closely resemble contemporary clothing than the simple, unpretentious fashion of tradition.

Degrees of mechanization within the colonies provide another identifying characteristic of the more conservative Leut. The liberal Schmiedeleut are distinguished by a greater degree of mechanization, especially in the newer colonies, where labor is in short supply and newer more efficient equipment is preferred. However, the trend toward advances in technology can be observed throughout all branching Hutterite colonies. Start-up funds are allocated to new colonies, with particular specification made for new machinery and equipment.

Variations in traditional dress and degrees of mechanization are easily noticed. However, several more-subtle characteristics serve to distinguish the groups. Lehrerleut colonies are customarily more dedicated to thorough education in the German language. During Sunday worship assemblies, Lehrerleut preachers are the last to enter the service. In Dariusleut and Schmiedeleut assemblies the preachers enter first. Other differences can be observed in attitudes toward the rearing and schooling of children.

Growth patterns and branching of colonies are consistent across all Leut. Daughter colonies are planned twelve to twenty years before actual branching occurs, requiring careful saving and management of capital assets in preparation for the process of division. Birthrates are high, and division takes place when a colony reaches approximately 130 to 150 members or, on average, about every fourteen years. Although problems often occur with redistribution of authority during the time prior to division, the growth process enables the Hutterites to maintain small, manageable, more personalized domestic groups.

The Schmiedeleut and Lehrerleut are more cohesive than the Dariusleut in their requirements for branching. The former require consensus among their own Leut before approving plans for a new colony, while latter do not. Consensus is insurance for the new colony, since all are committed to its well-being. Hardships sometimes require assistance, and colonies that have given their consent are more likely to offer aid. The Dariusleut have been more likely to experience branching due to conflicts among members before optimal conditions for growth have been reached. Although internal conflicts can often be resolved by branching, greater long-term risk is involved in establishing a new colony without the support and consent of the other Leut.

Branching requires more than investment in land and equipment. New colonies are carefully chosen to maintain age and sex distributions. In a colony of sixty members, about half are younger than fifteen years of age, with approximately fifteen male members capable of bearing major work and managerial responsibilities. Usually, only five of the male members are aged twenty-five or older, with only married men being eligible for positions as foremen. There is much work to be done early in a colony's life, with many married men holding a combination of several positions until the younger men mature and marry. Careful planning ensures the availability of potential jobs and positions with a minimum of struggle.

As colonies mature, however, opportunities for young married men become limited as competition in the labor force increases. As more men mature, positions cease to overlap, resulting in a more specific division of labor and greater opportunity for older members to influence the appointments of favored young men for available positions. Thus, branching also serves the function of channeling the friction of competition into a productive new venture.

New colonies are typically established about thirty miles from the parent colony. Rarely does a newly established colony begin with all of the land it will ultimately need. It must first pay off 50 percent of the debt incurred in start-up, with the remaining 50 percent of the costs paid by the parent colony. Only then can the new colony expand its land holdings and purchase the new equipment needed to provide jobs for its steadily increasing population.

The arrangement of the buildings in Hutterite colonies reflects the attitude of maintaining people's proper relationship to God and the world. Buildings are carefully set in relationship to each other, with angles determined by a compass. The houses, which run due north and south, reflect the Hutterite discipline of walking a straight and orderly path while in a temporal world. The central communal kitchen likewise runs due north and south and is the center of activity and work for the Hutterite women. Everything is classified and orderly, symbolizing strength of belief. The floor plans of the houses and relation of buildings one to another serve as outward manifestations of unchanging beliefs and social patterns in a changing and often hostile world. To the Hutterites, orderly external appearances are a reflection of internal stability.

Orderliness can be observed in other phases of life, as well. Daily work schedules are well planned, with the schedules and work patterns of all members integrated for smoothness and the efficient operation of the entire community. The day is broken into small units of time revolving around work and meals. Great emphasis is placed on the efficiency and speed with which one works, and status is gained accordingly. Concerted efforts and goals leave little time or need for private decision making or free choice in secular matters. Getting the job done quickly and efficiently takes precedence over enjoyment or fulfillment in performing the task.

Spiritual time is, however, a different matter. Each evening the entire community gathers for a church service and a time of spiritual renewal and motivation. In contrast to the busyness of the day, time seems suspended as the preacher unhurriedly recites memorized prayers and reads the sermon. Finally, the congregation sings long traditional hymns slowly and deliberately. Communal living is evident even in the organization of the Hutterite worship service. Ritualized prayers and hymns are repeated in unison in just the right way to bring glory to God, never in a manner for personal enjoyment or just making a pleasant sound. Separate voices blend with the whole, leaving little opportunity for individual assertion. However, the responsibility for developing a spiritual relationship with God is entirely individualistic. Either the individual accepts the absolute authority and unchanging wisdom of God, or he does not. There is no negotiation of the written Word (the Bible) by the individual.

In the past, defection to the outside world has not been common, although its increasing tendency has concerned leaders. From 1918 to about 1960, of 106 men and 7 women who left permanently, 98 men and all 7 women were from the more liberal Schmiedeleut colonies, and most were unmarried. A large percentage of those defecting left weak or dying colonies, where disrupted socialization processes led to discontent and unresolved internal problems. Some who left gave other reasons, such as curiosity about the outside world, desire for their own possessions, dislike for the colony rules, or romance with someone outside the colony.

Since custom does not permit a member to move from his home colony to a more desirable one, unresolved internal problems tend to leave the discontented with no solution other than defection. Abandonment is a serious matter and usually is in response to antagonisms with leadership or other superiors. Inequality of opportunity, due to favoritism shown by members of high position, and inequitable distribution of traditional roles among siblings are often causes of dissension. In a declining colony laxity of discipline usually leads to loss of the traditional respect for authority and produces problems with younger members, as does allowing children freedom to be individualistic. Both of these situations pose potential threats to the collective welfare of the group.

Women traditionally assume submissive roles and tend to marry at a fairly young age if they are born to a family of good reputation. Therefore, opportunities for contact with the outside world are less likely for women than for men. Roles within the colony are characterized by a strong sense of dependency, especially for women. When women have difficulty accepting the traditional roles, their chances for finding an alternative within the colony are even fewer than for the dissatisfied men.

The Hutterites have historically envisioned themselves as a people chosen by God yet destined to endure persecution as a result of their beliefs. After an individual has made the commitment to accept the authority of God, the individual is then accountable to God for his own actions and behavior, providing an internal source of stability and conscience. The structure of organization within the Leut and separate colonies themselves provides a means for imparting God's will for the good of the group, who liken their pattern of living to the protection of Noah's Ark in the midst of a world that is beyond any hope of redemption.

CHAPTER ELEVEN

Jewish Agricultural Resettlement

The Hutterites were not alone in being forced out of Russia. Jewish emigrants began arriving in America in large numbers in the 1880s. Aid societies attempted to settle some in agricultural settlements, inspired by the communal utopian tradition and inspiring, in turn, the kibbutz as the primary means by which Jews would resettle Palestine. In contrast to those of the Hutterites, few of the Jewish agricultural settlements lasted for very long.

Russia's Jews lived in the "Pale of Settlement" created by Empress Catherine II in 1791–92 in the southwestern territories that had been annexed from Poland in 1772. Jews were forbidden to live or travel outside the Pale, which by the nineteenth century included all of Russian Poland, Lithuania, Byelorussia, most of the Ukraine, Crimea, and Bessarabia (Herrscher, 1981, p. 15). They were literate—frequently intellectual—primarily involved in industrial and commercial pursuits, urbanoriented and bourgeois in aspiration, maintaining their wealth in liquid form. There was continuing conflict with an ignorant, oppressed Russian peasantry and continuing oppression by the Russian government.

The 1870s saw a rising tide of racial hatred in Europe. In his *Essai sur l'inégalité des races humaines* (1853–55), Comte Joseph-Arthur de Gobineau advanced the theory that the fate of civilization is determined by racial composition. He held that Aryan societies flourish just as long as they remain "pure," free of black and yellow strains. The more a culture is diluted through miscegenation, he said, the more likely it is to lose its creativity and vitality and sink into corruption and immorality. These ideas were converted into the pseudoscience of *Rassenkunde* by Adolph Stöcker Heinrich von Treitschke, German proponent of authoritarian power politics and herald of German unification via Prussian military might. The new doctrines of racial superiority found their way into Russia, paving the way for atrocities after the assassination of Czar Alexander II in 1881. False rumors aroused Russian mobs to attack Jews in more than two hundred cities and towns. One of the czar's ministers argued that the "Jewish problem" could be solved by triage—the disappearance of one-third of the Jews, the enforced emigration of another third, and the pauperization and starvation to death of the remaining third (Davidson, 1943, p. 7). Although the Russian government did not organize the pogroms, official persecution and harassment of the Jews led the anti-Semites to believe that their violence was legitimate. The massacres and terror precipitated wild, chaotic, disorganized Jewish emigration (Herrscher, 1981, p. 21).

In the United States the Hebrew Emigrant and Aid Society (HEAS) was formed "to aid and advise emigrants of the Hebrew faith coming from countries where they were suffering due to oppressive laws or hostile populace" (ibid., p. 23). The founders of HEAS, influenced by social critic Henry George's *Progress and Poverty* (see Chapter 15), were devoted to providing opportunities for agricultural land ownership and settlement for the emigrant Jews. One of the aims was to prevent the new arrivals from crowding into the large cities. To the emigrant "Jews agriculture was not solely a means of livelihood . . . but the visual and tangible sign of religious liberty and political emancipation" (Davidson, 1943, p. 36). The same idea was deeply embedded in the Zionism of Theodor Herzl and Martin Buber. In *Paths to Utopia* (1949), Buber, reflecting on the Israeli kibbutz, said that such agricultural communities, in which members work in the natural environment and live together in voluntary communion, have proved that utopian socialism can work. Today, the kibbutzim have some 160,000 members in Israel.

These views were consistent with those of the earliest emigrants, who were members of the Ad Olam, an organization that developed in southern Russia, principally Odessa, after the pogroms of 1881. Ad Olam was founded by intellectual youths with socialist convictions. The earliest Ad Olam emigrants, arriving in New York in January 1882, were committed to the development of model communitarian colonies. They believed that farming was a noble occupation, a solution to the Jewish predicament.

HEAS, formed to help them, prepared plans for settlement in the frontier states, proposing Jewish farming colonies in the newly opened Minnesota and South Dakota territories. HEAS insisted, however, that "no colony should be organized on a communistic and cooperative plan, and the refugees should not be disposed of collectively, but individually. Communist colonies have succeeded in this country but in very few instances. . . . Colonization must be conducted strictly on business principles and not on charity" (quoted in Oved, 1988, p. 223). The seeds of ideological conflict were set.

Table 5

Community	Started	Ended
Sicily Island, La.	1881	1882
Rosenhayn, N.J.	1882	1889
Bethlehem Yehudah, S. Dak.	1882	1885
Beersheba, Kans.	1882	1885
Cremieux, S. Dak.	1882	1889
Painted Woods, N. Dak.	1882	1887
Alliance, N.J.	1882	1908
Ad Olam, Ark.	1883	1883
New Odessa, Oreg.	1883	1887
Woodbine, N.J.	1891	1903

In all, nine Jewish farm settlements were planted in the years 1881–83. See Table 5 and Figures 27 and 28. Of these settlements, only New Odessa was communitarian from the start, although some of the others were communitarian for a while. None survived long.

Herman Rosenthal was the first to settle East European Jews in America. He was a successful merchant and litterateur from the Ukrainian city of Kiev and an Ad Olam organizer. Coming to the United States in 1881 as an Ad Olam agent, he persuaded the Alliance Israelite Universelle (AIU) to assist 124 colonists. AIU had been established to promote educational, industrial, and agricultural work among needy Jews and had been engaged in emigration work between 1869 and 1872. It was responsible for the establishment of Mikveh Israel Agricultural School near Jaffa in Ottoman Palestine. In 1881, AIU provided a loan of $5,000 for a tract of approximately twenty-eight hundred acres on Sicily Island in Catahoula Parish, upriver from New Orleans and Baton Rouge in Louisiana. The land was three days journey from the nearest city, swampy and malarial.

The group consisted of twenty families and several single men. In Eastern Europe they were students, teachers, artists, merchants, craftsmen, and peddlers. These people had not farmed before and were not accustomed to manual labor. On 16 November 1881 the *chalulzim* (pioneers) incorporated themselves in Louisiana as the First Agricultural Colony of Russian Israelites in America. The colony was given the power to purchase and apportion lands and to erect dwellings, farmhouses, and a school for the education of their children. They established a library for the use of the colony, as well as supplying money, farming utensils or other articles of husbandry, household furniture, and stock. They were to provide for the furtherance of the aims and purposes of the colony. A board of seven members was set up to administer the business and settle disputes.

All supplies sent to the colony by the Immigrant Aid Association were charged to the colony and the members receiving them. The association

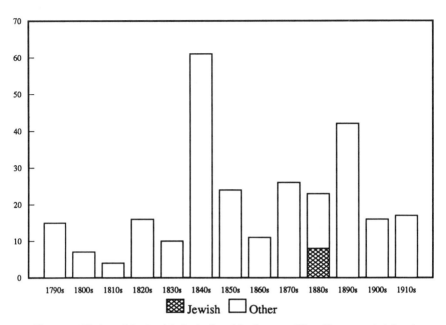

Figure 27. Timing of the Jewish Agricultural Settlements. The 1880s saw a brief and un-successful attempt to resettle Jewish refugees from the Pale on agricultural communes. Although unsuccessful in the United States, the idea took root in Jewish colonization of Palestine.

was charged with carrying out the socialist ideals of the Am Olam group. Article 7 of their constitution states:

All money belonging to individual of the colony which had been deposited with the Immigrant Aid Society of New Orleans [the committee of the New Orleans community set up to deal with the problems of the new arrivals] will remain as a general fund for the benefit of the colony; but each member will be entitled to a special credit on the book of association for the amount deposited less the cost incident to his voyage and support. (quoted in Herrscher, 1981, p. 34)

Members were not allowed to sell, barter, or offer for sale anything within the boundaries of the colony. Any commercial enterprise would require approval by two-thirds of the colonists.

The tract of land was divided into three sections to facilitate coopera-tive work—an echo of the feudal three-field system. "All resources were pooled" (ibid., p. 35) The business and profits were divided on an equal basis. In the beginning, individuals had no shares of their own, but when the colony achieved strong foundation "each person was to be established on an individual basis" (ibid.).

Figure 28. Locations Chosen for the Jewish Communities.

The local committee of AIU dealt with the basic problem of supplies by furnishing the colonists with lumber for their houses, farm implements, cattle, and poultry. They had an advisor and tilled the soil and planted corn, cotton, and vegetables. Ten houses were built. There was a general store. Evenings were devoted to discussions and debates. Borowick, a Russian opera star, entertained with songs. Herman Rosenthal read his poems to an appreciative audience. There was a weekly news bulletin.

In the spring of 1882 the colonists complained of the heat. Snakes and mosquitoes added to their discomforts. Then, in the spring of 1882 a Mississippi flood washed everything away, and Sicily Island was abandoned.

One group, under Rosenthal, left for South Dakota to try again at Cremieux, named for Adolphe Cremieux, late president of AIU. Each colonist settled a 160-acre quarter section of a deserted Indian reservation in the Dakota Territory. The hope was that the enterprise would enable them to "become independent men" (citation from the *American Israelite*, quoted in Herrscher, 1981, p. 49). Rosenthal returned to New York to arrange for other relocations, leaving the task of colonization to Benoir Greenberg, who with Rosenthal organized the Montefiore Agricultural Aid Society (MAAS) as a successor to HEAS.

At Cremieux, land ownership was individual, but implements, lumber for housing, and livestock were bought from a common fund. The settlers lacked agricultural skills and were afflicted by a number of disasters. A prairie fire destroyed the standing hay in 1882. The winter of 1882–83 was unusually severe. An 1884 hailstorm destroyed the flax crop, the Hessian fly destroyed the wheat, and many of the livestock died in the summer heat and drought. The financial resources were inadequate to withstand these losses, and, unable to meet mortgage payments, Cremieux was abandoned in 1885.

A second Dakota Territory settlement was organized near Bismarck by St. Paul Rabbi Wechster in 1882. There were twenty families initially and fifty-four within a year. At first, things went well, but again financial resources were inadequate to withstand losses from crop failures, a prairie fire, and the drought of 1886. Painted Woods was abandoned in 1887.

Also established in the Dakota Territory in 1882 was Bethlehem Yehudah, organized by the Kremenchung party of Am Olam known as the Sons of Freedom. There were thirty-two members, all unmarried men, who settled on government land near Cremieux. Unlike other Jewish colonies, they refused outside support from American Jewish philanthropists because they were interested in staying away from the traditional Jewish petty trades. Financed by AIU, they aimed at a full collective life. According to Okugawa (1980), this was the best example of a Jewish communal society whose purpose was to demonstrate to the anti-Semites of the world that Jews were capable farmers. Women were to "enjoy equal rights with men" (Herrscher, 1981, p. 52). Rabbi Wechsler, one of the founders, said that it was, however, "characterized by difference of opinion, quarrels and confusion. There was no law and order" (ibid.). Add to this the lack of experience and the malaria and yellow fever epidemics in which twenty settlers died in 1883; the colony was liquidated in three years.

In 1882 the Cincinnati Hebrew Union Agricultural Society planted the Beersheba Colony in Kansas. Other attempts were made to establish settlements at Lasher, Gilead, Touro, Leeser, and Hebron in southern Kansas, but apparently these efforts did not take hold. At Beersheba, there was progress for two years, but then disputes emerged between the settlement manager and the colonists. Cattle and implements were confiscated. Without other funds, the colony disintegrated.

Two more settlements were established in 1882, Alliance and Rosenhayn in New Jersey. There also were attempts to establish settlements in the state at Carmel, Montefiore, Figa, and Ziontown, but those evidently were false starts.

Alliance was founded by HEAS and AIU some thirty-five miles from Philadelphia and included an area five miles away called Vineland. Forty families from southern Russia, mostly from Kiev and Elizabetgard, formed the settlement. The 1,150 acres were owned in common by the settlers. The families were charged $300 to be repaid in thirty-three years without interest. There were twenty-five families who were storekeepers and small traders. Alliance paid transportation expenses, built temporary structures, and taught farming. Wages were paid by HEAS on a weekly basis. Some worked part-time for Christian farmers who preferred Jewish workers over non-Jews.

Later, the Baron de Hirsch Fund took over the farms. The farmers received a stove, furniture and household goods, and each spring, tools, furniture, cooking utensils, plants, and farm utensils to the value of $100. Initially, the colonists worked four farms on a cooperative basis to save on the expenses of horses and farm tools, but this was not successful, and each farmer became responsible for his own. The colonists were encouraged to set up factories. Their success brought more immigrants. Alliance ended as a distinct community around 1908, but many of the settlers remained on their land.

Rosenhayn was established as a cooperative farm by HEAS for a group of six families. A successful shirt factory was built nearby that attracted some three hundred settlers (Brandes and Douglas, 1977, p. 61). The communal farming enterprise was abandoned by 1889.

In 1883 two additional Ad Olam settlements were established, one of 150 individuals near Newport, Arkansas, and one at New Odessa in Oregon. The Ad Olam settlement in Arkansas did not last long. The area settled was plague-infested and generally unsuitable for agriculture, and plans to provide timber to the railroads did not work out.

The New Odessa community was located on Crow Creek (near Glendale) in Douglas County, Oregon, on a tract of about 780 acres. Upon their arrival in America the settlers landed in New York, but their reception was not cordial because of their "socialist convictions, their radicalism and atheistic attitudes" (Oved, 1988, p. 224). There were about sixty young members between the ages of twenty-one and thirty.

Later, help came from banker Jacob Schiff, who contributed a large sum of money for the purchase of the land (ibid., p. 225). The project began in a systematic way, unlike other groups. Some worked as farm laborers to gain experience as farmers, and others worked at jobs for which they had the requisite skills in order to gain funds for the establishment of their own farms. Those who worked in the city lived together and organized "The Commune" (Herrscher, 1981, p. 38). Household tasks were divided and earnings pooled, and educational meetings were held at night to formulate plans for the future.

According to Herrscher (1981), about forty to fifty people occupied the colony in the spring of 1883. They built a large two-story frame building. The upper story was a dormitory, and the lower one was a communal kitchen, dining room, and assembly hall. They raised wheat, oats, peas, and other crops, but marketing and transportation of their produce was a problem. William Frey (formerly Vladimir Konstantinovich Geins) was the leading spirit among the colonists (Okugawa, 1980, p. 212). He was a non-Jewish Russian who had established several communes in the Midwest. He believed in the humanist positivism of the French philosopher Auguste Comte, professing simplicity in thought and deed. He settled in New Odessa together with his wife, Maria Slavinskya, and his mistress, Lydia Eichoff (Herrscher, 1981, p. 45). Odessa was soon known for its dances, and Mari Frey, a musician, entertained once a week.

The colony aimed at "pure communism": equalization of wealth and income. The Marxist creed "from everyone according to his ability and to everyone according to his need" was applied consistently. The hours of labor were fixed, and tasks were assigned on the farm, in the forest, and in the kitchen. The colonists emphasized Comtean discipline by confining their diet to beans, peas, and coarse bread, refusing to live lavishly while millions starved. They aimed at inspiring the world with an example of equality and brotherly love (ibid., p. 46).

The colony lived in harmony. The divisions that developed were mainly intellectual, coming from their nightly discussions, debates about Auguste Comte's philosophy of positivism and the religion of humanity. The meetings were aimed at self-criticism and mutual criticism in order to provide reciprocal examination of individual morals, thus cleansing the colony, but this brought opposition. Sexual jealousies emerged because there were insufficient women. Two schools of thought emerged, bringing a schism between adherents of Frey and Paul Kaplan. Kaplan, one of the Odessa group founders, engaged in administrative matters and was a firm believer in communism (Oved, 1988, p. 228).

Frey and fifteen of his followers left Odessa. He and his wife settled in London, where he died in 1888. Others returned to New York, where they established a common household with a cooperative laundry that lasted about five years. Kaplan was unable to improve conditions after Frey left. Matters were made more difficult by the burning of the library, the colony's most valuable possession, and the colony dissolved.

A final settlement was planted at Woodbine, New Jersey, after new persecutions in Russia. The noted German financier-philanthropist Baron Maurice de Hirsch had proposed an agreement with the czar's government to assume the cost of education of his fellow Jews in agriculture and mechanical pursuits if the government would stop the harsh discriminatory legislation that denied Jews equality (Herrscher, 1981, p. 84).

Talks broke down when Hirsch realized that the government preferred the removal of the Jews from Russia.

Hirsch aimed at an orderly emigration in order to "help the immigrant adjust quickly to his new home." The fund later turned over the activities to the Jewish Agricultural and Industrial Aid Society, which later became the Jewish Agricultural Society. The fund appointed Dr. Julius Goldman to establish a colony (others included Herman Rosenthal and Paul Kaplan). The colony was established with industrial activity to supplement farm income. Woodbine, in Cape May County, was fifty-six miles from Philadelphia.

A corporation to manage Woodbine known as the Woodbine Land and Improvement Company, was created. The directors were the trustees of Baron de Hirsch Fund, and its capital was $50,000. Goldman was elected president and Hirsch L. Sabsovich, an agricultural chemist, was named president of the colony. Fifty-three hundred acres of land was purchased for $37,500. Herman Rosenthal was assigned to select the colonists. Each family was to invest some of its own money and to pay an additional $200. By 1893, 650 acres of farmland had been cleared, 100 miles of farm roads had been built, and farmhouses had been erected. Jonasson Clock factory was in operation. There were cutlery, knitting, and cigar factories. A hotel was built, and a railroad was in operation. By spring, problems developed, however. All building in the colony stopped because there was a failure of communication between the colonists and the trustees. The trustees felt that the colonists did not need any assistance because the clock factory was in operation, and they decided to discontinue aid; but this was premature. The farms were not successful. Sabsovich soon admitted that the farmers were inexperienced and had been given their seeds and too many acres too soon.

Colonel John B. Weber investigated the situation after much publicity and made some concessions and recommendations. Within seven years there were a number of new industrial ventures. Woodbine became a town, and the population created a market for farm products. Agriculture and industry complemented each other. In 1903, Woodbine became a borough with political autonomy. It failed as an agricultural colony but was a success as an experiment in agro-industrial colonization.

CHAPTER TWELVE

Religious Sectarianism, the Social Gospel, and Theosophy

Elements of the Transcendentalists' philosophy—the unity of all creation, the preeminence of individual insight as the source of knowledge and of spiritual fulfillment, and social reform by collective means to ensure material welfare—appeared and reappeared in a variety of religious experiments in the second half of the nineteenth century and helped shape the Third Great Awakening after 1890. Through the 1850s the religious communes that were established outside the principal movements reflected the diversity of sectarianism. Most of these were established in the surge of the 1840s (see Fig. 29). Later, religious communes were predominantly Social Christian, but some became imbued with the mysticism of Asian religions.

Among the earlier sectarian initiatives, the Pilgrims (1817–18) originated in Lower Canada and settled in the Woodstock district. Their stay there was brief, and they continued their search for their Promised Land as far west as New Madrid, Missouri. Sholem (1837–42) was a small group of New York Jews of German and Dutch descent who established a colony in virtually inaccessible mountainous land in the state of New York. Finding it impossible to support themselves, many sold their holdings and moved back to the city. Henry Ginal, a radical Lutheran minister from Philadelphia founded Teutonia (1842–44), also in the northern wilderness, attracting four hundred settlers to a colony that went bankrupt in two years. Friedens-Verein (1843–45) was established by Andreas Bernardus Smolnikar, a Benedictine monk from Austria. The Brotherhood, or Spiritualist Community (1847) was another creation of John Wattles (see Chapter 14). Ephraim, at Green Bay (1850–53), was a Moravian religious commune organized by Nils Otto Tank, an affluent Norwegian convert. A group of twenty-five poor Norwegians under A. M. Iverson broke away and formed another Wisconsin Ephraim (1853–64). The St. Nazianz

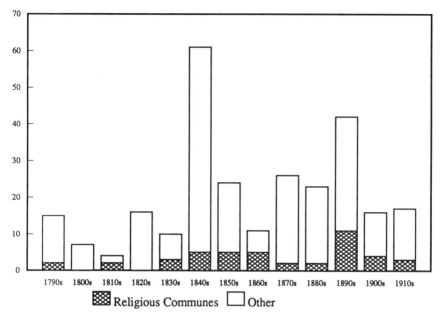

Figure 29. When Other Religious Communes Were Developed. A wide variety of experiments, beyond the principal religious surges, is included in this chart. There is long-wave rhythmicity, with the heightened activity in the 1890s associated with liberal Protestantism's turn to a social mission.

Community, the only Roman Catholic communal society established in America before World War I, was formed by 113 German immigrants from Baden led by Father Ambrose Oschwald. St. Nazianz was taken over in 1874 by the Catholic Society of Our Divine Saviour.

It was during the last quarter of the nineteenth century, especially during the depression of the 1890s, that new themes appeared.

Hine (1953) comments that "certain clusters of ideal communities, especially in the first half of the nineteenth century, drew from clearly definable sources . . . with the last half of the century, however, the thought patterns resulting in communitarian experiments became far more numerous . . . portions of the religious world, moved by industrialization and urbanization, produced a Social Gospel and a Christian Socialism" (p. 4).

"What the proliferation of religious groups did was provide ways for many people to invest their lives with a significance that eased their sense of frustration" (Fogarty, 1990, p. 6). The Third Great Awakening brought the Social Gospel movement, committed to the notion of planning to achieve a just society. The Awakening also reinforced interest in spiritualism and psychic and occult phenomena as well as provoking a

Fundamentalist reaction, epitomized by Billy Sunday's urban revivalism. Sunday extolled "old time religion" and inveighed against Darwinism, Progressive ideologies, social action, and the destruction of the American way of life by "new" immigrants. The Fundamentalists were responsible for another millenarian upsurge during the depression of the 1890s, as they and the Pentecostals held conferences to discuss the imminent end of the world.

During the decade, the resulting utopian experiments took many forms. In 1896 about twenty-five families responded to Ralph Albertson's series of articles in *The Kingdom* (1895–96) on the relationship of Christianity to social problems. They settled on the 934 acres of an old plantation in west-central Georgia, creating the Christian Commonwealth Colony. The Commonwealth lasted four years and had the usual problems with membership and economics (most came empty-handed, and few added much to the financial strength of the colony) and eventually with the courts. Their noteworthy success was their periodical, *The Social Gospel*, with a circulation of two thousand and so widely known that it became the accepted name for Social Christianity.

Texan Baptists established the Commonwealth of Israel in Texas (1899–1900). Jacob Beilhart, a Second Adventist and faith healer, gathered thirteen followers into the spiritualist Spirit Fruit Society in Lisbon, Ohio, later relocated to Lake County, Illinois (1899–1908). John Alexander Dowie organized Zion City (1901–6) in Illinois to house his Christian Catholic Apostolic Church. The Israelite House of David (1903–28) was founded by "Queen Mary and King Benjamin" Purnell, based on their reading of the Hebrew Scriptures.

A group of dissatisfied Methodists in Chicago, who founded the Metropolitan Church Association with headquarters in Waukesha, Wisconsin, purchased 1,520 acres in east Texas. The Burning Bush community (1903–19) had 375 members, whose occupational backgrounds varied widely, from farm laborers to professionals. "All wealth was held in common, and everyone who lived on the land ate from the common table." Although the "Holy Jumpers," as neighbors called them because of their religious rituals, prospered for several years, the end came abruptly after World War I, when the colony's financial backer lost his bond business in Chicago.

A growing number of utopian experiments were started in California (for an overview, see Hine, 1953). They came in a variety of "flavors." Following the charitable activities of the Pisgah movement, directed toward the downtrodden on the back streets of Los Angeles and elsewhere, Finis E. Yoakum, a physician, established Pisgah Grande (1914–21), a Pentecostal Christian commune on a thirty-two-hundred-acre cattle ranch in the Santa Susana Mountains. Among the three hundred residents were some recruited from the mission in Los Angeles, plus farmers, teachers, nurses, and artists. After Yoakum's death in 1920 the colony slowly crumbled. The Pisgah movement remained in Los Angeles for several years, and later the headquarters was moved to Pikeville, Tennessee.

With a proposal to rid California of "negroes and orientals," William E. Riker established a colony with thirty followers of the Perfect Christian Divine Way. The new Zion, Holy City (1919–58) was situated on two hundred acres in the Santa Cruz Mountains in central California. The community provided housing, clothing, meals, and the means of production. At its peak there were over two hundred converts. Riker's notoriety in court and the press eventually caused a decline in the membership, however. Only twelve residents remained in 1952 after he was charged with sedition.

Among the stranger, and ultimately unsuccessful, developments of the 1890s were the Koreshan Unity communes of Cyrus R. Teed. Teed was born in Moravia, New York, in 1840. A physician, his first experiment was a small communal household in Moravia. When he was thirty, he took the name of "Koresh," announcing that God always so addressed him, because Koresh was the Hebrew equivalent of his name, Cyrus. He argued that the universe was all one substance, and he defied the Copernican system. Christening his new system "Koreshamity," he said "amity" was added to Koresh to designate the new heaven and new earth and the new philosophy that would "replace all churches and government." Koreshamity consisted in part of his "Cellular Cosmogony." He was able, he thought, to demonstrate the contradictions of the Copernican system with instruments such as a hollow globe, which "demonstrated" that people lived on the outer shell of a hollow earth. He established a "scientific staff" among disciples, who preached his doctrine for fifteen years or so. In 1878 he visited Economy, still one of the most prosperous communal enterprises, to research the organization of this successful commune.

In 1886 he and his disciples moved to Chicago and established a church called the Assembly of the Covenant and an educational institution called the World's College of Life. The two organizations combined in 1888 into a cooperative home for his seventy-some disciples, Koreshan Unity, Chicago. Teed established a cooperative business organization, the Bureau of Equitable Commerce, to attract the working class. The membership began to increase. His new religion stressed his cosmogony, alchemy, reincarnation, celibacy, and communal life, mixing classical utopian themes with concepts from Asian religions.

In 1890 another community of Koreshans was formed in San Francisco by the Chicago group. It was called the Golden Gate Assembly of the Koreshan Unity. The San Francisco community had branches of the College of

Life, the Bureau of Equitable Commerce, and the Guiding Star Publishing House. This colony disintegrated late in 1891, and the remainder joined the Chicago community.

In the Chicago community three-fourths of the followers were female; all agreed to abstain from sex just as they freely gave Teed their property. He was reputed to have four thousand followers who also gave him large sums of money. The *Chicago Herald* criticized him as a dictator, but in spite of such criticism the Koreshan Unity was active in Chicago until its one hundred members moved to Florida in 1903.

When a disciple named Dampkohler gave Teed 320 acres of land in Estero, Florida, in 1903, he began to establish his third community, to be called New Jerusalem. Teed thought the site appropriate enough to create the greatest city on earth. By 1904 the entire Chicago group had migrated to Florida, to be joined by a hundred new recruits. They obtained two thousand more acres of land and built a sawmill, printing establishments, and other shops. There were contributions from distant members of the "Church Triumphant."

However, recusants blamed Teed and a few of his favorites with inappropriate use of funds. The departing members sued Teed for the return of their property, but the courts rejected their suit. When Dampkohler, who donated the original 320 acres, wanted the return of his land, the courts provided him with half.

Meanwhile, Teed was regarded as a corrupt and foolish man by many people. Even though he recommended celibacy for the members, he enjoyed relations with many young women in the community. Various Florida papers criticized him, and the national press picked up the story. The prophet, who had promised that he would take all believers directly to heaven, wilted under the pressure.

When Teed died on 24 December 1908, the members gathered around the body for a prayer meeting until officers, four days later, ordered them to bury him. The prophet was put into a bathtub and carried to a tomb on Estero Island.

Two groups attempted to create new communities. Mrs. Annie G. Ordway, who was pro-Teed, led a small group of followers and established a Koreshan community in Hillsborough County, Florida, which quickly disintegrated. An anti-Teed group formed a new colony, the Order of Theocracy, in Fort Myers, Florida. This lasted until 1931.

About 130 remaining members stayed at Estero, subsisting largely by farming and fishing. The membership declined to sixty in 1928 and to twelve in 1948. The Unity donated the major part of the land to the state, which became Koreshan State Park in 1967.

The full list of thirty-four "miscellaneous" religious communes appears

Table 6

Community	Started	Ended
Pilgrims, Vt.	1817	1818
Community of United Christians, Ohio	1836	1837
Sholem, N.Y.	1837	1842
Teutonia, Pa.	1842	1844
Friedens-Verein, Pa.	1843	1845
The Brotherhood, or Spiritualist Community, Ohio	1846	1847
Ephraim at Green Bay, Wis.	1850	1853
Ephraim, Wis.	1853	1864
St. Nazianz Community, Wis.	1854	1874
The Christian Republic, Ohio	1865	1866
Cedarvale Community, Kans.	1875	1877
Bible Community, Miss.	1878	1879
Esoteric Fraternity, Calif.	1887	1973
Koreshan Unity, Ill.	1888	1903
Koreshan Unity, Calif.	1890	1891
Koreshan Unity, Fla.	1894	Present
New House of Israel, Tex.	1895	1920
Christian Commonwealth, Ga.	1896	1900
Fort Amity, Colo.	1898	1910
Romie, Calif.	1898	1910
Fort Herrick, Ohio	1898	1910
Point Loma, Calif.	1898	1942
Commonwealth of Israel, Tex.	1899	1900
Christian Social Association, Wis.	1899	1904
Spirit Fruit Society, Ohio/Ill.	1899	1908
Zion City, Ill.	1901	1906
House of David, Mich.	1903	1928
Temple Home, Calif.	1903	1913
Order of Theocracy, Fla.	1910	1931
Lopez Community, Wash.	1912	1920
Krotona Community, Calif.	1912	Present
The Burning Bush Community, Tex.	1903	1919
Pisgah Circle, Calif.	1914	1921
Holy City, Calif.	1919	1958

in Table 6. For their locations, see Figure 30. Special attention must be given in this list to the Social Christians of the Salvation Army, as well as to the California Theosophists, who reached out to Eastern philosophies and religions.

The Salvation Army

The Salvation Army was organized in England in 1878 to battle poverty in the slums of London. Under the stringent and zealous leadership of General William Booth, the Salvation Army took the Social Gospel to the poor in an effort to save the soul by saving the body. The organization

Figure 30. Locations of the Miscellaneous Religious Communes. Before Reconstruction the other religious communes that were constructed were confined to the Northeast. The locus of activity moved west and south thereafter.

made its way to the United States in 1898, and three experimental colonies were established to relieve urban poverty in a subsidized back-to-the-land movement.

General Booth was a controversial figure in nineteenth-century England who had experienced poverty as a child. He made the decision to become a Methodist minister dedicated to redeeming the degraded poor who were ignored by other factions of society. In 1861 he abandoned the pulpit to become an evangelical preacher. Four years later his calling led him to London, where he organized the Christian Mission in the worst slums in that city. The name was changed to the Salvation Army in 1878 when a semimilitary framework was adopted for waging war against the forces of evil. Booth expected unquestioning obedience from his officers as orders were issued in the style of the British army. Consistent with the mission, uniforms were worn. The Salvation Army began seeking out the poor by taking its religion to street corners or wherever the forgotten segment of society could be found.

Booth's vision of reforming society was influenced by the back-to-the-land efforts of Irishman Feargus O'Connor, who, during the Hungry Forties, had lectured in Nottingham on the need to break up large estates to provide settlements for industrial families. Booth developed the idea further. His book *In Darkest England and the Way Out* laid out a visionary scheme for creating a concentric system of colonies where the poor would be redeemed, trained, and mainstreamed into productive lives. At the center of the system would be sources of basic provisions—inexpensive food centers, shelters, labor yards, rescue homes for women, retreats for discharged convicts, and temporary employment. After a period of training and betterment those ready to assume permanent jobs would return to their families, while others would contribute their labor to the Farm Colony, where unused farmland would sustain the colonies with no waste.

As early as 1886, Booth's attention turned to the possibility of emigrating to North America to build farm colonies. Plans included acquiring a private ship manned by Salvationists. The Salvation Ship would be used to transport emigrants to the newly established utopian colonies.

Before branching out to the United States, the Salvation Army experienced opposition from middle-class critics, who considered its militancy fanatical and its mission unrealistic and simplistic. The critics argued that the nonworking poor could not be transformed into productive members of society and that Booth's harsh discipline and dictatorial leadership would undermine the family and encourage oppression and tyranny. In spite of insult, incidents of open violence, and arrests for disturbing the peace, Booth persisted. The movement spread throughout the British Isles.

During the depression of the 1890s a number of Protestant groups in America were convinced of the need to do practical missionary work in city slums as the ranks of the unemployed swelled in the wake of economic crisis. The Salvation Army thus was able to make a substantial impact. Agricultural colonies ultimately were established at Fort Amity in Colorado, Fort Herrick in Ohio, and Fort Romie in California.

The American venture was led by Booth's daughter and son-in-law (who assumed the name Booth-Tucker). Their goal was to further Booth's cause by establishing a chain of farm colonies that would form a network across the entire United States. Capital was in short supply, however, and the Salvation Army was entirely dependent on donations of land and capital from sympathetic citizens. Booth-Tucker was well received by several standing-room-only crowds when he announced that, with the army's plan and conviction, 3 million paupers could be resettled and rehabilitated. Finally, enough donations were received to support the establishment of the first farm colony.

Land was acquired in 1898 at Fort Romie, California. Colonists were carefully screened and typically were the unemployed from urban areas who had no previous experience in agriculture. Upon arrival each colonist was required to enter into a contract with the Salvation Army, which included paying rent on buildings and land with an option to purchase at the end of ten years if the moral and financial requirements set forth by the manager of the colony were met. Colonists were expected to work hard, be responsible, and refrain from alcohol consumption. If a colonist was deficient in any of these areas, he abdicated all rights to property. At first, Fort Romie appeared successful, and by March 1898 eighty people, representing sixteen families, had settled in the colony.

Drought and water shortages, along with internal problems, threatened the viability of the colony only three years after its establishment, however. Leadership factions arose over financial matters, culminating in the resignation of the head of the fund-raising committee. Other leadership changes were made, resulting in a tightening of control and a commitment to cut costs. With shrewd planning and reorganization through a general bond issue, Fort Romie was reestablished on a more solid financial base. Meanwhile, most of the colonists had left.

The leadership recognized its error in bringing families with no agricultural background, so the second wave of settlers brought families with farming skills. Each family was to be allowed to settle on twenty acres at $100 per acre, payable at 5 percent interest over a twenty-year period. By 1905 twenty families were living at Fort Romie.

Most of the families, in fact, came with very limited capital and questionable farming experience and, due to an oversight among leadership, without signing a formal contract with the Salvation Army. When the omission was recognized, the leadership drew up a document they believed to be fair to the settlers as well as to the army. However, settlers requested compromises regarding consumption of alcohol and restrictions on disorderly activity. An agreement was reached, and by 1906 the colony was apparently on its way to success. Most colonists were able to gain title to their land between 1910 and 1917, and Fort Romie ceased to be a communal settlement.

After establishing its first colony, the Salvation Army began pouring its resources into a second colony, located in the Arkansas Valley at Fort Amity, Colorado. The key figure in selecting and settling colonists was Thomas Holland. Those chosen to settle in Fort Amity had to possess honesty, industry, sobriety, ability, and experience in farming. A contract was required as an agreement to farm ten acres at a yearly rental of $2 per acre, with the title to be transferred at the end of eleven years, when the payments would total $22.50 plus the interest charged. Each man was provided with a house according to the size of his family and equipment needed to begin farming.

The first crop raised for sale at Fort Amity was cantaloupe. Extreme price fluctuations, followed by an untimely frost, resulted in a total loss the first year. Fortunately, enough other vegetables had been harvested to provide food for the settlers during the winter. Loans from the Salvation Army supplemented outside jobs long enough to help the colony expand and diversify the crops to be planted.

By 1905 only thirty-eight families were living at Fort Amity, although Booth-Tucker had predicted there would be over one hundred. Frequently assisted by the Salvation Army, a number of colonists eventually branched out from agriculture to become small-town businessmen. Just as the colony was on its way to becoming well established, a build-up of salt in the soil due to poor drainage caused severe crop failures. Engineers were consulted, but solutions were costly and improvements came too late. An expensive drainage system was installed, but results were disappointing. Debts rose, and soon the settlers began withdrawing. Settlement payments were made but were relatively small, since debts owed to the Salvation Army were large. By 1909, Fort Amity had been sold, and the colony was completely abandoned.

In 1898 a third colony, named Fort Herrick, was established twenty miles from Cleveland, Ohio, on a 288-acre tract of land purchased from Myron T. Herrick and his brother-in-law James Parmalee, two prominent Ohio politicians. Booth-Tucker saw in Fort Herrick the opportunity to build a model colony that would serve as a training ground for future colonies in the West. With much fanfare and excitement the site was opened publicly, and plans for its phenomenal growth were announced.

Selection of colonists was similar to the process used for settling Fort Romie and Fort Amity. Each farmer was to get five to ten acres with a title transfer occurring upon completion of a ten-year lease. Booth-Tucker established a Colonization Finance Council to monitor the financial activities of Fort Herrick. Organizationally, it appeared Fort Herrick would be successful. However, settlers soon began noticing that the poor drainage of the land caused the foundations of the poorly built houses to settle, resulting in leaking roofs, shifting chimneys, and doors that would not open correctly. Immediate repairs were ordered, the number of houses was increased, and drainage improvements were requested.

Leadership fell to Charles W. Bourne, a young Salvationist who had arrived in America in 1887. His lack of leadership ability soon became apparent in his inability to work well with the Colonization Finance Council appointed by Booth-Tucker. The majority of his requests for improvement funds met with disapproval on the grounds that Bourne was wasteful and needed to be more economical in his expenditures. In spite of the friction among leadership, the Salvation Army continued pouring funds into the newly formed colony.

High land prices constrained expansion of Fort Herrick, and settlers became discontented when their requests for additional land were denied for reasons of cost. Meanwhile, the colonies at Fort Romie and Fort Amity were given priority, since Booth-Tucker had realized irrigation and intense cultivation of cheap land were the key ingredients to successful colonization. Because high prices limited expansion, the Salvation Army soon decided to reorganize Fort Herrick's farm colony concept into a drying-out facility for drunkards, and the few remaining colonists were relocated. The new mission was short-lived, and the colony was again reorganized, this time into a camp for children. It was used for this purpose until 1974, when the property was sold.

Although Booth-Tucker's plans were noble, the colonists were slow to meet their obligations, delinquencies were frequent, and army expenditures greatly outweighed income received from the colonies. Initial heavy outlays usually included building costs, equipment, wages, fencing, and livestock. Other expenditures included subsidies, travel expenses for colonists when necessary, and loan support for settlement. Booth-Tucker's unwillingness to enforce foreclosure on any settler resulted in loss to the Salvation Army and caused friction among leaders of the monitoring Colonization Finance Council, some of whom accused Booth-Tucker of treating the colonies as charities when they were actually business agreements.

In addition to internal disagreements over financial matters, fundraising was difficult, and those who could have afforded to support the Salvation Army's colonization efforts were unconvinced of its likelihood of success. Much of the support pledged was in the form of loans that required repayment at inconvenient times. The colonization scheme was attractive to American society in general, an expression of back-to-the-land efforts that reappeared again in the federal government's New Deal programs, but large donations depended on the success of Fort Romie or Fort Amity. Expansion on a large scale was impossible without further funds, and the breakthrough needed to establish a chain of farm colonies was never realized.

The California Theosophists

Although the Theosophists established only three communes in California—Point Loma (1898–1942), Temple Home (1903–13), and the Krotona Community (1912–)—they had a profound influence on later radical thought. The Theosophists popularized Asian religious and philosophical ideas in the West, influencing many other movements, for example Rosicrucianism, with its interest in transmutation, psychic development, and meditative/yogic disciplines, as well as sections of the metaphysical/New Thought movement, putting into place the ideas underpinning many of the communes that were formed during the 1960s—ideas that coalesced as the New Age Paradigm (Chapter 18). J. Stillson Judah (1967) traces a direct lineage from Theosophy to Alice Bailey's Arcane School, which, in the 1960s, was among the sources of the doctrine that we were about to leave the Piscean Age and enter a new Aquarian Age. Many occultists believe that this New Age will terminate the Christian period. Alice Bailey advanced the idea that the Age of Aquarius will mark the fusion of Christianity and Buddhism and the advent of the Messiah (Judah, 1967, pp. 122ff.).

Theosophy (*theos* [god], *sophia* [wisdom]—i.e., divine wisdom) is identified in modern times with the doctrines of Helene Petrovna Blavatsky but is a religious philosophy with roots in third-century Neo-Platonism. Blavatsky, daughter of Russian nobility, escaped conventional responsibilities as a young woman via an unconsummated marriage, traveling widely thereafter in Eastern Europe, Greece, and Egypt. Originally, she was inspired by the Kabbala, with its Jewish esoteric mysticism, and by Gnosticism, with its notion of esoteric salvatory knowledge, plus other forms of occultism. In 1851, in London, she met the Tibetan Master Morya and followed him to the Himalayas. Thereafter she was variously in India and elsewhere in Asia and the Middle East until 1873, when Master Morya ordered her to travel to New York. There she offered to the West her version of Theosophy (Blavatsky, 1966). In New York she made contact with American lawyer and student of spiritualism Henry Steel Olcott and with the Irish lawyer W. Q. Judge. In 1875 they founded the Theosophical Society, committed to advancing Theosophy's three basic doctrines—the universal brotherhood of man, the study of Eastern religion, and the investigation of psychic phenomena—in the West.

In 1878, Blavatsky and Olcott returned to India, and in 1882 they bought an estate at Adyar, near Madras, which became and remains the international headquarters of the Theosophical Society. After conflict at Adyar, Blavatsky moved to London, where she died in 1891.

While Blavatsky and Olcott were in India, William Q. Judge had kept the American movement alive during the 1880s, supporting Edward Bellamy's reform movements. After Blavatsky's death, conflict between Judge and Olcott led to secession of American Theosophy from Indian control, however. Judge remained in power in America, and Olcott retained control in India.

Judge died in 1896, and Katherine Tingley succeeded him. Tingley, a reformer who had worked in prisons, hospitals, and children's organizations, had been converted by Judge. Assuming leadership, she explored religious and occult centers in the United States and then in 1898 moved the American headquarters to a theosophical school and community she established on 330 acres of land at Point Loma, near San Diego, California (Hine, 1953, p. 33ff.) The community was supported by a fee-paying Raja-Yoga school that emphasized the Montessori method and by gifts from wealthy Theosophists. In 1910 there were five hundred inhabitants, of whom three hundred were students in the school. The community flourished under Tingley but declined after her death in an automobile accident in Europe in 1929. The property at Point Loma was sold in 1942, and the remaining Theosophists moved to Covina, California. In 1950–51, the American movement's international headquarters was moved to Pasadena.

One group of Theosophists in Syracuse, New York, led by William H. Dower, rejected Katherine Tingley as Judge's successor. Relocating to San Luis Obispo County, California, in 1903, they formed the Temple Home Association on three hundred acres north of Santa Barbara. By 1906 they had 140 members and owned the Halcyon Sanatorium and Hotel. The cooperative venture failed in 1913, although the temple still exists.

Olcott died in India in 1906 and was succeeded by the dynamic Annie Besant, who actively located branches of the movement throughout India and Europe and later back in the United States. In 1912 a friend of Besant's, Albert P. Washington, established the Krotona Community of Adyar Theosophists in Hollywood, California. In 1924 the commune was moved to the Ojai Valley in Ventura County, where it remains with its school of Theosophy. There are branches in many countries around the world.

What is Theosophy? It has several basic characteristics:

Belief in *mystical experience*, emphasizing that a deeper spiritual reality exists and that people can establish direct contact with that reality through intuition, meditation, or some other state transcending normal consciousness.

Emphasis upon *esoteric doctrine*. Esoteric or inner teaching concerns hidden meaning, in contrast to exoteric, or outer, teaching of overt meaning.

Interest in the *occult*, the supernatural, and higher psychic and spiritual powers.

Assertion of *monism*, the notion that reality is made up of one principle, such as mind or spirit, thus affirming an all-encompassing unity that subsumes all differences.

Blavatsky emphasized one supreme First Cause, from which all manifestation comes. She also proclaimed universal brotherhood and promoted exploration of the occult. Modern Theosophists subscribe to an elaborate theory of the universe (cosmogony), heavily imbued with religious and philosophical conceptions derived from Asian thought. These include the idea that there are seven worlds or planes through which the universe evolves, in ascending order: (1) the physical, (2) the emotional (astral), (3) the mental, (4) the intuitional (Buddhic), (5) the spiritual (Atmic), (6) the monadic (Anupadaka), and (7) the divine (Adi). Man goes through the same progression, eventually reaching perfection via a series of reincarnations, each determined by karma, the rule by which rewards and punishments are meted out for actions, desires, and thoughts in the present life. "Right thought is necessary to right conduct, right understanding to right living" (Besant, 1897/1969, p. 1). Because there is a supreme moral arbiter, central to the Theosophists' system of belief is the notion that proper behavior in this life is necessary for progress in future lives.

These were ideas that reappeared in the 1960s, ultimately helping form the New Age Paradigm, as we shall see in Chapter 18.

CHAPTER THIRTEEN

Secular Alternatives: From Free Love and Vegetarianism to the Cooperative Commonwealth

Just as many religious sects built communes in response to economic crises in the nineteenth and early twentieth centuries, so did secular communards in surges that were concentrated in the economic crises of the 1840s, the 1870s, the 1890s, and athwart the Crisis of 1907. Again one sees the pattern of multiplicity of source but common timing of the reaction. The long list of communities includes the forty-eight listed in Table 7.

What is impressive about this list is the extraordinary variety of the initiatives, the long-wave rhythmicity (Fig. 31), and the brevity of most of the experiments. Within the variety, several threads are evident, however. Fogarty (1990, pp. 14–16) says he can discern three broad groups between the Civil War and World War I: (1) the "cooperative colonizers" who believed that secular salvation could be attained by establishing groups in new settlements that, with collective responsibility, would lead to moral and material improvement; (2) the "charismatic perfectionists" who, following a forceful leader, sought perfection in a confined community that molded the dreams and visions of that leader and that offered the opportunity for spiritual or sexual experimentation; and (3) the "political pragmatists" who advanced the cooperative commonwealth as a means to implement socialism in hard times. Some of these groups were discussed in Chapter 12. The socialist experiments will be considered in Chapter 14. Here, after listing the communes that mixed spiritualism, free love, and vegetarianism, we turn to the attempts to establish cooperative communities, many of which, started after 1880, were on the West Coast (Fig. 32).

Numbered among the former are Harmonia, New York (1853–63), a spiritualist and staunchly feminist community organized around springs thought to have special magnetic healing qualities; the "long-haired sleek-looking" free love spiritualists at Davis House, Ohio (1854–58) and their

Table 7

Community	Started	Ended
The Union, N.Y.	1804	1810
Oberlin Colony, Ohio	1833	1841
Marlborough Association, Ohio	1841	1845
Northampton Association, Mass.	1842	1846
Abram Brooke's Community, Ohio	1843	1845
Bishop Hill, Ill.	1846	1862
Modern Times, N.Y.	1851	1863
Jaspis Kolonie, Iowa	1851	1853
Old Bull's Colony, Pa.	1852	1853
Rising Star Association, Ohio	1853	1863
Free-Lovers at Davis House, Ohio	1854	1858
Harmonia, N.Y.	1857	1863
Harmonial Vegetarian Society, Ark.	1860	1864
Point Hope, Ohio	1861	1861
Union Colony, Colo.	1869	1872
German Colonization Company, Colo.	1870	1871
Progressive Community, Kans.	1871	1878
Warm Springs, N.C.	1871	1871
Chicago-Colorado Colony, Colo.	1871	1873
Western Colony, Colo.	1871	1872
Dawn Valcour, Vt.	1874	1875
Women's Commonwealth, Tex.	1874	1906
Investigating Community, Kans.	1875	1875
Modejska Community, Calif.	1877	1878
Societas Fraternias, Calif.	1879	?
Thompson Colony, Kans.	1880	—
Joyful, Calif.	1884	1884
Shalam, N. Mex.	1884	1901
Columbia Cooperative Colony, Oreg.	1886	1892
Puget Sound Cooperative Colony, Wash.	1887	1890
Lord's Farm, N.J.	1889	1907
Union Mill Cooperative, Oreg.	1891	1897
Glennis Cooperative Industrial Colony, Wash.	1894	1896
Magnolia, Tex.	1896	1896
American Settlers Association, Ga.	1898	1899
Mutual Home Association, Wash.	1898	1921
Straight Edge Industrial Association, N.Y.	1899	1918
The Roycrofters, N.Y.	1900	1915
Fellowship Farm Association, Mass.	1907	1918
Little Landers Colonies, Calif.	1909	1916
San Ysidro		
Runnymede		
Hayward Heath		
San Fernando		
Cupertino		
Los Angeles Fellowship Farm, Calif.	1912	1927
Bohemian Cooperative Farm Association, Tenn.	1913	1916
Ferrer Colony, N.J.	1915	1946

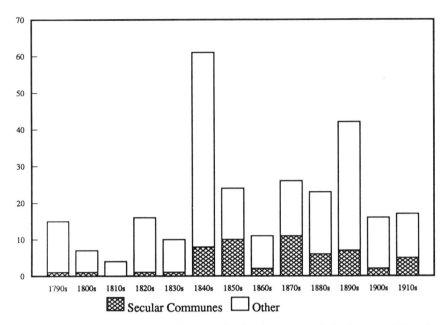

Figure 31. Timing of the Miscellaneous Secular Communes. As in the case of the miscellaneous religious communes, a wide variety of settlement initiatives are represented here. Despite the variety, clear surges are to be seen, although in the 1890s many of the secular initiatives were dominated by socialist ideologies (Fig. 33).

offshoot at Point Hope, Ohio (1860–61); the Harmonial Vegetarian Society, Arkansas (1860–64), which practiced vegetarianism and free love; Dawn Velcour, Vermont (1874–75), the "Head Center of Advanced Spiritualism and Free Love"; Women's Commonwealth, Texas (1874–1906), a celibate group of Pentecostal feminists; the vegetarians of Societas Fraternia, California (1879–), and Joyful, California (1884); the spiritualists at Shalam, New Mexico (1884–1901); and the vegetarian celibates and anarchists at Lord's Farm, New Jersey (1889–1907).

Cooperative experiments actually came very early in the history of utopian community building. The first American cooperative experiment whose community theory was not based on religious doctrine was The Union, started near Potsdam, New York, in 1804. Some twenty-four hundred acres of land were farmed cooperatively. After a constitution was adopted in 1807, the "virus of self interest" took over, however, and the land was divided in 1810. Most members stayed on, farming their land individually. This was followed by the Oberlin Colony, established in Loraine County, Ohio, by eight immigrant Yankee families under the leadership of John Shepherd in 1833 to create "as perfect a community

Figure 32. Locations of the Secular Communes. Note, once again, the restriction to the North before the Civil War and the diffusion after Reconstruction. Note also that whereas California was the location of a number of communal religious communities between the Civil War and World War I, the secular communards (other than the socialists) avoided that state—compare with Figures 30 and 34.

of interests as though we held a community of property." A school was established that became Oberlin College. The college absorbed the colony in 1841.

The next cooperative experiments came in the depression of the 1840s. A number of secular communes were established in New York, Massachusetts, and Ohio: Marlborough, Northampton, and Abram Brooke's Experiment. Okugawa (1980) describes them as follows:

> *Marlborough* . . . consisted of two separate farms, donated by Edward Brooke and his brother Abram Brooke. . . . Many of the members were Freethinkers, who did not practice religion. After death of one of the leaders . . . the members adopted a constitution. For the first time, they realized that they differed radically on the basic questions of communal property and the principles of government. Torn by internal dissension, the group dissolved in the latter part of 1845. . . .
>
> *Northampton*, perhaps the most thoroughly industrial secular communal enterprise, originated in a silk company as early as 1835 and was gradually transformed into a communal organization. It had strong ties with Garrisonism, with several former black slaves living in the community. . . .
>
> *Abram Brooke* . . . tried his own experiment in the community of ownership after he withdrew from the Marlborough Association. . . . [A]s indicated in his letter to *The Harbinger* [it comprised] only his own and his mother's family. (Pp. 183, 184, 187)

In 1851 there was the Modern Times experiment. Leaving Ohio and Indiana, Josiah Warren set up another community on Long Island with the support of Stephen Pearl Andrews, a veteran reformer. Like his earlier attempt, Utopia, the community advocated a cooperative, nonprofit system of labor and commodity exchange while each member owned a house and land. A group of the former members of Brook Farm joined in 1857; the community numbered two hundred inhabitants in total. Some members, including T. L. Nichols and his wife Mary, put into practice their ideas of free love. Although Warren went to Boston in 1863 and never returned to Modern Times, a few community residents were still in Brentwood after the turn of the century.

The descent into the primary deflationary trough of the 1870s brought, among others, the Union, Chicago-Colorado, and Western colonies in Colorado. Union Colony was founded by Nathaniel C. Meeker. The basic idea of Meeker's Colorado plan was to form a land-purchase cooperative through which easterners could amass sufficient capital to buy and to irrigate the cheap but dry land of the West. The land was then to be apportioned among the members of the cooperative as individual holdings. It was conceived to be a compact agricultural community centered around a town, where all could benefit from the advantages of cooperative life. Meeker's plan reawakened Horace Greeley's interest in creating cooperative communities to relieve American cities of their surplus populations. He thought that by setting up a network of colonies, opportunities could be provided for the jobless and the underemployed.

The Union Colony Association was formed in 1869 by Meeker with Greeley's support. There were 442 members at the beginning, mostly eastern farmers, artisans, and small businessmen. The cooperative colony recognized private ownership of land but shared community responsibilities. It had no saloons or billboards but constructed a school, library, and lyceum. By 1871 the colonists had voted to replace the community officers with an elected town government. Shortly thereafter, the land was made available to the general public. During 1871–72, an effort was made to establish a cooperative stock and dairy association, but it failed for lack of funds. By 1872 the Union Colony had merged into the town of Greeley, and its meager cooperative base had disappeared. Although its idealism was soon overwhelmed by its individualism, Greeley developed by 1900 into a prosperous town of three thousand people, with a strong sense of community centered on its tree-lined streets, its public park, its temperance character, and its schools. This "Garden City of the West" became a model for later colonies, which helped populate the dry lands of the West.

Okugawa (1980) says of the Chicago-Colorado and Western colonies:

[T]he Chicago-Colorado Colony was organized partly by the *Chicago Tribune*. The constitution was modeled after Union Colony's. . . . The majority of the four hundred members came from Chicago, but some ninety people already living in the vicinity also joined. As in the case of Union Colony, the communal features quickly disappeared when irrigation projects were completed. . . .

The Western Colony was first organized in Ayres Point (now Oakdale), Washington County, Illinois, by Andrew C. Todd, a Reformed Presbyterian minister, and his parishioners in 1870. The headquarters of the organization was moved to St. Louis before their westward migration. A former member of Union Colony who was also from Ayres Point, was instrumental in deciding the colony site, only four miles from Greeley. The colony had about five hundred members the first summer. Apparently, Greeley deprived the colony of its potential growth. (Pp. 204–5)

The depression years of the 1890s brought additional cooperative experiments in Oregon and Washington. (For descriptions of these I rely on Fogarty, 1980. Fogarty presents additional materials in his more recent book [1990]). The Columbia Cooperative Colony at Mist, Oregon (later the Nehalem Valley Cooperative Colony), had a communal constitution and in 1892 owned a sawmill. Also, in Tillamook County, Oregon, the Union Mill Company was held in common, lumbering was carried on cooperatively, and the members received equal pay. In the state of Washington, the nucleus of the anti-Chinese movement among the working class in Seattle established a model city based on cooperation, the Puget Sound Cooperative Colony. The colony published a newspaper called *Model Commonwealth*. The four hundred members in 1887 were mainly from Washington and the Midwest, including a dozen or so families from Union Colony. Disputes over management of properties caused constant turnover of leadership. By 1890 many members were drifting away, some to a recently opened reservation.

The Glennis Cooperative Industrial Company was inspired by the Bellamy national movement and occupied 166 homestead acres about seventeen miles south of Tacoma, at one time with thirty members. Because of communal bylaws restricting activities that were in reality private matters, the colony quickly disbanded. Many left. A few tried another experiment based on their experience at Glennis and founded the Mutual Home Association on the other side of Tacoma. The Home, an "anarchist colony" as contemporaries more commonly referred to it, was founded by the three who had participated in the Glennis Colony. Except that land was held in common, the organizational structure was not highly communal. It was incorporated as a landholding company in 1898, and the houses were considered private property.

Despite the founders' denial that it was a cooperative colony, it had communal features, especially in its ideology. Reconverted socialists arrived from the defunct Ruskin Colony in Tennessee, the Cooperative Brotherhood, the Puget Sound Cooperative Colony, and the Equality Colony. Visitors from other communes included the Koreshans in Chicago and Elbert Hubbard of the Roycrofters near Buffalo. There were forty members originally, ninety-one by 1900. Because of its anarchist leanings, the colony, which published a succession of anarchistic periodicals (*New Era*, *Discontent: Mother of Progress*, *Demonstrator*, and *Agitator*), was in constant trouble with local officials. Most notably, the Home became the target of public and press attacks following the assassination of President McKinley in 1901.

This colony of individualists had few cooperative institutions. A cooperative store was organized in 1902, and some construction projects were done cooperatively. It was an exciting and colorful community where a high degree of individualism was tolerated and where free speech, free love, and free ideas were encouraged. In 1909 the articles of incorporation of the Mutual Home Association were changed to allow property to be held privately. Before that time all land was held in trust and could never be sold or disposed of. This change in the articles signaled the end of the Home as a cooperative colony, but it continued as a center for anarchist agitation.

In the environs of New York, the more notable of the secular communes included the Straight-Edgers, the Roycrofters, and the Ferrer Colony. The Straight-Edge Industrial Settlement was an experiment in cooperative enterprise. In the beginning, for economic reasons only, a small group of a dozen or so Straight-Edgers participated in communal living. Wilbur F. Copeland, who, though not a resident, had been associated with the Christian Commonwealth, started A School of Methods for the Application of the Teachings of Jesus to Business and Society. It was a school of cooperative industry in various fields of trade. The settlement also ran cooperative farms on Staten Island and later in Alpine, Bergen County, New Jersey. Communal life disappeared around 1906, although the industrial organization continued to exist until 1918.

The Roycrofters were a unique case of a profit-sharing "semi-communistic corporation," as it was described by its founder Elbert Hubbard. Between three hundred and five hundred people worked on a farm, in a bank, printing plant, bookbindery, furniture factory, and blacksmith shop. Some lived in the quarters called Roycroft Phalanstery. All of the company's proceeds, including a considerable profit from the multimillion sales of the inspirational and patriotic pamphlet published after the Spanish-American War, *A Message to Garcia*, went, according to Hubbard, "into the common fund of The Roycrofters—the benefit is for all." During one of his lecture tours around the country, Hubbard visited the Home in Washington, and one of the Roycroft families joined the Home. With the death of Hubbard aboard the *Lusitania* in 1915, the community became a purely commercial enterprise.

Ferrer Colony was organized in August 1914 in New York City. It was an anarchist community led by Harry Kelly, Joseph Cohen, and Leonard Abbott. Cohen later created the Sunrise Colony in Michigan (see Chapter 16). The Ferrer movement, named after the Spanish freethinker and anarchist Francisco Ferrer, was the force behind development of the colony. It was thought that a colony located outside New York City could be a more effective force for social change than one within the city, however, and in May 1915 the group moved across the Hudson River to Stelton, New Jersey, where eventually 90 homes were built and 120 children were enrolled in the school. Consistent with anarchist beliefs, land was owned by individuals. The Ferrer Colony was an odd mixture of anarchists, socialists, and communists, who inhabited the same ground for more than twenty years. By the 1940s and after two decades of community and conflict, many of the colonists sold their homes and moved to warmer sites in the Los Angeles and Miami areas. By 1946 it ceased to exist as a distinct entity.

In California there were five Little Landers Colonies, plus the Los Angeles Fellowship Farm. With support from the California Promotion Committee, William E. Smythe, renowned leader of the national reclamation movement, organized a settlement of the Little Landers. He believed that large tracts of land could be purchased cooperatively, irrigated, and subdivided into small plots, "little lands," and made productive. The colony's land, originally 120 and later 500 acres, was at San Ysidro in the Tijuana Valley, fourteen miles south of San Diego, facing the hills of Mexico. Besides San Ysidro, there were at least three other Little Landers colonies: Runnymede near Palo Alto, Hayward Heath in the San Fernando Valley, and Cupertino near San Jose. Each settler held his own land, usually an acre, but community living was carried on cooperatively as much as the members were willing, without any formal structure. Membership expanded, and by the fourth year there were 116 families at San Ysidro, 300 people in all, largely middle-aged and elderly. A cooperative store was established in the heart of San Diego to sell produce. The Little Landers were confident that their social ideal and settlements would become permanent features of the San Diego area, but in 1916 a flood destroyed all of the colony's houses.

Los Angeles Fellowship Farm was patterned after the Fellowship Farm Association of Westwood, Massachusetts. Settled on a seventy-acre tract about twelve miles southwest of Boston, the farm was organized by George E. Littlefield, a Unitarian minister. Each of the forty members was assigned an acre; the rest was common land. Most members were skilled tradesmen, who cooperated in house building. A simple one-room house cost only $16. Following this model, a group of twelve families settled on seventy-five acres in the La Puente Valley, about twenty miles east of Los Angeles. Each family had an acre for farming, and six central plots were used for communal activities. The colonists, finding cooperative farming unprofitable, dissolved the colony in 1927 and reorganized into the Maple Water Company.

Other cooperative communes included the American Settlers Association of Duke, Georgia, and Magnolia at Shepherd, Texas. The Settlers Association was organized in Dayton, Ohio, by a group of poor farmers and originally consisted of nine families who moved to Okefenokee land in southeastern Georgia. At first there was no communal aspect in its organization, but when it became necessary to clear 760 acres of timberland, the work became cooperative. "Each for all and all for each" was the colony's motto. It was joined later by several families from Indiana. In 1899, Duke Colony merged with the Ruskin Commonwealth following the latter's reorganization from the Ruskin Cooperative Association and relocation from Tennessee. The short-lived Magnolia at Shepherd was also known as the East Texas Cooperative Association. It started with 479 acres and began "practical operations" on 1 April 1896. One reason given for its failure was a low membership fee of $300, according to *Coming Nation*.

There was also the Bohemian Cooperative Terminal Company in Cumberland County, Tennessee. A group of economically depressed Bohemian immigrants residing in urban centers of the North during the difficult years following the Panic of 1907 settled on a wooded tract of fifty-three hundred acres of the Cumberland plateau in Tennessee. They attempted to set up the village life they had known in their homeland. Instead of scattering houses on individual tracts, according to the prevailing American pattern, they grouped them in one spot. All land was held in common, and a common treasury and a common storehouse were maintained. With dissension between Camp 1 and Camp 2 and the return of prosperity in northern industrial areas, the settlement was abandoned.

What might be said about this diverse set of cooperative experiments? Economic crisis in what was perceived to be a corrupt world provided the impetus to reorganize social life on the basis of some form of brotherly cooperation, where a harmony of interests would assure all a share of the benefits of progress. Having rejected politics, government, and the other institutions of society, many reformers adopted some form of cooperative organization as their instrument of change, with the hope that by forming one successful cooperative community they could begin the conversion of a troubled world. Each community viewed itself as an experiment, testing principles that could later be used as instruments of broader social and economic change. But few survived the passing of the crisis and the reemergence of individual opportunity. Typically, the mainstream prevailed.

An Epidemic of Socialism?

Responding to the same long-wave rhythms that influenced other secular communards, "scientific socialists" also developed their alternatives to capitalism in the same succession of nineteenth-century surges: the 1840s, the 1870s, the 1890s, and after the Crisis of 1907 (Fig. 33). Each surge coincided with a period of capitalist crisis: two deflationary depressions and the primary trough of the 1870s. Each took socialist development to another region (Fig. 34). And each waned as the economic mainstream moved back on track and individuals were once again able to work and to prosper.

The socialist communities are listed in Table 8.

In the 1840s—repeated in the 1870s—some of the socialist communes were established by foreign immigrants with a strong background in European socialism. Paraphrasing Okugawa (1980, pp. 194, 208):

Communia was organized in 1847 in Clayton County, Iowa, by a group of German socialists, including a Swiss who earlier had attempted to form New Helvetia in Osage County, Missouri. It occupied 1,240 acres and later merged with Wilhelm Weitling's Arbeiterbund, which had twenty chapters in large eastern cities. The union led to a schism. Communia ended in 1856, and some of the settlers joined the Icarians at Nauvoo.

Bettina (1847–48) was established by thirty-three radical students from Darmstadt, Germany, on the Llano River in Gillespie (now Llano) County, Texas, with the aid of the Society for the Protection of German Immigrants to Texas. Okugawa (1980) notes that their "motto friendship, freedom and equality soon created an idle atmosphere without governing rules, and the community went to pieces like a bubble at the end of the following summer" (p. 194).

Hays City Danish Colony (1877) was established by a group of eighteen Socialists from Denmark who emigrated to Ellis County, Kansas, under

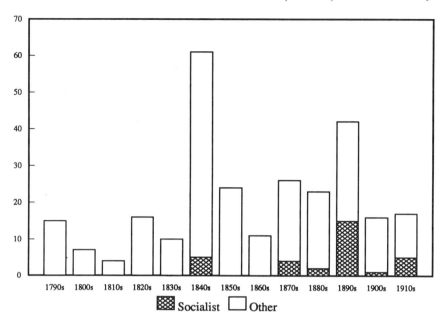

Figure 33. Surges of Socialist Community Building. Interest in socialist alternatives is clearly associated with capitalist crises: the depressions of the 1840s and 1890s and the trough of the 1870s.

the leadership of Louis Albert François Pio, principal leader of the Danish Socialist party and a participant in Karl Marx's First International. Their well-planned colonization scheme in the New World soon disintegrated, due to constant arguments among the colonists' wives over domestic task allocations. It lasted less than two months.

The first American socialist initiatives resulted from the attendance by John O. Wattles at a socialist convention in New York in 1843. Wattles was, like a number of other promoters in American utopian history, a "Music Man" who, despite failures, went on to establish a whole chain of communal societies. Inspired by what they heard at the 1843 convention, Wattles, Valentine Nicholson, and others organized the Prairie Home Community (1844) in Logan County, Ohio. Orson S. Murray, the editor of *Regenerator*, also was interested in this community and was on his way with his printing establishment to join it and publish his paper under its auspices when he was wrecked on Lake Erie. The members numbered about 130 farmers, nearly all of whom were Hicksite Quakers. Property was held in common, and there was joint ownership of the means of production, particularly land.

The group worked with a number of mottos rather than with a ruling

Figure 34. Locations of the Socialist Surges. Although Wattles's first experiments were in Ohio and Indiana, after Reconstruction socialist experiments were located throughout the South, the Middle Plains, and the West. The maps show the locations of the frontier in 1850 and 1890, respectively.

government and constitution: "The land is free to all, let those who want, come and use it." Animals were allowed to go where they pleased. Those who wanted them were free to take them. The organization of production was on a voluntary basis. There were social meetings about community affairs, but the meetings had no chairman, no secretary and no consti-

Table 8

Community	Started	Ended
Skaneateles, N.Y.	1843	1843
Prairie Home, Ohio	1844	1844
Highland Home, Ohio	1844	1844
Union Home, Ind.	1844	1846
Bettina, Tex.	1847	1848
Communia, Iowa	1847	1856
Grand Prairie Harmonial Institute, Ind.	1853	1854
Friendship Community, Miss.	1872	1877
Bennett Cooperative Colony, Miss.	1873	1877
Social Freedom Community, Va.	1874	1880
Hays City Danish Colony, Kans.	1877	1877
Mutual Aid Community, Miss.	1883	1887
Kaweah Coop. Commonwealth, Calif.	1885	1922
Cooperative Brotherhood, Calif.	1893	1898
Hiawatha Village Association, Mich.	1893	1896
Altruria, Calif.	1894	1895
Ruskin Cooperative Association, Tenn.	1894	1899
Home Employment Cooperative Colony, Miss.	1894	1906
Christian Corporation, Nebr.	1896	1897
Freedom Colony, Vt.	1897	1905
Equality, Wash.	1897	1907
Cooperative Brotherhood, Wash.	1898	1908
Ruskin Commonwealth, Ga.	1899	1901
Friedheim, Va.	1899	1906
Niksur Cooperative Association, Minn.	1899	1899
Kinder Lou, Ga.	1900	1901
Freeland Association, Wash.	1900	1906
Southern Cooperative Association, Fla.	1900	1904
Helicon Hall, N.J.	1906	1907
Fruit Crest, Mo.	1911	1912
Llano del Rio Company, Calif.	1914	1918
Army of Industry, Calif.	1914	1918
Llano del Rio Company, Nev.	1916	1918
Newllano Cooperative Colony, La.	1917	1938

tution or bylaws to preserve order. Individuals could rise and state that there was a certain thing to be done on the following day and "if it was thought best by the brothers and sisters, they would do it." In addition to collective production there was collective consumption. Their only principle was to endeavor to practice the Golden Rule: "Do as you would be done by." The virtue was felt to be the amicable, harmonious life-style, free of rules or compulsion. The problem was the tragedy of the commons: no one took responsibility; the arrangement fostered freeloading. Prairie Home lasted less than a year, like its sister community, Highland Home (1844), in nearby Logan County, which also lasted less than a year.[1]

Another 1843 initiative was the Skaneateles Community in Onondaga County, New York. This experiment, according to Okugawa (1980, p. 186), originated in Syracuse, New York, when John Collins, a salaried abolition agent from Massachusetts, visited with Frederick Douglass to promote the abolition cause. He instead organized a socialist community and forbade the practice of all organized religion. The community published a paper called *The Communist*. Several members who were dismissed because of religious quarrels joined the Oneida perfectionists.

Socialist community building then waned until the 1870s, when, in addition to the Hays City Danish colony, four other socialist communities were planted, and the Icarians at Corning flirted with Marx. But this "wave" was more apparent than real. Friendship Community (1872–77) in Missouri was one of Alcander Longley's efforts, and the Bennett Cooperative Colony (1873–77) was a schismatic offshoot from it.[2] The later Mutual Aid Community was another Longley creation, and the Social Freedom Community (1874–80) in Chesterfield County, Virginia, was small and insignificant. The 1870s did not really see a socialist surge; after the tentative beginnings of the 1840s, the real outbreak of socialist community building came in the depression of the 1890s, with a continuing carryover that lasted until World War I.

Between 1847 and 1893 the only genuine socialist initiative was the Kaweah Cooperative Commonwealth (1885–92), located near Visalia in Tulare County, California. Okugawa (1980, p. 203) notes that, organized by James J. Martin and Burnett Haskell, two labor leaders of the International Workingmen's Association in San Francisco, this socialist colony sprang up from Laurence Gronlund's *Cooperative Commonwealth*, a book that attempted to translate Marx into practical American terms. Taking advantage of the Timber Act of 1878 and the Homestead Act of 1862, more than forty men, mostly skilled laborers from trade unions, filed claims on six hundred acres of timber in the Sierra Nevada in northeastern Tulare County. In the course of its seven years' existence there were altogether about four hundred members, most of whom were affiliated with the Bellamy movement. The colony survived the mass withdrawals of fifty members and an internal split until the U.S. government evicted the colonists to found Sequoia National Park.

A socialist revival did occur in the 1890s, however, when another deflationary depression was viewed as signaling the terminal capitalist crisis. Between 1893 and 1900 fifteen communities were started and six in the ensuing years before World War I. Many were seen as experiments, providing the experience in cooperation needed to prepare people for the coming of the cooperative commonwealth. Most turned out to be dead ends, but at least one had great significance for socialism. It was the Ruskin Colony, the brainchild of Julius A. Wayland (1854–1912), established in Dickinson County, Tennessee.

In the early 1890s, under the influence of populism and nationalism,

Wayland adopted what he believed was socialism, although most of it was derived from a reading of Bellamy's "wonderful book." Wayland also studied many of Ruskin's works. More than any others, Ruskin and Bellamy were the philosophical giants in Wayland's vision of socialism. The correct anticipation of an economic collapse following the Panic of 1893 convinced him that the time was ripe for socialist action. He made efforts to found a colony by means of a joint-stock company that would provide homes and employment in a "cooperative village" for those who had purchased its stock.

Ordinary members could adapt the corporate form to their needs, protecting their interest from the wealthy by instituting the rule of "one man, one vote" in corporate decisions regardless of the amount of stock owned by any particular individual. In association they could pool their labor to create for themselves good homes, scientifically constructed and supplied with every convenience that the rich enjoy. They could also enjoy permanent employment at wages higher than ever dreamed of by laborers, with the advantages of good schools, free libraries, a gymnasium, lecture halls, parks, and playgrounds. Under the influence of the collective ownership and operation of economic and social institutions, members would work and live in an atmosphere of equality and brotherhood, protected from the poisons of competitive capitalism and the profit motive.

By the end of 1894, Wayland and associated enthusiasts had begun to organize a colony open to all persons pledged to socialism. Each charter member received one share of stock in the corporation, regardless of the amount he actually had paid in. Wives as well as husbands received shares, and the stockholders met once a month to transact the business of the colony. They elected a board of directors and officers and organized the activities of the colony under elected superintendents. The settlers enjoyed collective production and consumption. They worked together to build individual homes for each family. All meals were provided in a common dining facility. Agricultural and manufacturing activities were initiated, and a steady stream of new residents came to share in the arduous but productive undertaking. All work was of equal value. Supported by an array of machines beyond the dreams of most colonists, the Ruskinites worked a ten-hour day in the various departments to which they were assigned, generally on the basis of personal preference. In exchange they received free meals, housing, medical assistance, shoe repairing, laundry work, and education, along with a dollar each per week for incidentals.

They believed that a new socialistic society was being born, raising the usual expectations for the regeneration of the world. For a time, the vigorous growth and vital life of the Ruskin Cooperative Association raised the familiar hope that some Americans had finally discovered a successful secular formula for a cooperative village life in which the insecurities, class disharmonies, and degradations of urban-industrial society would be eliminated. But soon, as the population grew, disagreements surfaced, leading to Wayland's angry departure in the summer of 1895. This was followed by a series of conflicts among the members, which belied the hope that brotherhood could be found in collective ownership. Its problems, as Wayland had said they would be, were internal, and they were multiple and complex.

There was a pronounced division between the charter members and most of those who came after them. For the most part, the original colonists were middle-class urbanites with an intellectual and philosophical interest in socialism. They were not radicals but romantics, gentle people who believed in the principle of cooperation but opposed the theory of the class struggle. The later arrivals came from rural areas or from the hard-hit ranks of the depressed working class. They were less disciplined, less well educated, and more radical than their predecessors. They sensed an attitude of superiority among the charter members—a feeling that was reinforced by some who expressed the view that a higher value should be placed on "brain" work and "thinking" jobs than on "hand" work and "common" labor.

Education was another bone of contention. From the beginning great emphasis had been placed on the school program and on cultural and intellectual activities for all ages, as well as on the teaching of socialist principles. But as time passed, the interest began to diminish, and educational pursuits were given a lower priority.

The colonists also had serious quarrels about religion. In time the membership included some who practiced spiritualism and faith healing, others who came from the major Protestant denominations, and still others who were militantly antireligious. Emotional religious conflicts sometimes erupted, and they were seldom tempered with brotherly love.

Finally, the most visible and outwardly controversial dispute was about sex. A few of the latecomers to Ruskin were advocates of free love. Their well-publicized arguments with the monogamous colonists created in the minds of many outsiders a false impression of rampant immorality. The free love dispute was actually a minor matter, concerning only a few Ruskinites, but it became yet another strain on the already weakened cord that bound Ruskin together.

By the middle of 1897, Ruskin's internal crisis was building rapidly. There now were quarrels over the adherence to Ruskin's principles. Even in their publication *The Coming Nation* a columnist wrote: "[w]e can't change human nature in four years." Conflict not only undermined commitment and the willingness to work but also resulted in battles over the property that led some of the dissidents to force the colony into bankruptcy in 1899. Some of the colonists then formed a new Ruskin Commonwealth in Ware County, Georgia, and continued publishing *The Coming Nation*. These colonists resumed many of their old businesses. Yet the same problems emerged in the new location, and the colony closed in 1901. Other Ruskinites moved on to the single-tax community at Fairhope (Chapter 15), and others moved to a socialist settlement at Burley in the state of Washington.

The kind of community socialism practiced at Ruskin was viewed as experimental, an attempt to develop the prototype for a universal communal organization to come. But this attempt to create socialism in microcosm failed, largely because the communards were unable to isolate themselves from society at large. There was continual movement of members in and out of the new settlements and difficulty in transmitting a singular set of goals and maintaining a value system.

The Cooperative Brotherhood of Winters Island, California (1893–98), founded by Erastus Kelley, leader of the Oakland Nationalist Club, failed because members were unable to pay their dues ($5 per month for 100 months) after the Crash of 1893. Hiawatha Village Association in Schoolcraft County, Michigan, an attempt to realize the concepts spelled out in Walter T. Mills's book *The Product Sharing Village*, failed when community members objected to equalization. Altruria, established by Edward Biron Payne in Sonoma County, California, closed when the community's farm and logging operations failed to make a profit.

As the Ruskin Cooperative Association disintegrated, two other socialist ventures were the Freedom Colony (1897–1905) in Bourbon County, Kansas and Equality (1897–1907) in Skagit County, Washington.

Freedom was organized as Branch 199 of the General Labor Exchange Organization with headquarters in Independence, Missouri. Fourteen families purchased 160 acres on the Osage River bottom, a short distance from the Missouri state line. Only members of the General Labor Exchange organization were admitted to membership. To avoid conflicting with currency laws, the exchange scrip issued by the colony was printed in denominations of "one-half," "one-quarter," "one-tenth," and so forth, without the mention of dollars. The colony was important enough to warrant a visit by Eugene Debs, the perennial Socialist presidential candidate and labor leader. One member, Carl Browne, ran unsuccessfully for the U.S. Congress while at the colony. A fire in 1905 ended the colony.

A precursor to Equality was organized by eastern reformers in 1895 as the Brotherhood of the Cooperative Commonwealth, with a plan for a socialized state. *The Equality Colony*, named after Edward Bellamy's novel of that name, was the first of numerous colonies the Brotherhood was to establish in Washington. For a short period the Brotherhood of Cooperative Commonwealth No. 2 colony existed at Edison. Another planned colony by a small group of Populists in Lewis County, called Harmony Colony, failed to develop. The membership increased rapidly during 1897, from 115 in March to 300 in November, and came from the Midwest, South, Pacific Coast, and nearby northwestern states. At its peak there were over three thousand nonresident members who paid dues to the brotherhood. Prior to the colony's publishing *Industrial Freedom*, the Ruskin colony's *Coming Nation* was used as the colony's mouthpiece. Frequent contact was maintained with nearby colonies, especially with Burley, the socialist colony on Puget Sound. When the membership declined to thirty-eight in 1904, the colony came under the influence of a small band of newly arrived anarchists from New York. Revising the constitution along the lines of Theodor Hertzka's Freeland movement, the colony quickly divided into two factions. After two years of bitter legal fights, it was dissolved by court order.

Other socialist ventures at the end of the decade included the Niksur Cooperative Association (1899) in Mille Lacs County, Minnesota, formed by fifteen Minnesotan socialists who were discouraged when Ruskin failed; Kinder Lou (1900–1901) in Lowndes County, Georgia, established by migrants from Ruskin; and the Freeland Association (1900–1906) on Whidby Island, Washington, formed by a group leaving Equality. The major socialist community-building effort in the World War I period was that of the Llano del Rio Company, however.

In 1914, Job Harriman, who had first attracted notice in 1891 as an energetic organizer of socialist clubs in San Francisco and Cincinnati, formed the Llano del Rio Corporation in Los Angeles County, California, capitalized at $2 million. The corporation was to guarantee a house and employment to anyone who invested $1,000 in it. Located in the Antelope Valley, forty-five miles northeast of Los Angeles, by 1916 the place proclaimed itself "the World's Greatest Cooperative Community." In 1917 this socialist paradise had a population of over a thousand people and the beginnings of what was claimed to be a new civilization. Recruitment of new members was through the magazine *The Western Comrade*. But Harriman's colony soon encountered shortages of both money and water. While the colony's industries proliferated in much the same way as its social life, many members were hired as day laborers by neighboring farms because the colony's operations were small and unprofitable. Financial difficulties, conflict between nonresident directors and the resident members, and lawsuits against the colony ended the California site. In 1917 forty remaining members moved to a new location in Louisiana.

Meanwhile, the Llano del Rio Company of Nevada (1916–18) was founded in Churchill County, Nevada, by C. V. Eggleston, formerly a fiscal agent of the Llano colony in California. The Llano del Rio Corporation of California repeatedly repudiated its connection with the Nevada colony, however. The colony's 1,640 acres were not contiguous, being scattered twelve miles east, twelve miles west, and thirty-five miles north of the colony headquarters. The membership reached nearly two hundred at its peak in 1918. Financial mismanagement sent the colony into receivership in May 1919.

The successor to Llano de Rio was, in fact, the Newllano Cooperative Colony (1917–38), located in Vernon Parish, Louisiana. Newllano grew out of Job Harriman's experiences at Llano del Rio. He had believed that the consolidating trends of modern society were preparing the way for the Cooperative Commonwealth, especially by engendering a cooperative spirit among the members of the producing class. At Llano del Rio, however, he and his followers found little of the cooperative temperament they had expected from the New Socialist Man. Harriman, in particular, was upset by what he saw as sheer human nastiness, particularly in the form of an organized "brush gang" perversely hostile to his leadership. Both the experience and the conclusion led Harriman to make a new experiment along more traditional communitarian lines. In 1918 he and a small band of followers made a trek from California to northwestern Louisiana, where they converted an abandoned mill village into the Newllano Cooperative Colony. Having decided that a truly brotherly disposition would come only when the present generation had "undergone a long period of ethical or spiritual training," he placed his hopes in the educational and conditioning influence of communal living. Common work, common property, and the intimacy of communal life would gradually rework the psychology and behavior of individuals into cooperative dispositions with the assistance of "man's fundamental gregarious urge." The self-contained community would be the cradle of the New Socialist Man. He aimed at developing "a social spirit, a spirit of fellowship, and we are doing it in this colony and doing it magnificently."

Pulling through many hardships, the colony grew from a handful of dedicated families to over 150 inhabitants. The character of the population indicates that it had become something of a rallying ground for the dispersed and depleted forces of the old idealism. Beside the main force of socialists, there were anarchists, communists, pacifists, and radical feminists. The colony adopted the joint-stock principle of property ownership. Llano was a corporation, chartered in Nevada, whose stock was available to anyone willing to put up $1 per share. Anyone could buy as many shares as he pleased, but to prevent the community from falling under the control of wealth no one could vote more than two thousand shares in corporate elections. In order to be admitted to membership, each head of a family was required to purchase two thousand shares, part of which was to be paid in cash. Every member was expected to contribute eight hours of work per day to the community in exchange for full access to everything available in the community. Along with its familiar ideal of "the good of one is the good of all," Newllano also had the usual range of industries and institutions required for a miniature commonwealth.

The inhabitants were satisfied with their isolation from the turmoil and uncertainties of the larger world. It was an island of peace through socialism and full of hope for "cooperation the world over." In 1924, however, the new cooperative experienced a crisis of authority that developed out of a struggle for control of the colony between Job Harriman and his chief lieutenant, George T. Pickett, a former insurance man whose business talents had kept the colony going. Harriman left Newllano that year and died the year after. But Newllano was not ended by this loss, in part because of the practical business talents of George Pickett. To gain members who paid the admission fee of $2,000, the community became less selective in its admission standards and instead became a producer's cooperative. Unlike the earlier cooperative structure in California, all household goods, houses, automobiles, and the like remained private property. The colony went bankrupt in 1936, and after it failed to obtain financial support from the federal government it was dissolved in 1938.

Newllano was the last stand of the Cooperative Commonwealth. The Great Depression did revive some interest in cooperative colonies, but this was overshadowed by the policies of the national government, which adopted "socialistic" programs as part of an effort to save the old order from the terminal capitalist crisis that socialists were quick to proclaim, as we shall see in Chapter 16.

CHAPTER FIFTEEN

Henry George and the Single Tax

Another influence came upon the national scene in the last decades of the nineteenth century, that of Henry George (Fig. 35). Whereas the communards and the socialists tried to create experimental communities in microcosm to serve as models for the voluntary restructuring of society, George was "one of the first to impress upon the American people that poverty and depressions could bring down the established social order, yet this need not be so if the government took the proper legislative steps" (Cord, 1965, p. 7). His *Progress and Poverty* and Edward Bellamy's novel *Looking Backward* contributed to the millenarian visions of the Populists who envisioned "sudden destruction or slow strangulation [lying] in wait for a rotten civilization" (Jaher, 1964, p. 7). To George and Bellamy, the millennium lay not in the supernatural but in the remote hands of capitalist economics; yet if economic forces were refocused, they might bring back an Edenic world of egalitarian abundance. Such thinking influenced the millenarians of the 1930s and helped form Roosevelt's New Deal cooptation of their proposals.

Born in Philadelphia in 1839, Henry George left school before he was fourteen. After two years clerking in an importing house, he went to sea, traveling to India and Australia. On a second voyage he jumped ship in San Francisco in 1857, intending to join the gold rush in western Canada. But he arrived too late. Returning to San Francisco in 1858, he had multiple printing-industry jobs and was active in Democratic party politics. Working as a reporter for the *Alta California*, he began to focus on issues in economics, criticizing much of the generally accepted theory of political economy of the day and becoming involved in debates on the effects of Chinese immigration on the wage rate, on the benefits of the railroad, and on the effects of inflation.

He made a number of unsuccessful attempts to found newspapers be-

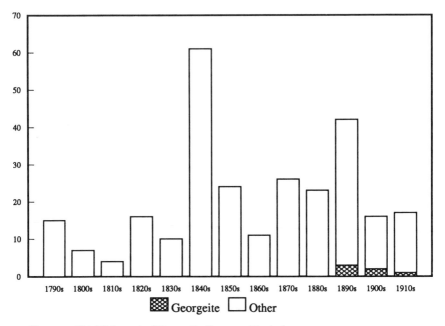

Figure 35. Establishment of Georgeite Communities before 1920.

fore he published, in 1871, a pamphlet entitled *Our Land and Land Policy* that struck a responsive chord. The years 1873–78 were difficult ones, the primary trough of prices after the 1865 inflation peak. Growth rates sagged after rushing upward in the years 1866–73. The book had massive sales in many languages, and George was much sought after on lecture tours in Britain and the United States.

In the pamphlet George took the Ricardian theory of rent and land use and gave it new meaning. Land, he said, is scarce. As economic progress occurs and the demand for land increases, the idle landowner reaps economic rents at the expense of capital and labor. This unearned rent should be taxed away by the state. The "single tax" would be so large that there would be a substantial surplus for public works.

Stimulated by the reception of the pamphlet and reacting to the economic hardships of 1873–78, he took his ideas one step further in *Progress and Poverty* in 1879. In this book he attempted "to harmonize the individualism of capitalist economics with the communalistic goals of Christian charity" (Rose, 1968, p. 64). "His hope and his vision were irresistible, and they reflected the general utopian dreams of many late nineteenth century essays and books as much as they described the need for social reform that also characterized a large body of the literature of the same period" (ibid., p. 63). The essential ideas of the book, reiterating the themes of *Our Land and Land Policy*, were

1. The progress of industrialization has resulted in making the individual less self-sufficient.

2. There is a high degree of exchange in mobility between capital and labor. Capital is, however, nothing more than another form of labor, the savings of accumulated labor from the past.

3. Land rents absorb the gains made possible by economic progress, and keep wages and interest near the subsistence level, making poverty the "inevitable concomitant" of progress.

4. During times of prosperity, the "seeds of the coming depression are spread." As speculation in land value increases, production is curbed and credit only postpones the "evil day."

5. The immorality of poverty among progress derives from private ownership of land, which is "unethical . . . because labor is the sole justification of private property . . . only things produced by labor should be privately owned, thus excluding land."

6. Taxation of land is the cure. As land prices approach zero because the government collects land rent through taxation, labor will have free access to land, and therefore unemployment will disappear. (Cord, 1965, pp. 23–26)

The single-tax idea emerged from George's belief in the progressive monopolization of land ownership. This implied that unearned economic rents were concentrated in fewer and fewer hands, resulting in growing inequality. The solution was to "make land common property" (George, 1879, p. 326). "Let the individuals who now hold it still retain, if they want to, possession of what they are pleased to call their land. . . . It is not necessary to confiscate land; it is only necessary to confiscate rent. . . . What I therefore propose . . . is to appropriate rent by taxation . . . to abolish all taxation save that upon land values" (ibid., pp. 403–4).

The implementation of land value taxation should take place in several stages, he said. First, land would be assessed separate from its improvements; then, the tax rate on the "raw land" would be increased by increments until the full ground rent was recaptured as public revenue. To reduce administrative costs and dislocation, "the landowners retain title to their land, and in return for their collection services be given . . . a percentage of rent which would probably be less than the cost and loss involved in attempting to rent lands through state agency" (Andelson, 1979, pp. 36–37).

George was confident that the effects of his proposal would reach into every sector of the economy. This would eliminate increased costs to the industrial sector, freeing production to meet the needs of the population. As prices fell, purchasing power would increase, stimulating economic

Table 9

Community	Started	Ended
Colorado Cooperative Co., Colo.	1894	1910
Fairhope, Ala.	1895	
Arden,* Del.	1900	
Tahanto, Mass.	1909	1934
Free Acres, N.J.	1910	1950
Halidon, Maine	1911	1938
Shakerton, Mass.	1921	
Gilpin's Point, Md.	1926	
Trapelo, Mass.	1927	
Wall Hill, Miss.	1932	

*Including Ardentown, 1922, and Ardencroft, 1950.

growth. However, the primary benefit would be to reduce speculation, the primary cause of depressions, and to eliminate social inequality.

His ideas were both praised and condemned. Conservative mainstream economists called him a radical, but Karl Marx referred to George's remedy as "the capitalist last ditch," saying that George was synonymous with the "repulsive presumption and arrogance that invariably distinguish all such panacea-mongers." George's reaction to Marx was equally unfavorable, saying that like "most superficial thinkers" he was "entangled in an inexact and vicious terminology" (Marx's criticism cited in Andelson, 1979, p. 196; George's response cited in Barker, 1955, p. 564).

Meanwhile, when the depression of the 1890s hit hard, some turned to his formulas to build alternative communities. By 1933 fifteen such settlements had been constructed, ten in the United States.

All the enclaves are identical in the principle of taking the economic rent and using it for the payment of taxes; in all of them, therefore, improvements are exempt; thus in essence the single tax prevails; but, on the other hand, in no one of them has there been any attempt to pay either the customs or the excise or the national income tax, or to atone to the enclavians for the artificial increment in the prices of domestic goods due to the "protective" policy. (Geiger, 1933, pp. 442–43).

Each community was an "area of land where, under the terms of the leases, the economic rent is collected, as contrasted with the surrounding region, or exclave, where it is not collected, such economic rent being used for communal purposes. The ownership of the land may be either public, as in Canberra and Labuon, or private as in the other enclaves" (Huntington, 1934, p. 26).

The single-tax enclaves constructed in the United States are shown in Table 9.

The first six of these communities are described in Okugawa's (1980) inventory. Several, Fairhope and Arden in particular, have been successful at microscale. Set within a larger capitalist environment, however, the single-tax communities have been unable to address the larger social issue of the role of speculation in the boom-and-bust economy and the continuing problem of social inequality.

The State Takes Over: New Deal Communities

Utopian community building waned in the Roaring Twenties. The last few single-tax settlements were built. In his *Dictionary of American Communal and Utopian History*, Robert Fogarty (1980, p. 143) lists only one other community, Heaven City, as being started in the decade after World War I, although there undoubtedly were others. Heaven City was built in 1923 near Harvard, Illinois, by Albert J. Moore, an apocalyptic millenarian who predicted an impending global catastrophe: a money panic in 1923; universal labor strikes in 1924; a reactionary worldwide revolution in 1925, leading to a world war and the destruction of three-quarters of the world's population in 1926. His was a religious colony organized by the Humanity Trust Estate. Thirty-six members joined, gave over their property to the community, and consumed in common. Each family had a separate home and worked its own farm. Moore's religion emphasized doing good works and cooperating; the reward was reincarnation. A forward-looking Montessori school was opened. But absent the 1926 Armageddon, the community dissolved.

Then came the stock market crash of October 1929. "A malaise [seized] Americans, a sense at once depressing and exhilarating, that capitalism itself was finished" (Schlesinger, 1960, p. 205). "Traditional conceptions of the moral order appeared to lose validity. *Laissez-faire* economics had been sanctified as part of the natural order and condition in which individuals were expected to reap the benefits and bear the burdens of economic decisions, yet as the ratio of winners and losers shifted, this no longer provided solace" (Barkun, 1986, p. 152).

[D]isaffection surfaced in a move towards new alternative lifestyles. In this country and elsewhere people sought to fashion new societies that would allow greater mass participation. In Russia, Germany, and Italy this communitarian reform spirit was perverted. In England, the rise of the collective will manifested itself constructively in government regulation and planning for urban growth. The concept of controlled growth spread to Scandinavia and migrated to the United States, where Roosevelt's "Brain Trust" was zealously trying to introduce a socialist esprit to a land where every man still fiercely guarded his castle. . . . American intellectuals were enthralled by the credo of communism. (Cutler, 1985, p. 116)

"The government operated against a backdrop of rabid unrest, as turmoil spurred an onslaught of demagogues preaching their personal cures" (ibid., p. 8). Huey Long, Dr. Francis Townshend, and Father Charles Coughlin offered "economic cures for the Depression [that] had a way of drifting from reform into local transformation, as though the magnitude of economic collapse had of necessity to engender cures as sweeping as the disease" (Barkun, 1984, p. 40).

Huey Long, governor of Louisiana and then senator (1932–35), sought national power through a radical Share-the-Wealth program ("every man a king") that proved exceedingly attractive to the Depression-afflicted population. Dr. Francis Townshend authored an Old Age Revolving Pension program. The poor in northern cities were attracted to a Roman Catholic priest, Father Coughlin, who used his "Golden Hour of the Little Flower" radio program to demand nationalization of the banks. Coughlin later turned antidemocratic and anti-Semitic; his magazine *Social Justice* was banned in 1942 for violating the Espionage Act.

Their proposals and the following they attracted, Barkun (1984) writes, "elevated economic tinkering to the position of master-lever in the construction of a virtuous society" (p. 40). The federal government assumed an unprecedented role in communal organization. New Deal agencies established communities that were conceived as fundamental departures from existing American social and economic patterns, although they were quite consistent with many of the utopian experiments that had gone before. In addition, there were a number of private initiatives that, like the government projects, involved the return of urbanites to the land. Barkun adds:

The dialectic between [this] utopian wave . . . and the coincident millennialism was evident. The economic crisis placed secular millennialists such as Long and Townsend in competition with the New Deal for the allegiance of voters, a political threat that could be most effectively dealt with if their ideas were co-opted. Thus, Roosevelt was only too happy to speed passage of the Social Security Act as a way of holding the Townsendites at bay. The permeable ideological boundaries of the New Deal allowed at least some millennialists (Tugwell, for example) to rise to positions of influence. Hence the New Deal community projects subsumed the views of a diverse "back-to-the-land" movement and genuinely reflected some in the Roosevelt Administration who believed that only through self-sufficient rural communities could the new society of cooperation be built. (pp. 40–41)

Was this another utopian wave in the deflationary depression formed by a Kondratiev trough? The answer to this question, which was a matter of great concern to Barkun, is negative. The Great Depression originated in a primary trough of prices, like the dislocations of the 1820s and 1870s. What began as a stock market crash at the end of an epoch of rapid deflationary growth was translated into a deep and prolonged crisis by ill-advised governmental actions—protectionist trade barriers, reductions in money supply—that dried up credit, brought economic growth to a standstill, and fed a widening wave of bank failures that destroyed personal wealth. When the secondary recovery came, backed by the power of the federal government, it was sharper and steeper than those of the 1830s and the 1880s.

This heightened effect carried over to utopian community building. The Owenite surge of the 1820s that introduced secular presocialism to the menu of utopian alternatives planted some ten utopian settlements. The miscellaneous movements that surged in the 1870s planted a dozen. Between 1933 and 1937, the federal government established ninety-nine new settlements. There was then a community-building sag during World War II that lasted through the end of the Korean War. The Kondratiev wave that began as the economy moved out of the depression of the 1890s peaked in 1920, dropped into the primary trough of 1929, and finally ended in the Kondratiev trough of the mid-1950s. This 1950s trough was unlike those of the 1840s and the 1890s because the New Deal introduced an environment of permanent inflation and an accompanying array of safety-net protections for the elderly and the unemployed. Instead of being a period of deflation, the 1950s were a period of relative disinflation. Prices kept increasing but at a slower rate. There was neither the massive loss of personal wealth nor the widespread feeling of an imminent economic Armageddon that had occurred in the earlier deflationary depressions. Millenarian thinking focused instead on the Holocaust and the nuclear arms race. The accompanying utopian wave lagged, gathering speed in the 1960s and rushing to a peak in 1973 amid widespread civil unrest.

The ninety-nine new communities that the U.S. government built between 1933 and 1937 reflected a "conscious break with individualism" (Conkin, 1959, p. 7).[1] Thirty-four were built by the Division of Subsistence Homesteads (ibid., Appendix; derived from U.S. House of Representatives Select Committee of the Committee on Agriculture, *Hearings of the Farm Security Administration*, 78th Congress, 1st Sess., 1943–1944, pp. 1118–1127), as shown in Table 10.

Another twenty-eight communities were built by the Federal Emergency Relief Administration (Conkin, 1959, Appendix). See Table 11.

Table 10

Community	Location	Type
Arthurdale	Reedsville, W.Va.	Stranded community
Cumberland Homesteads	Crossville, Tenn.	Stranded community
Tygart Valley Homesteads	Elkins, W.Va.	Stranded community
Westmoreland Homesteads	Greensburg, Pa.	Stranded community
Jersey Homesteads	Highstown, N.J.	Cooperative industrial
Penderlea Homesteads	Pender County, N.C.	Farm community
Piedmont Homesteads	Jasper County, Ga.	Farm community
Richton Homesteads	Richton, Miss.	Farm community
Shenandoah Homesteads	Five counties in Va.	Resettlement
Cahaba (Trussville Homesteads)	Near Birmingham, Ala.	Industrial (small garden city)
Austin Homesteads	Austin, Minn.	Industrial
Bankhead Farms	Jasper, Ala.	Industrial
Beauxart Gardens	Beaumont, Tex.	Industrial
Dalworthington Gardens	Arlington, Tex.	Industrial
Dayton Homesteads	Dayton, Ohio	Industrial
Decatur Homesteads	Decatur, Ind.	Industrial
Duluth Homesteads	Duluth, Minn.	Industrial
El Monte Homesteads	El Monte, Calif.	Industrial
Granger Homesteads	Granger, Iowa	Industrial
Greenwood Homesteads	Near Birmingham, Ala.	Industrial
Hattiesburg Homesteads	Hattiesburg, Ala.	Industrial
Houston Gardens	Houston, Tex.	Industrial
Lake County Homesteads	Chicago, Ill.	Industrial
Longview Homesteads	Longview, Wash.	Industrial
Magnolia Homesteads	Meridian, Miss.	Industrial
McComb Homesteads	McComb, Miss.	Industrial
Mount Olive Homesteads	Near Birmingham, Ala.	Industrial
Palmerdale Homesteads	Near Birmingham, Ala.	Industrial
Phoenix Homesteads	Phoenix, Ariz.	Industrial
San Fernando Homesteads	Reseda, Calif.	Industrial
Three Rivers Gardens	Three Rivers, Tex.	Industrial
Tupelo Homesteads	Tupelo, Miss.	Industrial
Wichita Gardens	Wichita Falls, Tex.	Industrial
Aberdeen Gardens	Newport News, Va.	Garden city for Negroes

An additional thirty-seven communities were developed by Rexford Tug-well's Resettlement Administration, which ultimately assumed responsibility for all ninety-nine (Conkin, 1959, Appendix). See Table 12.

A number of influences converged as these New Deal programs developed. One was a back-to-the-land movement that had existed in the United States at least since the Civil War. In the 1920s rural-to-urban migration had increased: between 1921 and 1929, the net gain in city population varied from 400,000 to 1,137,000 annually. Agrarianism survived the 1920s as a romantic movement that saw return to the land as an escape from the ugliness of urban life. Many of the agrarians were re-

Table 11

Community	Location	Type
Dyess Colony	Mississippi Cty., Ark.	Farm community
Cherry Lake Farms	Near Madison, Fla.	Farm and rural industrial
Pine Mountain Valley	Harris Cty., Ga.	Farm and rural industrial
Burlington Project	Burlington, N.Dak.	Stranded community
Red House	Red House, W.Va.	Stranded community
Albert Lea Homesteads	Albert Lea, Minn.	Industrial
Arizona Part-Time Farms	Phoenix, Ariz.	Industrial
Fairbury Farmsteads	Jefferson Cty., Nebr.	Farm village
Fall City Farmsteads	Richardson Cty., Nebr.	Farm village
Grand Island Farmsteads	Hall Cty., Nebr.	Farm village
Kearney Homesteads	Buffalo Cty., Nebr.	Farm village
Loup City Farmsteads	Sherman Cty., Nebr.	Farm village
Scottsbluff Farmsteads	Scotts Bluff Cty., Nebr.	Farm village
Sioux Falls Farms	Minnehaha Cty., S.Dak.	Farm village
South Sioux City Farmsteads	Dakota Cty., Nebr.	Farm village
Two Rivers Farmsteads	Douglas and Saunders Ctys., Nebr.	Farm village
Woodlake Community	Wood Cty., Tex.	Farm village
Ashwood Plantation	Lee Cty., S.C.	Farm community
Bosque Farms	Valencia Cty., N.Mex.	Farm community
Chicot Farms	Chicot and Drew Ctys., Ark.	Farm community
Irwinville	Irwin Cty., Ga.	Farm community
Roanoke Farms	Halifax Cty., N.C.	Farm community
Ropesville Farms	Hockley Cty., Tex.	Farm community
Scuppernong Farms	Tyrrell and Washington Ctys., N.C.	Farm community
Skyline Farms	Jackson Cty., Ala.	Farm community
St. Francis River Farms	Poinsett Cty., Ark.	Farm community
Wichita Valley Farms	Wichita Cty., Tex.	Farm community
Wolf Creek	Grady Cty., Ga.	Farm community

actionary: the Catholic Rural Life Conference, formed in 1923, took many of its ideas from Hilaire Belloc, whose "distributist" ideas were derived from the Catholic agrarian society of the late Middle Ages, "when the majority of men possessed, or had access to, wealth-producing property"; Belloc was opposed to the "modern, Protestant, industrial, capitalist society, in which only a few men owned real property" (Conkin, 1959, p. 25). With the deepening of the Depression, a back-to-the-land movement in fact began, although it was more for reasons of subsistence than for nostalgic idealism. In 1930, according to estimates of the Bureau of Agricultural Economics, the rural-to-urban trend reversed, with net gains to the country of 17,000 in 1930, 214,000 in 1931, and 533,000 in 1932.

A second concept that influenced the New Deal was "planning," which

Table 12

Community	Location	Type
Greenbelt	Berwyn, Md. (near Washington D.C.)	Garden city
Greendale	Milwaukee, Wis.	Garden city
Greenhills	Cincinnati, Ohio	Garden city
Ironwood Homesteads	Ironwood, Mich.	Small garden city
Drummond Project	Bayfield Cty., Wis.	Forest homesteads
Sublimity Farms	Laurel Cty., Ky.	Forest homesteads
Casa Grande Valley Farms	Pinal Cty., Ariz.	Cooperative farm
Lake Dick	Jefferson & Arkansas Ctys.	Cooperative farm
Terrebonne	Terrebonne Parish, La.	Cooperative plantation
Biscoe Farms	Prairie Cty., Ark.	Farm community
Christian-Trigg Farms	Christian Cty., Ky.	Farm community
Clover Bend Farms	Lawrence Cty., Ark.	Farm community
Desha Farms	Desha and Drew Ctys., Ark.	Farm community
Escambia Farms	Okaloosa Cty., Fla.	Farm community
Flint River Farms	Macon Cty., Ga.	Farm community
Gee's Bend Farms	Wilcox Cty., Ala.	Farm community
Hinds Farms	Hinds Cty., Miss.	Farm community
Kinsey Flats	Custer Cty., Mont.	Farm community
La Forge Farms	New Madrid Cty., Mo.	Farm community
Lakeview Farms	Lee and Phillips Ctys., Ark.	Farm community
Lonoke Farms	Lonoke Cty., Ark.	Farm community
Lucedale Farms	George and Greene Ctys., Miss.	Farm community
McLennan Farms	McLennan Cty., Tex.	Farm community
Mileston Farms	Holmes Cty., Miss.	Farm community
Mounds Farms	Madison and East Parish, La.	Farm community
Orangeburg Farms	Orangeburg and Calhoun Ctys., S.C.	Farm community
Osage Farms	Pettis Cty., Mo.	Farm community
Pembroke Farms	Robeson Cty., N.C.	Farm community
Plum Bayou	Jefferson Cty., Ark.	Farm community
Prairie Farms	Macon Cty., Ala.	Farm community
Sabine Farms	Harrison Cty., Tex.	Farm community
Saginaw Valley Farms	Saginaw Cty., Mich.	Farm community
Sam Houston Farms	Harris Cty., Tex.	Farm community
Tiverton Farms	Sumter Cty., S.C.	Farm community
Townes Farms	Crittenden Cty., Ark.	Farm community
Transylvania Farms	East Carroll Parish, La.	Farm community
Trumann Farms	Poinsett Cty., Ark.	Farm community

was understood to mean state planning of collective programs (ibid., p. 38). Two types were important to those who engaged in community building. Rural land settlement planning, which would create organized rural communities, was influenced by the ideas of Elwood Mead, a civil engineer who taught at the University of California from 1897 to 1907 and experienced rural community planning firsthand as head of the State

Rivers and Water Supply Commission of Victoria, Australia. In Australia, Mead developed his ideas about planned rural development, which included community settlement with cooperative institutions, advance land planning and preparation by agricultural experts, subsistence homesteads for laborers to eliminate the problems of migrant labor, location of small industries near the settlements, careful selection of settlers, and continuing direction of the project by agricultural experts.

The second type of planning was that embraced by the city planning movement, which emphasized the construction of towns or communities in a way that would preserve a healthy environment for the residents, with many of the advantages of rural life. Inspired by the ideas of Ebenezer Howard, "garden cities" were seen as a means of decentralizing urban industries and population into towns limited in size by a "greenbelt" of woods and meadows. The plan of the towns would include large open spaces and would be protected by community ownership of all of the land. Land would be leased for the construction of homes, businesses, and industries (Berry, 1973).

The first New Deal communities to be planned were the subsistence homesteads communities. In May 1933 funds were allocated in Section 208 of Title II of the National Industrial Recovery Act for the president to use "through such agencies as he may establish and under such regulations as he may make, for making loans for and otherwise aiding in the purchase of subsistence homesteads." Roosevelt gave the program to Harold L. Ickes, secretary of the interior. Ickes established the Division of Subsistence Homesteads, headed by M. L. Wilson. In October 1933, Wilson announced that three types of communities would be developed to be constructed and managed by local corporations. The most important would be located near industrial employment, with plots of land for part-time farming. For farmers resettled from submarginal land, there would be some all-rural colonies. Finally, and most controversially, there would be communities with newly decentralized industry, among them communities for stranded coal miners (Conkin, 1959, pp. 105–6).

The typical community was described as consisting of individual homesteads, from one to five acres each, for anywhere from twenty-five to one hundred families. Each family could have a vegetable garden and orchard, poultry, a pig, and perhaps a cow. The housing would be inexpensive but durable and convenient, with utilities provided. Settlers would be chosen from low-income applicants on the basis of character, agricultural fitness, and other qualifications. Control of the projects was to remain with local corporations.

From the beginning there was a difference in outlook between Ickes and Wilson. Ickes was an administrator who believed in tight control over expenditures and centralized decision making. To Ickes more control meant less graft and waste. Wilson believed that central control was undemocratic. He insisted that "the subsistence homesteads projects, if they were to become real communities, had to be wanted, planned, and managed by the people within the locality where they were to be constructed" (Conkin, 1959, p. 120). Wilson's view was the one originally followed, but by early 1934 expenditures on some of the projects had become so excessive and publicity so bad that Ickes's disapproval of Wilson's administrative methods deepened considerably. The project that gave Ickes the most frustration was Arthurdale, which had been virtually taken over by Eleanor Roosevelt and Lewis Howe, who were, according to Ickes, "spending money like drunken sailors" (ibid., p. 122).

In January 1934, Comptroller General John R. McCarl issued a ruling that required local subsistence homesteads corporations to use standard government accounting and disbursing procedures and to deposit all borrowed funds with the U.S. Treasurer. Ickes was furious at McCarl's intervention, which was only the first in a series of decisions that seriously hindered the operation of the Division of Subsistence Homesteads. He quickly realized that the local corporations would no longer be able to function except as advisory bodies. In March 1934, Wilson reluctantly issued a new administrative plan: the Federal Subsistence Homesteads Corporation would henceforth control local projects through project managers and accountants. The local corporations would no longer be policy-making bodies (Conkin, 1959, p. 119). Wilson decided to return to the Department of Agriculture, where he had previously served, as of 30 June 1934; most of his assistants left with him (ibid., p. 122).

By the time Wilson left, thirty-one of the industrial-type communities had been announced, of which twenty-three would eventually be completed. Over half of those that were completed were located in three groups in the South: five in the area around Jasper and Birmingham, Alabama; five in scattered locations in Texas; and four small projects in Mississippi. The industrial communities were in a sense the only true subsistence homesteads communities, in that they most closely approximated the official definition:

A subsistence homestead denotes a house and out buildings located upon a plot of land on which can be grown a large portion of the foodstuffs required by the homestead family. It signifies production for home consumption and not for commercial sale. In that it provides for subsistence only, it carries with it the corollary that cash income must be drawn from some outside source. The central motive of the subsistence homestead program, therefore, is to demonstrate the economic value of a livelihood which combines part-time wage work and part-time gardening or farming. (U.S. Department of the Interior, Division of Subsistence Homesteads, *Bulletin 1* [Washington, D.C.: 1934], p. 4)

Four communities of the stranded-worker type were built, all designed to house miners who had become unemployed through coal mine closings. These were among the most controversial of the communities and presented serious problems in that some form of industrial employment had to be attracted to the locations, since the plots of land were too small for full-time farming (Conkin, 1959, p. 108). Three purely rural communities were also planned: one sponsored by the University System of Georgia; Penderlea Homesteads, in North Carolina; and one at Richton, Mississippi, which was constructed by the Resettlement Administration. One project was planned for a homestead community in a national forest but was later turned over to the Forest Service (ibid., p. 110). Both the stranded-worker and the rural communities encountered legal difficulties, the latter type being declared illegal by the Solicitor of the Department of the Interior, so their development was quickly curtailed, leaving the industrial homesteads predominant (ibid., p. 131).

The first loan granted by the Division of Subsistence Homesteads went to Ralph Borsodi, a back-to-the-land and single-tax advocate who had begun subsistence farming personally near New York City in 1920 and was already developing a subsistence homesteads colony in Dayton, Ohio.

The second project, for stranded coal miners in Reedsville, West Virginia, was the most highly publicized and controversial. Arthurdale began in 1931 as a program of the American Friends Service Committee to feed children in the coalfields, but the project had subsequently developed to include subsistence gardening and handicrafts. The committee had set up a plan to resettle stranded miners on subsistence farms. Eleanor Roosevelt took a personal interest in the project; its original director, Clarence Pickett, became assistant administrator of the Division of Subsistence Homesteads, heading the program for stranded miners. The local sponsors quickly submitted plans to the division for a loan. The plan that was accepted called for two hundred five-acre homesteads, a cooperative store, and a school. Part-time employment was to be provided by a post office facility.

From the beginning, Mrs. Roosevelt and Louis Howe intervened. Howe ordered prefabricated homes that, when they arrived, proved to have paper-thin walls unsuited to the cold winters in the mountains; Mrs. Roosevelt selected an architect to remodel the cottages to include oversize furnaces, since parts of the dwellings still consisted of the thin prefab walls. Ickes and Mrs. Roosevelt were perpetually at odds over the project, with Ickes wanting to house as many miners as possible quickly and cheaply (a matter on which he had FDR's agreement) and Mrs. Roosevelt wanting an experimental showplace. She supervised the interior design and furnishings of the new homes, which included maple furniture from the Mountaineer Craftsmen's Co-operative Association, the group originally founded by the American Friends Service Committee. Settlers were chosen on the basis of a physical examination, an interview with a social worker, and an eight-page questionnaire. The final costs of Arthurdale homes and outbuildings averaged $8,665, much above the initial plan of $2,500. Mrs. Roosevelt obtained funds from Bernard Baruch and advice from John Dewey, among others, to begin the Arthurdale school system; she used her own money to pay the salary of Miss Elsie Clapp, of the Ballard Memorial School near Louisville, Kentucky, to serve as director of an experimental program. The six school buildings cost over $250,000 to construct and housed an ambitious program that provided pre- and postnatal care, a nursery school, a progressive elementary school curriculum without formal instruction or examinations, a vocationally oriented high school, and adult community activities. After two years the schools were turned over to the county school system, much to the relief of the parents, who were afraid their children were receiving little education. The nursery, however, was popular and continued to operate.

Arthurdale was to Roosevelt's critics a symbol of New Deal extravagance and mismanagement and served as a symbol of the entire subsistence-homesteads program whenever government-planned communities were under attack. The greatest problems the community faced were due to lack of jobs, despite the efforts of Mrs. Roosevelt to attract employers to the community. Several enterprises, from a vacuum cleaner factory to a tractor factory to cooperative poultry and dairy farms all proved unprofitable and failed to survive. The problem of employment frustrated plans to turn the community over to a homestead association, and after World War II began, the homes were sold to individuals rather than to an association.

Jersey Homesteads was a proposed colony of two hundred skilled Jewish garment workers that was to combine subsistence farming with community ownership of a cooperative garment factory. Other cooperative projects were to include a truck garden, dairy, poultry plant, and a community store. The proposal was submitted by Benjamin Brown, a Jewish emigrant from the Ukraine who had extensive experience in organizing rural cooperatives (Conkin, 1959, p. 261). Brown gained the support of several Jewish labor organizations in forming a new Provisional Commission for Jewish Farm settlements in the United States, which later included Albert Einstein, among others, as a member. The Division of

Subsistence Homesteads granted Brown's commission a loan of $500,000 in December 1933. Brown purchased a twelve-hundred-acre tract of land near Highstown, New Jersey. The announcement of the project brought in over eight hundred applications for two hundred homesteads, despite the requirement that each homesteader had to contribute $500 to the project.

By fall of 1934, when construction had begun, David Dubinsky, head of the International Ladies' Garment Workers' Union, objected to Brown's plan to get a private manufacturer to operate the garment factory until the homesteaders could take over, since that meant the loss of a factory and jobs from New York. Neither Brown nor Dubinsky would budge on the issue, and the situation remained stalemated until the Resettlement Administration took over the project in 1935.

The Jersey Homesteads settlers were required to be union members in good standing, to be skilled in their trades, and to show as a family evidence of good home management (Conkin, 1959, p. 264). As a group, they were highly committed, used to organizing to achieve results, prepared to struggle to reach their desired ends. They were also an ethnically homogeneous population with strong religious ties (ibid., pp. 264, 266). The pattern of the community was entirely cooperative, and they remained a cohesive group despite the failure of the project. The cooperative factory failed to make money "because of an inexperienced manager, because of production in excess of orders, and because of high labor costs and inefficient production" (ibid., p. 271). Many of the unionized homesteaders would not work for low farm wages on the Jersey Homesteads general farming, poultry, or dairy operations, even when unemployed (ibid., p. 270), though they wanted the low prices in the community stores. Many of the homesteaders had no interest in subsistence farming; 8 of the 120 families never used their plots, and 38 grew only flowers on them.

Nevertheless, Jersey Homesteads did function as a community. The failures cemented bonds rather than causing dissension, and those who had to move away did so reluctantly and sadly. The failed cooperative factory was taken over in the 1940s by a hat manufacturer. Many homesteaders commuted to work in cities nearby (ibid., p. 272). Eventually, Jersey Homesteads passed into the hands of the Public Housing Administration, which, after World War II, sold the homes to individuals, many of them original homesteaders. The name of the community was changed to Roosevelt, New Jersey (ibid., p. 276).

The second agency to build New Deal communities was the Federal Emergency Relief Administration. FERA funds were given to the states, which then distributed the money through relief organizations. In Texas, the relief administrator was Col. Lawrence Westbrook, a former state legislator, who thought that making farmers self-sustaining would be less costly than continuing to maintain them on relief. With David Williams, a Dallas architect, he developed a plan for a relief community. In June 1934, Westbrook and Williams took a group of former farmers from the Houston relief rolls to a location about one hundred miles north of Houston to begin the construction of the Woodlake community (ibid., pp. 131–33).

The Woodlake community served as the prototype for the rest of the FERA communities. At Woodlake, about 100 three-, four-, and five-room houses were built on three-acre plots. Each had a combination barn-garage-laundry, an orchard, a vineyard, and a chicken house. The homes cost about $1,500 each, included a modern bath, and were leased for $180 a year to relief clients. Rents were payable in crop and poultry surpluses. "The whole community jointly owned a 225-acre park, a school, a community house, a bathhouse, a trading post, and two cooperative farms of 600 acres each. Each family, in addition to farming the three-acre subsistence plot, was expected to participate in handicrafts and processing industries" (ibid., p. 132). The project was administered by the Texas Rural Communities.

Harry Hopkins, FERA administrator, asked Westbrook and Williams to come to Washington. By administrative order, Hopkins created the Division of Rural Rehabilitation and Stranded Populations of the FERA, headed by Lawrence Westbrook. Since the FERA had no authority to purchase land or build houses, the legal staff worked out a means for state rural rehabilitation corporations to handle loans and community development projects under the direction of the Rural Rehabilitation Division (ibid., p. 133). Forty-five states had rural rehabilitation corporations by June 1935 (ibid., p. 134). Each state corporation had a board of directors made up of a regional representative of the FERA, the state relief administrator, the director of the State Extension Service, a representative of the Land Policy Section of the Agricultural Adjustment Administration, and three outstanding citizens (ibid., p. 135).

The state corporations used most of their funds for loans to individual farmers, with only a small portion of funds going to community construction. There were other differences from the Division of Subsistence Homesteads. More local control was allowed, the houses were constructed quickly and inexpensively, all were planned to house relief clients, and the economic bases of the communities were planned to be cooperative farms or village industries, not the decentralized industry of the Division of Subsistence Homesteads. Almost all of the FERA communities were constructed by prospective settlers. One of the most publicized was the Dyess Colony, the largest farm colony ever built by a U.S. public agency. It and two others were not turned over to the Resettlement Administration in 1935 but were placed under the Works Progress Administration and so stayed under the supervision of Hopkins and Westbrook. Dyess consisted of 17,500 acres of cotton land. It contained about 500 twenty-acre farms and a community center comprising 100 acres of land, an administration building, a mule barn, a theater building, a twenty-two-bed hospital, a school for about sixteen hundred pupils, a seed house, a cotton gin, a store, and thirty-two subsistence homes. The colony failed financially, largely because the farm units were too small. Some of the farms were consolidated, but the project remained a financial failure and the local corporation lost over $750,000 from 1937 to 1939 and was threatened with an investigation by the State of Arkansas (ibid., p. 138).

Altogether the FERA initiated plans for twenty-eight communities, although many were actually built by the Resettlement Administration. Some migratory camps also were built in California.

By early 1935, Roosevelt was considering a reorganization of the New Deal land and relief programs. Since Ickes's and Hopkins's agencies were both constructing communities and Ickes was unhappy with the subsistence homesteads program, Roosevelt had considered turning the subsistence homesteads over to Hopkins. Ickes had tried to trade off the homesteads to the Department of Agriculture with the idea of attracting Rexford G. Tugwell to Interior to direct a coordinated conservation program, but Wallace refused to exchange, and Hopkins didn't want the subsistence homesteads. On 30 April, FDR established the Resettlement Administration under Tugwell, who also retained his position as undersecretary of agriculture.

Tugwell, unlike M. L. Wilson, was not a back-to-the-land enthusiast and did not subscribe to the idea of subsistence homesteads as a solution to the problems faced by poor farmers. He believed that the rural problem in America was one of poor farmers on submarginal land, which made the poor farmers even poorer, with the result that they used methods that further depleted the land in their desperation to survive (Sternsher, 1964, p. 267). He thought that the submarginal lands should be retired to forest or recreational use and that farmers should be resettled on better land. However, he did not believe that it was possible to resettle all of the displaced farmers on new land, and even if it were, it would not be desirable to do so because mechanization was making fewer farmers necessary. He also thought it was impractical to combine rural subsistence farms with decentralized industries, since industry was highly unlikely to return to rural areas in small units. Tugwell's chief concern lay in providing for the numbers of farm dwellers who would inevitably have to be absorbed into urban areas.

His position was not merely a response to the problem of rural-to-urban migration but a consequence of his economic and social philosophy.

Tugwell believed that the irreversible trend in industrial societies was toward concentration and cooperation but that so far in the United States this movement had been seen only in business, while government clung to outmoded Jeffersonian ideals. He "desired collectivism and called it by that name" (Conkin, 1959, p. 149) and deplored "misguided, rural-minded reformers who pressed for a return to more competition, less efficiency, and more struggle" (ibid., p. 150). He felt that the "most iniquitous institution was uncontrolled capitalism" (ibid.), which pursued its ends while the public was deceived by anachronistic rhetoric that glorified competition, individualism, and fragmentation, resulting in "struggle rather than co-operation, divisiveness rather than unity" (ibid.). Although the public was divided, business was consolidating into large, noncompetitive groups that were not controlled by the public interest; the myth of free enterprise, competition, and democracy concealed from the misinformed public what was really happening in business. The few who had spoken out for true reform had been labeled fanatics. As a result, "the apex of the capitalist structure glittered on a broad base of dirty factories, ravaged land, and miserable slums; but even the poorest faces were turned adoringly to its light" (Tugwell, 1955, p. 38).

Tugwell held that the Depression had been caused by inequity in income distribution, which had resulted in too little purchasing power for most people, causing scarcity in the midst of surpluses. He hoped that the Depression would awaken most people to the power and practices of the special interests and would discredit the privileged groups. Conkin (1959) calls Tugwell "a savior without a flock, constantly frustrated when people failed to respond to his ideas" (p. 151). His goal was to make people aware of the need for "an organic society, with a unity of purpose, with a co-operative and collective economy, and with a purposeful, functioning government" (ibid., p. 150). For Tugwell, the question of public or private ownership was beside the point: what was important was public planning for the purpose of reaching publicly oriented goals. He saw the unplanned sector of the economy as uncoordinated, working at cross-purposes. In prosperous times, businessmen, lacking inclusive information about their industry or markets, tended to think of the same things at the same time and make similar capital investments, resulting in optimistic overexpansion and, ultimately, overproduction and contraction (Sternsher, 1964, pp. 92–93). Tugwell was, in fact, an anti-trustbuster; he thought that antitrust sentiment came from an incorrect understanding of the problem, that cooperative impulses were bound to dominate and businesses to combine, and that the real problem was in directing these combinations so that they served the public rather than special interests (ibid., p. 93). This purpose was thwarted by "negative governments" and the promotion of individualism for the majority of people, while the major businesses operated collectively under the guise of competition.

Tugwell saw the Depression, then, as an opportunity to demonstrate the virtues of his collectivist principles. The Resettlement Administration was created in 1935 in part because of Tugwell's insistence that existing federal agencies were inadequate to solve the problems faced by poor farmers on poor land. As assistant secretary of agriculture from 1933 to 1934 and undersecretary of agriculture from 1934 to 1936, Tugwell had concluded that the Agricultural Adjustment Administration (AAA) was the "big staple farmer's agency" and that not enough was being done to help poor farmers, who had no comparable agency to turn to. At the same time, he criticized the government's role in land-use planning, which was fragmented among numerous agencies. Tugwell urged Roosevelt to create a single agency to consolidate programs in rehabilitation, land use, and resettlement. Roosevelt created the Resettlement Administration by Executive Order 7027 in May 1935 and named Tugwell as resettlement administrator. The Resettlement Administration had no Congressional authorization and was funded for only one year from the Emergency Relief Act of 1935; its continuation would be dependent on legislative appropriations.

The new agency had four principal tasks: suburban resettlement, rural rehabilitation, land utilization, and rural resettlement. Each was the responsibility of one of the Resettlement Administration's divisions. Rural Resettlement inherited the uncompleted farm communities from the Division of Subsistence Homesteads and the FERA and approved plans for additional rural communities. Land Utilization had over 9 million acres of optioned or purchased land to handle, as well as over two hundred projects to develop new uses for the land; many resettlement clients came from among those displaced by this program. The Rural Rehabilitation Division made loans and grants to farmers and adjusted farm debts; some of the loans went to resettlement communities, and many of its clients later joined rural communities. A separate Construction Division did all of the construction for both rural and suburban communities. The Management Division controlled completed communities, directing educational and community activities, developing economic opportunities, selecting settlers, organizing community governments, and seeing to the maintenance of the buildings in the communities. Suburban Resettlement had little connection with the other divisions; it had control over the inherited suburban subsistence homesteads and the greenbelt cities. The rehabilitation program was completely decentralized, in the manner of the FERA, and administered through eleven regional offices; rural resettlement was also handled through the regional offices, though with more supervision from Washington. Suburban resettlement, conversely, was controlled from Washington and had no connection with the regional offices (Conkin, 1959, pp. 156–60).

The division most closely identified with Tugwell's ideas was this Suburban Resettlement Division. The broad goals of the division were to contend with the problems of rural-to-urban movement and to provide alternative housing for urban slum dwellers.

The principal program initiative involved construction of greenbelt cities, the largest and most important of the New Deal communities. Tugwell believed that there should be three thousand greenbelt towns. The towns were to combine work relief for the unemployed, low-cost housing for the slum dweller, long-term community planning, and subsistence farming. Low-income housing projects in the suburbs would differ from the WPA slum clearance program, which was slow, worked too great a hardship on slum dwellers being cleared, and was expensive for tenants when completed. The problem with urban public housing was that assembling a large tract of land from many small parcels was expensive and time-consuming, resulting in housing that was impossible for the poor to rent without subsidization. Those in the Resettlement Administration believed that suburban projects could be built inexpensively before slums could be cleared, providing housing at a price with which slum housing would not be able to compete and thus correcting a fundamental error in federal slum clearance (Arnold, 1971, pp. 29, 37, 38).

Over one hundred cities were studied for greenbelt sites, and twenty-five were picked for additional investigation. Tugwell hoped for greenbelt towns for all twenty-five, but only eight projects were approved by Roosevelt. When funds were finally allocated, only $31 million was actually allotted, largely because of the intervention of Henry Morgenthau, the secretary of the treasury, who was an ally of Harry Hopkins, now with the Works Progress Administration. Hopkins and Morgenthau wanted relief money to go for jobs for the unemployed through quick-action projects (ibid., pp. 42–43). Furthermore, the Resettlement Administration was limited by the requirement that it had to get permission from the Works Progress Administration (WPA), based on the supply of relief labor in a locality, to begin work on a town; each worker hired then had to be certified by the WPA as being on relief, unemployed, or otherwise in need of a government job. The tightest restriction was on the time allowed; the land must be bought and construction begun by 15 December 1935 (the funds were approved on 12 September 1935) and the towns completed by 30 June 1936.

Ultimately, only three "Tugwell Towns" were built: Greenbelt, Maryland, near Washington, D.C.; Greenhills, near Cincinnati; and Greendale, near Milwaukee. The division modified plans of two subsistence-home-steads communities, near Newport News, Virginia, and Birmingham, Ala-bama, to more closely resemble garden cities; it also built one suburban community near Ironwood, Michigan, which had some resemblance to the greenbelt communities. The greenbelt towns were designed to provide housing for five hundred to eight hundred families each. They were sur-rounded by a greenbelt of fields and woods in order to prevent invasion by outside development; internally, they emphasized open space, parks, and paths for foot traffic and were to be ideal for families with children. Tugwell's enthusiasm for the greenbelt communities was expressed in a 1937 article, when he called them the "best chance we have ever had in this country for affecting our living and working environment favorably."

The majority of the Resettlement Administration's rural settlements were of one pattern: typically in the South, with either white or black tenants, but not both, living in frame houses with three to five rooms (and without plumbing). The houses were on farm units of from forty to one hundred acres. Tenants leased the farms for a percentage of annual crop production. The community typically had a school, a cooperative cotton gin, a warehouse, and a community building. Most communities had several cooperative enterprises operated by a cooperative association (Conkin, 1959, p. 168).

Three rural communities did not fit the pattern. At Lake Dick, Arkan-sas, and Casa Grande Farms, Arizona, the Resettlement Administration established large cooperative farms. Tenants lived in a village, with plots for individual gardens. Farming was done by a cooperative association of all of the tenants; individual tenants were paid wages and shared in cooperative profits at the end of the year. In Terrebonne Parish, Louisi-ana, a collective farm of twenty-eight hundred acres was leased to a co-op association for ninety-nine years; the association raised sugar cane, truck crops, and livestock (ibid., p. 169).

Selection of tenants, in almost all cases, was a rigid screening proce-dure conducted by social workers. Prospective settlers were assessed on the bases of age, health, economic stability, character, and number of chil-dren. Income limits for suburban families were set at $1,600, lower for rural families (ibid., p. 187). The average family contained 5.2 members; the husbands averaged 37.3 years of age; the wives, 33.3. The husbands had an average of 7.2 years of education; the wives, 8.1 years. The prin-cipal problem faced by the tenants was that, to afford a new home worth around $5,000 to $6,000, and a farm and outbuildings worth around $4,000, they would have to generate a good deal more income than they had previously. In addition to the home and plot, they frequently had to afford a larger heating bill and pay for electricity, which they might not have used before.

The problem of providing economic opportunities so that the tenants could afford the new projects was to be solved, in the Resettlement Administration, by two "magic ingredients": cooperation and supervision. Supervision meant the presence of home economists and agricultural advisers on every subsistence homesteads project and, on the rural projects, farm and home experts essentially responsible for the project's success (Conkin, 1959, p. 189). In each rural community a farm management expert guided each family in working out complete farm and home budgets and production plans for each year. In 1937 the homesteaders began to receive government loans; on some projects, to protect the loans, the project manager had joint bank accounts with the tenants, who could not sign a check without the manager's approval (ibid., p. 190).

> The real key to the new society was to be cooperation. The whole history of the New Deal communities could be related to the idea of co-operation, which was to replace competition and extreme individualism. From M. L. Wilson, who saw co-operation as the only means of retaining democratic institutions, to Tugwell, whose desire for a collectivized, co-operative society was almost a religion, the architects of the New Deal communities were attempting to develop co-operation as the new institution best suited for the modern environment. . . . Voluntary, democratic co-operation was to be the alternative to the economic insecurity and chaos of an individualistic, capitalistic past and to the involuntary, totalitarian collectivism of both fascism and communism. (Conkin, 1959, pp. 202–3)

The Resettlement Administration made loans primarily to producers' cooperatives, reversing the past government emphasis on consumers' cooperatives. Most of the early co-ops were for production or processing of agricultural products, consumer services, or medical care. Many co-op associations had ten or twelve different programs. A large number of the programs failed "because of poor management, resentment of government control, lack of understanding of the co-operative idea, nonbusinesslike practices, factionalism in the associations, and outside competition or opposition" (ibid., p. 205). Among the more successful were the medical co-ops, which won the support of many doctors and medical societies and in which over one hundred thousand families participated by 1941 (ibid., p. 198).

The need remained, though, for some type of industrial employment. Cooperative farms and consumer co-ops could employ no more than a few of the settlers at a time on each project. The Farm Security Administration financed several industrial projects. These involved contracting with private industry for the establishment and management of plants: a wood mill at Tygart Valley, a tractor assembly plant at Arthurdale, a pants factory at Westmoreland, and hosiery mills at five other locations. For a few years the ventures provided jobs for the settlers, but all of the plants lost money and none lasted past 1944 (ibid., p. 208).

The homesteaders entered the new projects enthusiastically, but their expectations often turned to disappointment. Expensive construction made the tenants fear they could never afford to own their homesteads. Cooperation was frequently a formality, with real community decisions being made by the project manager. Government policies changed, and tenants were informed of them only after the fact. Factions arose around strong community leaders, often in opposition to the appointed project managers. Most important, though, few of the tenants aspired to cooperation as a way of life; they accepted the idea only as a step toward achieving individual ownership.

From the beginning, the Resettlement Administration was under attack. Tugwell was already one of the most controversial figures of the New Deal, and the agency became almost synonymous with its administrator in the minds of Tugwell's critics. The press attacked the size and irresponsibility of the Resettlement Administration. One editorial described the purposes of the Resettlement Administrations as being "to arrange the earth and the people thereof and devote surplus time and money, if any, to a rehabilitation of the Solar System" (Conkin, 1959, p. 153). Congressional opponents attacked the Resettlement Administration for its high construction costs. These arose partly because of Tugwell's insistence that experimental methods in housing construction must be used on the projects but also in part because of the stipulation that relief labor must be used, resulting in a largely unskilled pool of workers, and because of further requirements that the maximum amount of relief employment had to be provided, which meant that labor-intensive methods were necessitated.

The real reason behind Congressional opposition, though, was that "Tugwell, with his broad authority under the executive order, set up a large administration and initiated an ambitious program without any clear mandate from Congress" (ibid., p. 176). Tugwell was "disdainful of Congressmen" and felt that his staff of planners and experts knew better than Congress "what the lower third of rural and urban America needed" (ibid., p. 177). Congress, on the other hand, had relinquished policymaking authority to the executive branch because of the national crisis and now regretted that loss; Tugwell, with his open distrust of legislators as "the instruments of special interests" (ibid.) was in line for retribution. Senator W. Warren Barbour of New Jersey led a campaign in the Senate for an investigation of the Resettlement Administration; this effort failed, but the Resettlement Administration was required to provide the Senate with a full account of its activities (ibid., p. 179).

Serious opposition also came from the courts. In New Jersey, a group of citizens filed an injunction against the construction of Greenbrook, a garden city planned for construction near New Brunswick, on the grounds that "the whole Emergency Relief Act of 1935 was unconstitutional, that the order creating the Resettlement Administration was not under the scope of any United States statute or law, that the proposed community was not for the general welfare or the common defense, and that the Resettlement Administration was exercising powers reserved for the states" (ibid., p. 173). This injunction was denied, but a second was filed, and in May 1936 the Court of Appeals of the District of Columbia declared the Emergency Relief Act of 1935 unconstitutional and further ruled that the Act, though unconstitutional, did not authorize a resettlement policy or the building of model communities (ibid., p. 174). The Resettlement Administration, rather than appealing to the Supreme Court, abandoned the Greenbrook project and proceeded with the other greenbelt cities.

Under attack, Tugwell urged that the Resettlement Administration be given a more permanent place within the Department of Agriculture. In November 1936, Tugwell announced his resignation; in December 1936 the Resettlement Administration was transferred to the Department of Agriculture, with Will Alexander as its administrator. In September 1937 the Resettlement Administration was renamed the Farm Security Administration. The greenbelt cities were completed in June 1938, and the Suburban Resettlement Division was abolished. In 1942 the three towns were transferred to the Public Housing Authority. The housing in Greenhills was sold in 1949 to a cooperative homeowners' association; the greenbelt remainder was sold in 1952 to the Cincinnati Park Service and the Cincinnati Development Corporation. Greendale's housing was sold to tenants and the greenbelt to the Milwaukee Community Development Corporation. Greenbelt was sold to a number of purchasers, most of the housing units being bought by a veteran's group in 1952. Although none of the towns was occupied under Tugwell's administration, Tugwell himself took up residence at Greenbelt in 1957.

Alongside the New Deal:
Catholic and Black American
Movements

The New Deal settlements were not the only alternative communities built in the 1930s. There also were private initiatives such as Shiloh Trust, the Rev. Eugene Crosby Monroe's self-sustaining Pentecostal commune located on a farm near Sherman, Texas, and the Rev. Harry Miller's People of the Living God group that located first in Kentucky, then in the mountains of Tennessee, and subsequently in New Orleans. Most were small. Among them, Sunrise, a Jewish anarchist community founded in 1932 at Saginaw, Michigan, has received most attention. More important, however, were the communal groups that were formed during or grew in response to the Depression. These included the Catholic Worker movement's communes, the communities of Father Divine's Peace Mission movement, and the Koinonia community.

The Sunrise Community

The prime mover at Sunrise was Joseph Cohen, who earlier had helped organize the anarchistic Ferrer Colony (1915–46) at Stelton, New Jersey. By 1932, Cohen was editor of the anarchist publication *Freie Arbeiter Stimme*. He saw cooperative living as a solution to the conditions of the Great Depression and in 1933 published his prospectus *A Project for a Collectivist Cooperative Colony*. In June 1933 he bought a working farm of ten thousand acres and was ultimately joined by one hundred families. No one was accepted who was older than forty-five, encumbered by children, or a professing Communist. The collectivists were spread over the farm in three separate settlements.

Early tensions developed because the largely urban settlers lacked agricultural skills and because hired hands were required. Whether the hands should be paid a going pittance or a professional wage was one source of friction, especially since the farm's profits had to be kept up to meet stiff mortgage payments. Loans from the Rural Rehabilitation Corporation (RRA) kept them afloat. But then conflicts arose over Cohen's leadership, about how a group of anarchists could work collectively, and between the anarchists and the Yiddish members of an organization called Poalei Zion, who demanded that their language rather than English be spoken and that the tradition of Jewish unions and party cells be maintained.

Cohen and the anarchists were ousted. A harvest failure made it difficult to meet obligations. The RRA stepped in and agreed to buy the farm and to discharge the community's obligations. Those wanting to return to the city would receive compensation and could do so. Those wanting to remain would be given priority in renting land from the government as individuals. The RRA purchased the land in 1936. By 1939 the group had completely dissolved (Fogarty, 1980, pp. 167–68; Oved, 1988, chap. 16).

Cohen later said that the failure was due to the fundamental contradiction between anarchist ideology and the need for authority and regulation to manage a profitable large-scale farming enterprise. Yet there was another reason, too. In 1932 the need was for security and social harmony in the depths of an increasingly fractious Great Depression. The contradictions produced disharmony, and as the New Deal recovery took hold and economic opportunity reappeared, the need for security waned.

The Catholic Worker Movement

The Catholic Worker movement, which introduced the reformist activities of the Social Gospel movement into the Catholic church, developed a number of communal settlements.

The movement arose from the collaboration of Dorothy Day and Peter Maurin in the publication of the radical newspaper *Catholic Worker*. Day was a journalist and Catholic convert who, in the early days of the Depression, reported on topics such as rent strikes, political meetings, and the condition of the unemployed for the Catholic journals *Commonweal* and *America*. In the winter of 1932, while covering a Communist hunger march in Washington, D.C., she found that her growing dissatisfaction with her role as uninvolved reporter had become a clear desire for social action. Maurin, a French peasant and social agitator with an extensive knowledge of Catholic social thought, introduced himself to Day on the recommendation of George Schuster, an editor of *Commonweal*, who recognized the affinities between Maurin's outlook and Day's. This, apparently, was more than Day recognized at first, for she was unimpressed with Maurin's outward eccentricity and his conversational manner of shouting monologues at close range. Only after several weeks of exhausting conversations did

Maurin suggest to Day that she should begin a Catholic newspaper for the unemployed, and she see the possibility of a collaboration.

Even so, the partnership was lopsided from the beginning; Maurin was irretrievably impractical, so the fund-raising, reporting, and circulation were Day's responsibility from the outset, while Maurin wrote articles expounding his theories and traveled around the country promoting the *Catholic Worker* and his "program." In fact, Maurin's contribution to the movement may have been chiefly as a symbolic figure whose ideas were interpreted and whose life as a poor holy man was described in *Catholic Worker* articles by Dorothy Day; as a middle-class, female convert, she used the European peasant Maurin to increase the following of her movement within the sexually conservative Catholic church.

Maurin's program had three points, as he described it:

> We need round-table discussions
> To keep trained minds from becoming academic.
> We need round-table discussions
> To keep untrained minds from becoming
> superficial.
>
> We need Houses of Hospitality
> To give to the rich the opportunity to serve
> the poor.
> We need Houses of Hospitality
> To bring social justice back to Catholic
> institutions.
>
> The unemployed need food.
> They can raise that
> In an agronomic university.
> The unemployed need to acquire skill.
> They can do that in an agronomic university.

The Houses of Hospitality were formed when it became clear that a newspaper advocating radical social action to help the poor and unemployed would have to serve as an example. The first House of Hospitality was the newspaper office itself. Maurin began to bring transients to the office, and the editorial staff of the newspaper served soup to the hungry at what was soon named St. Joseph's House of Hospitality. The original offices were rapidly outgrown, and St. Joseph's moved to a larger building that provided editorial offices, a print shop, and dining rooms, as well as three floors of apartments (two for men and one for women) where *Catholic Worker* staff and "guests" slept. By 1938 approximately 1,200 people ate at St. Joseph's twice a day, and around 150 slept there.

As *Catholic Worker* staff reported their experiences in the paper, readers wrote asking to join the movement, and the editors put them in touch with other like-minded readers in their own cities. Day and Maurin visited newly formed groups, and before long, Houses of Hospitality opened in other cities, beginning with Boston and St. Louis in 1934, followed by Chicago, Cleveland, and Washington, D.C., in 1935. Over a dozen houses opened in 1936, and by 1942 thirty-two were operating. Most of the groups published their own local versions of the *Catholic Worker* in order to raise funds, but otherwise the groups differed in character to a remarkable extent. They varied in size from fewer than a dozen members to several hundred. The St. Louis House fed twenty-seven hundred people in the bread line every day and took meals to seven hundred more. The houses varied in the stability of their leadership and in their relations with local Catholic institutions, whose attitudes ranged from encouragement to indifference to hostility. Moreover, each group emphasized different activities, with some involved in labor organizing and rent strikes, others having an intellectual focus, and others performing more traditional works of mercy.

The link between houses was Dorothy Day's leadership and her interpretation of Maurin's radical Gospel ideals. The principles that guided the movement were few and general. Each individual had to reach a personal understanding of "Christian love," then express this understanding, initially through helping those in immediate need of assistance and ultimately through societal change. Within the Houses of Hospitality the emphasis was on personal discovery, as opposed to indoctrination, anticipating a theme that became much stronger in the 1960s. The communities were considered to be "the imperfect external expressions of the interior lives of those who inhabited them" (Piehl, 1982, p. 98). In practice this translated into "free anarchist commune[s] held together only by shared commitment, religion, friendship, experience, and the spiritual leadership of Day and Maurin" (ibid., p. 98).

Although the Houses of Hospitality had no formal meetings, constitutions or bylaws, or elected officers (the leaders were appointed by Day), there were nevertheless some practices that were near-universal. Primary among these was the practice of "voluntary poverty," which was distinguished from "destitution," or involuntary poverty, and described as "a state of simple sufficiency of food, clothing, shelter, or other goods, with nothing superfluous" (Piehl, 1982, p. 98). Providing food was a central concern of all of the houses, and some maintained a perpetual soup pot to which anyone could add ingredients. Most houses also distributed secondhand clothes. Food, rent, utilities, and clothing were obtained through donations because Day maintained that part-time jobs held by Workers violated the principle of poverty, even when the wages were turned over to the movement. Wealth was held as undesirable for the group as for the individual, and whatever small surpluses might accumulate were given away.

The inner effects of this mild asceticism on individuals are of course difficult to assess, but its consequences for the movement as a whole are easier to see. The invitation to live a morally exacting existence in accord with radical Gospel ideals attracted many highly motivated persons to the movement. Poverty created an immediate sense of identification with the downtrodden that greatly intensified radical commitment, while the sense of sharp departure from the whole cluster of American values surrounding abundance and consumption constituted a significant critique of American society. The group's indifference to material considerations also made it less vulnerable to distraction and compromise. (Piehl, 1982, p. 100)

However, poverty as a source of solidarity was counterweighed by the stresses of a slum existence. The commitment to poverty precluded any form of ownership, but this inevitably resulted in conflicts. The *Catholic Worker* reported: "We hold on to our books, radios, tools such as typewriters, and instead of rejoicing when they are taken away from us, we lament." Competition also arose from the attempt to be less material and more selfless, a kind of spiritual competition that rewarded those who could come closest to achieving the movement's ideals. Disputes arose over work because there were no rules governing labor and each Worker was supposed to work at communal tasks from a sense of responsibility. Conflict did not generally arise from the principal activities of the house, such as putting out the paper, preparing food, or feeding the bread lines. The idea of teaching by example carried Workers through conflicts over other chores, since "if nothing else, it gave you a glow of self-righteousness that could sustain you for days." Piehl (1982) continues: "That so much difficult work was accomplished under this system argued against the cynics, some within the movement itself, who said it was impossible and bound to fail. That it was done at a price proved the difficulties of utopia" (p. 101).

The Catholic Worker movement grew rapidly during the early Depression years, in part because, despite its radical ideals, it appeared in practice to be part of the Catholic mainstream. The most obvious features of the movement were support for labor and provision of food and shelter for the destitute. The American Catholic church, unlike many Protestant denominations, was largely working-class, and its leaders were tolerant, if not actually supportive, of labor organization. The membership and executive board of the AFL were dominated by Catholics by 1918, and in 1919 the National Catholic War Council (later known as the National Catholic

Welfare Conference) published the "Bishops' Program of Social Reconstruction," which called for minimum wage laws, collective bargaining legislation, public housing, social insurance, and worker participation in industrial management and ownership. Furthermore, the ideal of charity combined with a fear of Protestant proselytizing among the impoverished led to the formation of a vast network of Catholic charities, helped by groups like the St. Vincent de Paul Society and the Sisters of Mercy, which largely provided aid to distressed parishioners. In the 1860s some New York parishes provided day care and employment counseling. Therefore, for those who knew the Catholic Worker movement through the houses rather than through the *Catholic Worker*'s articles on Catholic social thought and Maurin's Gospel interpretation, there was no apparent split between the movement and the church.

Day supported labor unions in the *Catholic Worker* despite Maurin's medievalist agrarianism and dislike of industrial proletarianism, and the movement supported them on the picket lines. The paper also reflected the national Catholic support of Roosevelt and the New Deal. From the time of the 1929 stock market crash, Catholic leaders had called for the replacement of the acquisitive, individualistic, capitalistic "Protestant ethic" with a new social order (Piehl, 1982, p. 113). While rejecting Marxism, they called for government intervention in national economic recovery, direct aid to the unemployed, and overhaul of the economic structure. By 1932 the church leadership was nearly unanimous in support of the New Deal. The *Catholic Worker* supported the NRA, although Day privately criticized the NRA as probusiness and antilabor, largely because those in the movement realized that private relief was inadequate to solve the nation's relief problems. Day probably appeared most part of the mainstream when, in 1935, she joined 130 other prominent Catholics in signing *Organized Social Justice*—the National Catholic Welfare Conference's statement denouncing the Supreme Court's decision in the case of *Schecter Poultry Co. v. United States*, which invalidated the National Industrial Recovery Act that had set up the NRA—and putting forward the Catholic case for new social reforms.

From 1935 onward, the national "Catholic consensus" began to fall apart, however. The first threat came from opponents of the proposed Child Labor Amendment to the Constitution, which was eight states short of ratification in 1935. The amendment was seen as a threat to parental prerogatives in child rearing; most of the Catholic hierarchy and a number of Catholic journals came out in opposition (Piehl, 1982, p. 121) Further splits between liberal and conservative wings within the church developed over the direction of the New Deal, the rise of militant CIO unionism, and anticommunism at home and abroad (ibid., p. 122). The split became greater with the Spanish civil war: American Catholic leaders supported Franco fervently and almost unanimously. *Commonweal*, which declared its support for the republic, lost almost a quarter of its circulation as a result, and the *Catholic Worker*'s call for neutrality also left it isolated (ibid., p. 123).

Internal conflicts also occurred in the Catholic Worker movement. The Campion Propaganda Committee—a caucus within the New York and Boston houses—was a militant group that "specializ[ed] in direct street-corner confrontations with pro-Nazis, scabs, and anti-Catholics" (ibid., p. 124). Campionites were allegedly nonviolent and refused to fight back when attacked, but it became obvious that they were, in fact, provoking violence. They also tried to increase the politicization of the Catholic Worker movement and eliminate some "soup-line" types of activities. After attempting to take over the paper, they left in 1936 to set up their own movement, led by Thomas Coddington.

Labor involvement also produced conflict. The CIO was formed in 1935 and was supported by the Catholic Workers. The New York House of Hospitality was the site of the formation of the Association of Catholic Trade Unionists (ACTU) in 1937 (Piehl, 1982, p. 125). ACTists were effective in getting Catholic moral prestige behind certain strikes and in persuading Catholic ethnics to join unions; for example, Polish and Italian Chrysler workers in 1939 joined the CIO because of ACTU persuasion (ibid., p. 161). The major split with the Catholic Workers came post-1940. The Catholic Workers said that ACTU was "tied to narrow union ideology that ultimately promoted the very bourgeois materialist values that caused social injustice in the first place" (ibid., p. 162). Even in the mid-1930s, though, Day saw the labor involvement as having more effect on the Catholic Worker movement than on labor, so she began to reemphasize utopian ideology (ibid., p. 125).

Farm communes were held up as the answer to the social crisis. They were promoted in particular by younger members of the movement with children:

Single persons under the influence of a powerful religious motive can live happily in a communal society where everything is shared in common. . . . But we soon learned that marriage and our attempts at communal living were incompatible, for no matter how devoted to the work, the moment they married their relationship gradually and imperceptibly and then frankly and strongly veered away from the community to take care of their own. . . . This fact, that the family seeks its own because it is a natural community, is the fundamental reason why a complete plan of communal living was bound to fail. (Stanley Vishnewski, quoted in Piehl, 1982, pp. 128–29)

The issues of families became a major problem by 1936. Some Workers proposed excluding families altogether, making the movement more of a lay religious order. Day opposed this suggestion, and the solution was seen in agrarian communes. A twenty-eight-acre farm near Easton, Pennsylvania, was donated. The next year, another forty acres was added. Individual families lived in a common house with single workers and guests, but eventually separate dwellings were to be constructed for the families. Each family was given a three-acre plot.

About a dozen other farm communes were established in the next few years; some became locally important. "St. Benedict's Farm in Massachusetts became an important Catholic art and liturgical center; Our Lady of the Wayside Farm in Ohio took in the retarded; St. Isidore's Farm in Minnesota was part of the same movement as Eugene and Abigail McCarthy's St. Anne's Farm" (Piehl, 1982, p. 130). A few of the farms survived into the 1940s. Most of these were midwestern, with better land and some experienced workers, but most failed nonetheless. Besides lack of sufficient land, capital, and experience, the reasons for failure include the movement's radical commitment to openness and personal sacrifice and a constant stream of visitors that consumed resources and caused controversy over what the *Catholic Worker* called "the conflict between workers and scholars." One Worker said, "Often the practice of the works of mercy distracted the Green Revolutionists from the soil. God bless them. It is better to try to be a Christian than a successful soil engineer" (ibid., p. 131).

The farms failed as communal utopias, but the New York Catholic Workers maintained farms near the city to serve as "retreat centers, halfway houses, and suppliers of vegetables" (ibid.). The urban houses made efforts to accommodate couples, sometimes finding them nearby apartments; many families with children were involved in the work weekends and summers, thus bringing up Catholic Worker children. There was a resurgence of Catholic Worker communal farms in the 1960s, but in the meantime the few remaining communities served mainly to keep the Catholic Workers in touch with other communities around the world. They established particularly close ties with Koinonia Farm (discussed below), where Dorothy Day spent time while it was under attack by the Ku Klux Klan.

The big split in the Catholic Worker movement came with the issue of pacifism. Day was intransigently pacifist. John Cogley, head of the Chicago House, denounced the draft at first, but as war began to seem inevitable, he dropped the subject from *Commonweal*, which he edited. The New York paper was vocally pacifist, so Catholic groups in some cities stopped distributing the *Catholic Worker* and sold the Chicago paper instead.

In July 1940, Day and other Workers testified in hearings of the House Military Affairs Committee against the proposed Selective Service Act. Day issued an open letter to all Catholic Workers in August 1940 stating that pacifism was central to the movement and demanding that the New York paper be distributed by all houses. Some houses closed immediately after her ultimatum, some tried to go along with her demands for a time, and others changed their names and carried on the work. But by 1942 only sixteen houses remained, only ten by January 1945. Houses that survived the war were those that had the strongest commitment to the radical Gospel ideology (Piehl, 1982, p. 197).

After the war, Day and her followers continued in the same way but with a much smaller movement. They were now strongly identified with pacifism though still involved in diverse social action, not a single-issue group. In 1946–47 they opposed a peacetime draft. They stayed off Senator McCarthy's lists in 1950s, perhaps because of their Catholic association. Although only eight houses were in operation by 1950, the paper's circulation rose from a low of fifty thousand during World War II to about sixty thousand during the early 1950s. It influenced Michael Harrington, a Worker from January 1951 to December 1952 (Piehl, 1982, p. 175), and the leaders of the Catholic Peace Fellowship, Thomas Cornell, James Forest, and Daniel Berrigan (ibid., p. 236).

The Catholic Worker movement was

not primarily . . . a movement for social change, but . . . a movement of utopian dissent. Such movements typically express their disaffection with the larger society not through direct social action but through attempts to criticize the values of that society, often by creating enclaves that are expected to serve as alternative social models. . . . Like most such ventures, the Catholic worker communities only partially lived up to their ideals, but they deserve a place in American history alongside other small but noteworthy American experiments such as the Shaker settlements, Brook Farm, and Oneida. (ibid., pp. 242–43)

"Dorothy Day's primary achievement . . . was to introduce the social perspectives of the radical Gospel into the American [Catholic] Church" (ibid., p. 244).

Father Divine

A second interwar movement that must be discussed was largely restricted to black Americans and pioneered the movement of black churches into the arena of civil rights and social reform. It was led by

"Father Divine," a cult figure who achieved national recognition as a social reformer (Weisbrot, 1983). His name originally may have been either George Baker or Frederick Edwards. Little verifiable information is available concerning his life until around 1900, when he lived in Baltimore and was drawn to the preaching of a man named Samuel Morris, also called Father Jehovia. Morris and Baker/Edwards became close associates and in 1908 were joined by a third preacher, John Hickerson, also called St. John the Vine. Baker/Edwards took the name "The Messenger." The three preached as a team until 1912, when Hickerson left for New York City. Morris faded out of the picture, and The Messenger went south. At Valdosta, Georgia, in 1913 he was arrested on grounds of insanity for preaching that since God was within him, therefore he was God; he was found guilty but not committed to a mental institution. He was ordered to leave Georgia and never return.

The Messenger and his southern disciples settled in Brooklyn by 1915. Baker got in touch with Hickerson, who had his own church, the Church of the Living God. Hickerson was still teaching that God was within every person, so although Hickerson claimed to be God, so could any number of others. The Messenger gained many of Hickerson's followers. His cult lived communally in Brooklyn. The Messenger operated an employment service, finding mostly domestic work and menial labor for his followers, who turned over their wages to him. He paid all of their bills, including rent and food. During this period he changed his name again, first to Major Jealous Devine and eventually to Father Divine.

In 1919, Father Divine and his followers moved to Sayville, Long Island. Although a black group in a white community, they encountered little trouble for several years, focusing on acceptance and tranquility. The group was quiet; no smoking, drinking, swearing, or "immodest behavior" were allowed. The house was kept neat, and Father Divine's employment service provided domestic workers to the community. "The transforming crisis came suddenly in 1929, from origins largely outside the ghetto's control. The Great Depression . . . crystallized a new militance among ghetto residents [and] the Negro church at last faced concerted community-wide pressure to contribute more vigorously to movements for social aid and reform" (Weisbrot, 1983, pp. 4–5). "Father Divine moved into the role of reformer through a transitional stage of philanthropist to poor and unemployed ghetto residents" (ibid.). On Sundays, enormous free meals, consisting of thirty to forty courses, were served to anyone who came, and many arrived on buses. In the 1930s private automobiles joined the buses, and the Sunday noise, crowds, and traffic became a problem to the other Sayville residents. Issuing large numbers of traffic tickets and parking citations had no effect; neither did an attempted infiltration of the movement to gain information about sexual practices (the only apparent sexual "practice" was celibacy). The angry residents of Sayville called a town meeting and chose a committee to put their demands before Father Divine. Father Divine listened to the committee, then pointed out his Constitutional rights, the legality of the group and its actions, and the contribution he and his followers were making to the local economy.

Shortly thereafter, Father Divine and eighty followers were arrested for disturbing the peace. Father Divine was indicted by the grand jury and held on $1,500 bail pending trial. The presiding judge, Lewis J. Smith, showed clear bias against the defendant; in his charge to the jury he called Father Divine a bad influence in the community and pointed out that he was not an ordained minister, that he was not legally married to the woman he called his wife ("Mother Divine"), and that he induced his followers to turn over their wages to him. The jury returned a guilty verdict but with a recommendation for leniency. Judge Smith ignored their recommendation and imposed the stiffest penalty allowed, a $500 fine and a year in jail.

Three days after the sentencing, Judge Smith, a fifty-year-old man in apparent health, died of a heart attack. Father Divine commented, "I hated to do it." The death of Judge Smith and Father Divine's comments made headlines in the black press. On the day after Father Divine's release from prison (as the result of an appellate decision overturning his conviction), over seven thousand persons attended a "Monster Glory to Our Lord" rally at the Rockland Palace in Harlem.

Father Divine's Peace Mission movement gained a considerable number of new followers as a result of the publicity surrounding the trial, but the attraction was sustained by the three parts of his program: "Food, jobs, and a joyous war against racism and alienation." Father Divine considered integration essential to racial harmony but believed that equality also had to exist in the economic sphere. His economic operations were widespread, but all operated on the same system. If Father Divine wanted to set up a business in a particular location, he first raised capital from his followers. The money was donated, not loaned, in cash. White disciples were used to circumvent restrictive housing covenants. His followers also staffed the businesses but received no wages; instead, they received room and board.

The most successful of the cooperative enterprises were hotels, which also housed many of the followers and provided facilities for meetings, rallies, and the enormous communion banquets that characterized the movement. Typically, the group renovated a run-down urban hotel and, through low overhead, was able to charge extremely low rates to paying customers. Several of the hotels, such as the Divine Tracy and the Divine Lorraine in Philadelphia, the Divine Hotel Riviera in Newark, and the Divine Fairmount in Jersey City, are still in operation. Other enterprises included apartments, rooming houses, restaurants, groceries, fish markets, shoemakers, tailors, jewelers, dry cleaners, clothing stores, and auto-repair shops. In 1935 Father Divine created a "Promised Land" of rural cooperatives in Ulster County, New York. He also found jobs for a large number of followers through his employment service. Those with outside jobs were not forced to turn over their wages to the movement, although many may have done so.

At the peak of the movement, there were over 175 "kingdoms, extensions, and connections," as the hotels and apartment houses where the most dedicated followers lived were called. "By the end of the Depression decade the Peace Mission had come to handle millions of dollars annually, accumulating savings reportedly in excess of $15 million" (Weisbrot, 1983, p. 6). Followers were not required to live in a kingdom, but those who did and any outsiders who stayed there had to follow strict rules of celibacy. Married couples were required to live apart, and children had to be reared away from their parents.

Father Divine was virtually the sole leader of the movement. With his declining vigor in the 1940s, the movement lagged, and he retreated to an estate near Philadelphia. Membership declined after his death in 1965, when his second wife, Mother Divine, became the movement's leader.

The movement is unusual because it was predominantly black. Although it emphasized its interracial nature, the membership during the 1930s and 1940s was probably 80 to 90 percent black. Mother Divine and her leadership were white, and black membership may have declined as a result. More important reasons for the decline may be that both the demand for unskilled labor and domestic servants and the supply of those looking for such work declined after World War II, that a new black leadership emerged with the onset of the civil rights movement, and that a new and different communal wave surged in the late 1960s.

Koinonia Farm

Koinonia Farm was not founded until November 1942, but inspiration for the community came from the experiences of its founder, Clarence Jordan, during the Depression. Clarence Jordan was a native of Talbotton, Georgia. His attitudes regarding racial issues had caused him great difficulty at the Southern Baptist Theological Seminary in the 1930s, especially his considerable involvement with black churches. He taught at Simmons University; one incident at the seminary arose from his invitation to a group of his students to speak at the seminary's weekly prayer meeting and then to take dinner in the dorm.

In 1939, Jordan took the position of director of a small mission, called the Sunshine Center, in the predominantly black area of Louisville's West End. He began to attend the black churches regularly and caused turmoil among the Southern Baptists when he asked that his church membership be transferred to one of them. Instead, his fellow seminarians dissuaded him through the offer of a new position as full-time superintendent of missions. One of his first proposals was to open an inner-city store, to be called "The Lord's Storehouse," which would obtain clothing, appliances, food, and fuel from donations and would distribute them to the poor, who would pay what (or if) they could. The store was never put into operation, but Jordan soon found followers among students involved in the mission work. A group met regularly to discuss Jordan's ideas, particularly concerning pacifism, racial equality, and complete sharing; they took the name "Koinonia," a term used in the Greek New Testament, meaning "communion," "collection," or "fellowship."

In 1941, Jordan became friends with Martin England, who had been a missionary to Burma. With Jordan's wife, Florence, and Martin's wife, Mabel, they discussed Clarence's ideas, particularly his dream of a farm in the South that could aid the rural poor who had been devastated by the Depression. Louisville and the missions were full of people who had left southern farms and were now suffering from unemployment and living in slum housing; welfare was their only source of income. Jordan wanted to teach good farming practices to small farmers and sharecroppers, who, he felt, were ignored by agricultural experts. He found a supporter in Arthur Steilberg, a businessman who was a pacifist member of the board of directors of one of the missions and who was interested in the idea of community. Steilberg offered Jordan and England money to help buy land and contributed the entire down payment on their mortgage.

Koinonia Farm was tiny at first, consisting only of the two couples and their five children. They had little or no agricultural experience; Jordan later said that he would get on the roof each morning to see what the neighbors were doing, and if they were plowing, he would plow. They also encountered hostility from the citizens of Americus, Georgia, from the beginning. This was partly because they let their black field hand take his meals with them and partly because, even during World War II, one of Martin England's children continued to receive mail with stamps for his collection from Burma and Japan, a suspicious circumstance that caused rumors that the Koinonia group were spies.

Some members of the surrounding community accepted the group, however. Their poultry business did extremely well. Koinonia helped local farmers establish their own flocks and then set up an egg-grading and marketing cooperative. They also set up a "cow library" from which poor families in the area could "check out" a milk cow at no charge and return her when dry to check out another. Other activities were less well accepted, such as their practice of providing transportation to school for poor black children.

By 1950 the group had a membership of fourteen adults and a large number of temporary visitors. Clarence insisted on "total community" for group members, with all goods and income held in common. On arrival new members had to turn over all property and cash to the group. Individual houses were built for families, but there was a communal house where single members could live with a communal kitchen where all members took the noon meal. At first the evening meal was prepared there and carried back to the individual houses, but later, kitchens were added to the family houses being built. Money and goods were distributed on the basis of need. These decisions, like all others, were made by the group, and the commitment to group decision making, time-consuming though it was, was strong. There was a work coordinator to manage the work teams, but this position shifted among the members when necessary. Members moved from one work team to another as the seasonal need for labor demanded. However, there was a division of labor between the sexes: women were assigned the work of cooking, child care, and housecleaning.

As membership grew, tensions developed. There was strain between the single members and couples, especially those with children, over the concept of the group as a family. Because of members who left after a short time or because of marriage outside the group, Koinonia tightened its membership requirements. Anyone wishing to join first had to spend three to nine months as a novice, participating in the work of the group but not, at that point, committed to stay. Three to nine months were spent as a provisional member, studying the scriptural bases of Clarence's communitarian ideals, which derived largely from the model of the early Christian church. Finally, the new member reached the point of total commitment and had to dispose of all personal possessions or convert them to community goods; if the possessions were too many or the amount of money too large, Clarence was known to require that they be given elsewhere than to the group, to avoid any feeling of indebtedness. The individual also had to make a personal commitment to the life of the group, which pledged in turn to care for the new member and any dependents.

Clarence Jordan had not studied other communal groups prior to Koinonia, but he became interested and made contact with a number of them in the early 1950s. Koinonia developed especially close ties with the Hutterites and the Bruderhof. The Bruderhof was a group founded in Germany on principles similar to those of the Hutterites after World War I. In 1937 the group moved to England, and when World War II began, they left England for Paraguay. After World War II the society wanted to move to the United States. They visited two groups, Koinonia and the Hutterites, that they thought could provide them with help and information, and in doing so they introduced Koinonia to the Hutterites.

In 1954, Koinonia suffered a severe drought and loss of crops. The next year the Hutterites raised money to help them and donated a tractor, a cultivator, and a truck to the group. Close ties were formed. In the winter of 1955, Clarence and another member drove to North Dakota in an unheated car; when they arrived, the Hutterites not only repaired the heater but invited them to preach, an almost unheard-of honor. Jordan actually changed the Hutterite practice of punishing young men who left the community and later returned by challenging them to show him a basis for the practice in scripture. Koinonia also sent a teacher to the Forest River colony, and there were many visits back and forth. Some members of the Koinonia group found that the practice of "admonishment" made Koinonia seem hypocritical in comparison, and eventually some members left Koinonia to join the Bruderhof.

By 1956, with national tensions high over school integration, the interracial aspect of the Koinonia community began to receive more local hostility and ultimately drew violence. Local residents boycotted Koinonia's egg business. The group received threatening phone calls. Their fences were cut. Garbage was dumped on their land. Corn was stolen from the fields. The signs for their roadside market were torn down. They lost their checking account at the local bank and were refused loans. No one would repair their vehicles or farm equipment. The children, verbally and physically abused in the public schools, were sent elsewhere to stay. Finally, local Ku Klux Klan members began shooting at buildings and bombing them. The roadside stand was destroyed, and Koinonia residents were beaten up, then themselves arrested and fined. One local businessman who opened his store to them had his business bombed and completely destroyed. All that was left of the farm enterprise was a mail-order pecan business, supported by sympathizers elsewhere in the country, of whom there were many. Dorothy Day came frequently during the virtual state of siege; Reba Place Fellowship, a group formed in 1957 by a number of Goshen College graduates—nine families and about a dozen single members who worked in the outside world but pooled possessions—sent its members to help with the farm work. Joe Maendel and Alan Baer of the Forest River community came to live at Koinonia during some of the worst violence. However, Koinonia was in trouble. Members came and left. Clarence was constantly on speaking tours and attracted followers through his strength of personality and powerful speeches; on the farm he became a member of the group, frustrated by problems and assigned to a work group like all the others, rather than the charismatic individual who had brought them there. The field crops were discontinued, and the cattle operations could no longer be maintained. The pecan business had grown to include fruitcakes and nut candies, but it was all that was left to support the community.

For a while the group hoped to begin over elsewhere. In 1940 five families had begun a community called Hidden Springs in central New Jersey. The community owned 140 acres there that it wanted to sell. Two Koinonia families, one black and one white, moved to the Hidden Springs farm. To their astonishment and sadness, the neighbors began to organize against them almost immediately, and the project fell through.

Koinonia kept going only because a wealthy lawyer, Millard Fuller, decided to keep it going. Clarence continued to travel and speak, and in those years he wrote the "Cotton-Patch" version of the Bible, a southern vernacular retelling of the Bible that brought him, once again, enthusiastic followers and hostile detractors. Only after his death in 1969 did Koinonia see an influx of new visitors, some of whom stayed for lengthy periods; but that was another time, and Koinonia came to fit the pattern of the 1960s communes discussed in Chapter 8, rather than Clarence Jordan's earlier vision. It survives today as the fifty-five-member Koinonia Partners, working six hundred acres, an "intentional community" committed to service to others (Fellowship for Intentional Community, 1991).

CHAPTER EIGHTEEN

Pathways to Self-Realization:
From Protest Movements
to the New Age Paradigm

A Fourth Great Awakening began to unfold after 1960 (McLoughlin, 1978, p. 179ff), amid an upwelling of millenarian excitation (Barkun [1985] provides a critical analysis of the relationship between millennialism and McLoughlin's "awakening cycles"). One manifestation was an upsurge of Fundamentalism, with evangelists such as Billy Graham sparking a new-wave of revivals. Both charismatic sects and new cults attracted growing memberships. Another expression was the emergence of a secular apocalyptic literature that, stressing the imminence of nuclear Armageddon, global famine, or environmental disaster, stimulated antiwar and environmental concerns. A third manifestation, growing out of the radical protest movements, was in the surge of countercultural communes after 1965.

The protest movements shared a common philosophy, the extension of the notion of human rights to embrace psychological well-being by filling needs for personal autonomy, a sense of belonging, and the development of self-identity (Carden, 1976, p. 14). Some protestors, advocating civil rights, black power, and feminism, sought to change the larger society by reform or revolution (ibid.). Other groups believed there was no hope of filling these needs within existing society and "dropped out" to create their own societies in hippie ghettos or isolated communes. After the excitement of protest abated, the New Age Paradigm emerged at the convergence of the cults and the communes, combining Eastern and mystical religions with the language of humanistic psychology.

Barkun (1984) found the relationship of this millenarian and communal surge to the long wave problematic:

no economic collapse . . . coincided with or directly preceded [this] . . . utopian wave. Almost alone among students of long-wave cycles, Walt W. Rostow does argue that the fourth Kondratieff [sic] downswing occurred at about this time, pointing in particular to the downward movement of commodity prices; but even he concedes that simultaneous low unemployment and high inflation made for a strange combination. (pp. 45–46)

But as we saw in Chapter 2, confirming Rostow's speculation, the late 1950s was indeed a Kondratiev trough that shared many characteristics with the 1840s and the 1890s, and if our hypothesis is correct, a major communal surge should have been expected. It differed from the 1840s and 1890s in that the New Deal had put into place, via Keynesian macroeconomics, an environment of permanent inflation. It therefore was not afflicted by the same kind of downwave psychology that emerged in the sharp deflations of the 1840s and 1890s, yet it nonetheless was one of those periods of sociocultural crisis within which charismatic movements and communes have characteristically emerged (Wagner, 1982, p. 12ff.).

The genesis . . . was the postbeatnik bohemian youth culture that developed in the early 1960s with the proliferation of psychedelic drugs . . . over the decade, college students became steadily more involved in political causes: first, the civil rights movement; later, anti-Vietnam War protests; and, ultimately, opposition to American capitalism and social institutions *in toto*. More than anything else, the conjunction of these two developments—visionary psychedelic and political defiance—led to the great commune surge of the late 1960s. (Gardner, 1978, p. 5)

Together, "the drug-based hippie culture and the student-based political movement joined in a shared vision of the apocalypse" (ibid., p. 9). "As disillusionment deepened into despair in the late 1960s, so too spread the general belief that the American system *in toto* was morally bankrupt, evil, and unredeemable . . . the counter culture had a way of defining itself in diametric opposition to the prevailing social order" (ibid., p. 13).

Perhaps as many as three thousand new and mostly ephemeral living groups were established in the decade ending in the mid-1970s. Some allege even greater numbers. Kern (1981) asserts that between 1965 and 1974 some 50,000 collective communities were created, with more than 750,000 members (p. 314), but such estimates lack credibility. Like the Fourierist outbreak of the 1840s and the socialist epidemic of the 1890s, the first wave of countercultural communes came in a surge that ended almost as quickly as it arrived; such appears to the response to a Kondratiev trough. The names and locations of many have not survived. "Many were little more than convenient ways of living cheaply or were exceedingly small" (Barkun, 1984, p. 44). Nonetheless the 1991 *Directory of Intentional Communities* does identify more than 750 defunct communities by name, plus another 120 founded in the 1965–75 decade that still are in existence (Fellowship for Intentional Community, 1991).

The early commentaries, coming soon after the crest of the wave, pointed to the great diversity and limited scope of many of the communes. Kanter (1972) identified several sources of inspiration: Timothy Leary's drug-centered "turn on, tune in, drop out" message to the hippie movement; Abraham Maslow's humanistic psychology, emphasizing self-actualization as the highest level of personal development; and B. F. Skinner's behavioral psychology, emphasizing principles of positive reinforcement (see also Fairfield, 1972). She concluded, however, that the communes of the late 1960s were of diminished scope, with fewer visions, hopes, people, or demands on members than those of previous waves.

Kern (1981) also pointed to the "bewildering range of ideological foci" in the communes, "from flying saucer cults to drug detoxification; from women's or gay liberation to tarot lore and occultism. Unlike the earlier communes," he said, "many contemporary . . . communities are self-consciously single-issue organizations; they do not concern themselves with a broad spectrum of issues, and therefore member commitment is frequently very limited and insufficient to sustain an ongoing community" (pp. 314–15). If there was any commonality, wrote Zicklin (1983) it "was the result of the relatively unorganized, anarchic response of thousands of individuals and groups to the hopes engendered by the counterculture for the creation of a new way of life" (p. 2). "The counterculture spread the idea that society had become a perversion of nature" (p. 10).

The defining characteristics appeared to many of the contemporary investigators to reside in the radicals' normative alienation (Melville, 1972). Kern (1981) noted:

Although today's communards are characterized by anomie and rootlessness, their alienation is that of a privileged class (upper middle, upper) rather than the dissatisfaction and bewilderment of a dispossessed class (lower middle, lower). The new communards are, indeed, in the words of a recent student, "the children of prosperity." Their revolt is grounded in disappointed expectations: American values, political and ethical, are hollow; the promise of prosperity and ease depends on mind-deadening, dehumanizing service to amoral corporate giants; and man in a materialist, technocratic, consumer culture has lost touch with his ability to feel and to respond spontaneously and, perhaps most importantly, with his desire, his need, for transcendence. It is not surprising, then, that the modern communitarian movement has been organized around three themes: political activism, psychedelic drugs, and the importance of self-realization. Thus, although both the classic nineteenth-century communitarian movement and its modern counterpart originated in a crisis of belief, an essentially normative alienation, their perceptions of the nature of cultural malaise and their methods of amelioration have been widely disparate. (p. 315)

A few investigators did, however, point to the communards' cultural radicalism, and it is on this that more recent reinterpretations have focused. Veysey (1978) suggested that what was critical was rejection of older established church organizations and of established institutions, the transferral of loyalty to new faiths that took on the character of social movements, substitution of a charismatic guru or rebel leader in the name of "liberation," and the return to romanticism via a post-Freudian view of human nature—the desire to form "communities based on beliefs that are radically at odds with those of the rest of society" (Melville, 1972, p. 23). Others added a reaction to scientific rationality and production-line capitalism, exemplified by the themes of individuality, decentralization, and simplicity, "attempts to effect radical change through small communitarian experiments" (ibid, p. 51).

With the advantage of hindsight, most now agree that what was ephemeral in the 1960s surge were the hippie ghettos, the antiwar movement, and many of the small collective housekeeping groups. Religious historians such as J. Gordon Melton argue that the "social innovations" (Bestor, 1950) that have proved to be most lasting have been a number of new cults and the crystallization of the New Age Paradigm that together have produced a set of "coherent lifestyles and social philosophies" (Wagner, 1982, p. 2). In addition, the seeds were sown for the Intentional Communities movement, to which we shall turn in Chapter 20.

New Cults

Religious historian J. Gordon Melton (1986b, pp. 3ff.) is careful to distinguish between churches, sects, and cults. *Churches* are large denominations characterized by their inclusive approach to life and their identification with the prevailing culture. *Sects* are groups that have broken away from the churchly denominations, becoming stricter in doctrine and in the behavioral demands placed on their members, and emphasizing their separation from the larger culture, even while they follow familiar cultural patterns. *Cults*, viewed neutrally, are groups that follow different religious structures that are alien to prevalent churches but represent a force of religious innovation within a culture. There are, however, other views of cults. For example, there are Christian countercult ministries that classify all "distortions of Biblical Christianity" as "perversions,"[1] and there is a secular anticult movement that views them as "destructive"[2] if they possess a majority of the following traits (Melton, 1986b, citing Marcia Rudin):

1. Members swear total allegiance to an all-powerful leader who they believe to be the Messiah.
2. Rational thought is discouraged or forbidden.
3. The cult's recruitment techniques are often deceptive.

4. The cult weakens the follower psychologically by making him or her depend upon the group to solve his or her problems.

5. The cults manipulate guilt to their advantage.

6. The cult leader makes all the career and life decisions of the members.

7. Cults exist only for their own material survival and make false promises to work to improve society.

8. Cult members often work full time for the group for little or no pay.

9. Cult members are isolated from the outside world and any reality testing it could provide.

10. Cults are antiwoman, antichild, and antifamily.

11. Cults are apocalyptic and believe themselves to be the remnant who will survive the soon-approaching end of the world.

12. Many cults follow an "ends justify the means" philosophy.

13. Cults, particularly in regard to their finances, are shrouded in secrecy.

14. There is frequently an aura of or potential for violence around cults. (p. 5)

The new cults that emerged out of the social unrest of the 1960s, Melton (1986b) says, continued the history of growth of metaphysical, occult, and Eastern religions in the United States that had its initial expression in New England Transcendentalism and was carried forward by the Theosophists; coincided with the 1965 rescinding of the Asian exclusion laws and the rapid influx of immigrants who brought with them their swamis, Zen masters, and gurus; and was stimulated by new interest in parapsychology, the discovery and spread of mind-altering drugs, and the rise of humanistic psychology and Jungian psychotherapy.

Sixteen cults, the majority of which have developed communes or other residential arrangements, are featured in Melton's (1986b) *Encyclopedic Handbook of Cults in America* as emerging out of the turmoil of the 1960s. I paraphrase:

1. *The Christian Foundation* was formed in 1969 by country singer Tony Alamo and his wife, Susan, who, in the 1960s, began to evangelize among the Hollywood street people. In 1970 they moved from Sunset Strip to a ranch near Saugus, forty miles from Los Angeles, which grew from a retreat to a permanent commune. As they spread their word, they recruited upward of three thousand members, and at the peak of their activities had communal groups living in ten different states, including Nashville, Tennessee. The ministry headquarters was moved to a commune at Dyer in the Arkansas Ozarks in 1973. Members were forced to sign over their assets to Alamo, who preached a virulent anti-Catholic doctrine. After Susan Alamo died of cancer in 1982, Alamo said she would rise from the dead, and he kept her body on display in a mausoleum for six months while his followers prayed. Alamo's cult became a target of the anticultists, who charged deceit and brainwashing and persuaded the

Department of Labor to file suit to pay back wages to members of the group. In 1985 the Internal Revenue Service revoked the sect's tax-exempt status and seized and sold the Arkansas commune for back taxes. When they took it over, Susan Alamo's body and one hundred communards had gone. Charges of child abuse followed, and California authorities removed several children from the Saugus commune in 1988. Alamo, who had fled California, was arrested by federal officials in Florida in 1991. Members of the cult still live communal lives in locations hidden from state and federal authorities.

2. *The Church of Scientology* was founded by science fiction writer L. Ron Hubbard, who had advanced a new way to understand and treat mental health, "Dianetics," and who developed the notion of "exteriorization," the separation of the consciousness from the body. Hubbard created his Association of Scientologists in 1952 and in 1959 established a headquarters in Washington, D.C. Scientologists seek to elevate the self to the spiritual realm and to achieve a "clean planet" free from war, pollution, drugs, insanity, and crime. Like the Christian Foundation, the Church of Scientology has been the object of countercult activity and of federal litigation involving fraud and the tax-exempt status of the organization.

3. *The Church Universal and Triumphant* emerged from the Summit Lighthouse, founded by Mark L. Prophet in Washington, D.C., in 1958 as an outgrowth of Theosophy (Chapter 12). After his marriage to Elizabeth Clare in 1965 (after which she too was anointed a Messenger), the headquarters was moved to Colorado Springs, Colorado, where Mark died in 1973. Elizabeth became Guru Ma and in 1974 incorporated the Church Universal and Triumphant, with the Summit Lighthouse as its publishing arm. Communicants were given the option to reside in spiritual communes, where they could live according to the tenets of the church. Church centers offering such communities (which average twenty members each) are located throughout the country. In 1976 the church moved its headquarters to Southern California, purchasing a former college near Malibu and naming it Camelot and subsequently acquiring the thirty-thousand-acre Royal Teton Ranch in Montana. Guru Ma later had apocalyptic visions. In 1990 two thousand members of the church streamed onto the ranch in the belief that nuclear Armageddon was imminent, selling their homes, closing their bank accounts, and heading to the Paradise Valley, where the church had constructed an elaborate system of concrete and steel shelters. Many paid up to $10,000 to reserve a spot guaranteeing them a role in planning the future after most of the world was dead.

4. *The Divine Light Mission* was brought to the United States in 1971 by thirteen-year-old Guru Maharaj Ji; it espouses Sant Mat, a variant of the Sikh religion. Yoga and meditation are used to link the individual with

"the eternal principle of unity in diversity." The mission had an immediate and massive impact. By the end of 1973 there were several hundred centers and over twenty ashrams, but then there were financial setbacks, retrenchment, and retreat to a much less visible position. Today there are more than twenty branches and several thousand members, with social outreach via hospitals and nursing homes.

5. *ECKANKAR*, founded by John Paul Twitchell in California in 1965, also is a Sant Mat offshoot, emphasizing "soul travel" to higher spiritual planes. There are centers throughout the country, offering classes. An offshoot is the Church of the Movement of Spiritual Inner Awareness that believes in "mystical traveller consciousness." It has educational facilities and an alternative health center and offers training programs throughout the United States.

6. The *Family of Love* (*Children of God*) emerged out of Pentecostal missionary activity directed to Los Angeles street people. David Brant Berg, who had been associated there with the Soul Clinic, moved in 1967 to take over the Teen Challenge activity of the Light Club Mission in Huntington Beach. He called for withdrawal from worldliness and a total commitment to a Jesus Revolution. After taking their message across the United States and assembling at a retreat in Canada, Berg gathered the group in Virginia and announced his "Old Church/New Church" revelation—that God had abandoned the old denominational church and embraced his new church, the Children of God, and its principles of inner leadership and communal sex. The group spread to forty colonies around the United States, and for some time the group's women were urged to go "flirty fishing," using sex to attract new members, much as Charles Manson's women had attracted men to his desert commune. However, there were setbacks. Venereal disease swept the group, and there were increasing countercult attacks after the Jim Jones Jonestown tragedy. Berg reorganized the group as the Family of Love and in 1979 disbanded the colonies and replaced them with a network of small family groups. He subsequently left the United States to settle in England.

7. *The International Society for Krishna Consciousness* (*ISKCON*, or *Hare Krishna*) "became for many people the symbol of the invasion of Asian religion into American life in the 1970s" (Melton, 1986b, p. 159). ISKCON's traditions go back to a sixteenth-century Bengali Saint, Chaitanya Mahaprabhu, but the organization was founded in the United States in 1965. The movement combines ascetic monasticism with intense devotional activity, focused on dancing and chanting. The U.S. founder was A. C. Bhaktivedanta Swami Prabhupada, who came to the United States in 1965 at the age of sixty-nine, after the Asian Exclusion Act was rescinded. He

began by attracting hippies in New York's Lower East Side. By 1971 there were twenty-one centers in the United States and by 1982 more than fifty, including several farms, three thousand initiated members, and many lay members. Initiates accept an ascetic semimonastic life and a discipline derived from conservative Hinduism's practice of bhakti yoga. "While trying to project an image of a bona fide religion following the traditions of ancient India, it has been seen as a foreign and enigmatic group whose ascetic, communal, and separatist lifestyle opposes dominant American values (to which it offers a distinct alternative) and threatens common family patterns (which, in many cases, it does)" (Melton, 1986b, p. 163).

8. *The Local Church* (*Watchman Nee* and *Witness Lee*) was founded in the 1920s by Ni Shu-Tsu (Watchman Nee), who was influenced in China by a number of evangelical Christian groups, particularly the Plymouth Brethren. It was brought to the United States in 1962 by his disciple, Witness Lee. The movement spread rapidly, a network of local congregations in which there is spirited worship and equally spirited conflict over doctrine with other groups, such as the Jesus People, who labeled it a cult. To establish new congregations, church members migrate as small groups, but they appear not to have established communal settlements.

9. *Nichiren Shoshu Academy, Soka Gakkai* is the most successful of the Buddhist groups that trace their origins to a thirteenth-century Japanese Buddhist reformer, Nichiven Daishonin. The faith was brought to the United States after World War II by Japanese immigrants, who established their headquarters in Los Angeles in 1963. Members abide by Buddhist ritual and can either become monastic, seeking enlightenment (Buddhahood), or can seek fulfillment while remaining in society. Today there are six temples in the United States, and twenty thousand to thirty thousand members.

10. *Rajneesh Foundation International* was founded in India by Bhagwan Rajneesh, a Sanskrit scholar who claimed to have achieved full enlightenment. His ashram at Poona attracted many Westerners, and centers espousing his views began to appear in the United States. He developed a combination of Jainism and Western techniques of inner transformation and therapy derived from humanistic psychology. The religion combines meditation and celebration via singing and dancing, vegetarianism, and individual freedom. In 1981 Rajneesh moved to the United States, first to New Jersey and then to the sixty-four-thousand-acre Big Muddy Ranch near Antelope, Oregon, to build a model community, Rajneeshpuram. Many followed, with sufficient voting strength to take over the Antelope city government in 1982. Conflicts with Oregon's local and state governments, with the Immigration and Naturalization Service, with the Internal

Revenue Service, and within the group led to his departure from the United States in 1985 and the closing and sale of the ranch. The movement remains a decentralized cult across the United States, however.

11. *Sikh Dharma* was brought to the United States via Canada by Yogi Bhajan in 1968, when he established his Healthy, Happy, Holy Organization and ashram in Los Angeles. He taught orthodox Sikhism, supplemented by various yoga practices. This movement also spread rapidly. By 1984 there were 125 ashrams and centers across the United States and, as part of the cult's social mission, a highly praised drug outreach program.

12. *Transcendental Meditation (TM)* and the *World Plan Executive Council* are creations of Maharishi Mehesh Yogi, who first introduced his ideas to the United States in the early 1960s. The spark to U.S. organization was acceptance of TM by the Beatles in 1967. The reaction was immediate and rapid, enabling the Maharishi to announce his World Plan in 1972, designed to share the Science of Creative Intelligence via a global network of thirty-six hundred centers. The plan is administered by his council; TM is the religious exercise that is promoted. There is active missionary activity and training at Maharishi International University in Iowa. There are more than three hundred World Plan Centers in the United States today, with some tens of thousands of active meditators and a new initiative to create a network of Cities of Immortals across the United States (Chapter 20).

13. *The Unification Church* was founded by the Reverend Sun Myung Moon, a North Korean Christian refugee who claimed revelations in 1936 and 1948. His movement, which centers on an apocalyptic hope of great changes, focuses on building the kingdom initiated by the Lord of the Second Advent. Members first join in the work of the church and practice absolute celibacy. The Rev. Mr. Moon then matches and marries couples, who become True Parents, their salvation expressed in their children, and who are part of the establishment of the Kingdom of God on earth. The church has an aggressive missionary activity, operates a theological seminary, and has a social action program. It also has been a target of the anticult movement, charged with brainwashing, and of the U.S. Treasury Department. The Rev. Mr. Moon spent 1984–85 in jail on income tax charges.

14. *The Vajradhatu, Naropa Institute,* has been responsible for spearheading the growth of Tibetan Buddhism in the United States, particularly that of the Kargyupa Sect, which was brought to the United States in 1970–71 by Chogyam Trungpa, Rinpoche. Trungpa, in bringing Kargyupa teachings to the United States introduced the language of humanistic growth-centered psychology that gave it broad appeal. There are major communities in Vermont and Colorado, as well as thirty-five other centers across the United States, serving two thousand students.

15. *The Way Intentional, Inc.*, is a "Pentecostal Ultra-dispensational Christian group" (Melton, 1986b, p. 206) founded by Victor Paul Wierwille. It began as a radio ministry and was built into an international organization in 1971. The group has five educational and administrative centers (New Knoxville, Ohio; Emporia, Kans.; Rome, Ind.; Gunnison, Oreg.; and Tinnie, N.Mex.) and over twenty-five thousand local community "fellowships." Emphasis is on education. The group has been a target of anticultists for brainwashing and mind control, as well as for its departures from orthodox Christianity, including adoption of Arianism.

16. *Wicca and Magick* arose from the development of contemporary witchcraft in England in the 1940s by Gerald B. Gardner, who created a new religion, Wicca, based on worship of the Mother Goddess. It was spread by initiates such as Alexander Sanders and Sybil Leek, who broke away from his coven. Each strand found its way to the United States—Sybil Leek established covens in Ohio and Massachusetts in 1966—and American forms developed. For example, one group of lesbians developed a militant feminist witchcraft called "Wimmin's Religion." Other groups did not accept the appellation "witch" and developed alternative rituals, calling themselves Pagans. All seek to use the cosmic power of the universe to effect "magick": "low magick," change in the everyday world; and "high magick," transformation of the individual. The groups organize into covens, ideally with thirteen members (Salem, Mass., has thirteen covens), and there are several overarching groups: The Church of Circle Wicca, Gardnerian Wicca, Saxon Witchcraft, the Covenant of the Goddess, and Feminist Wicca.

The New Age Paradigm

The growth of these cults was, J. Gordon Melton (Melton, Clark, and Kelly, 1990) argues, but one manifestation of the emergence of a New Age Paradigm, an attempt to find the social, religious, political, and cultural convergence between Eastern and mystical religions and the religious disenchantment of many Westerners. The roots of the paradigm are to be found, he says, in Transcendentalism, Swedenborgianism, Mesmerism, Spiritualism, Christian Science/New Thought, Theosophy, and Eastern Thought.

Transcendentalism, in the form expressed by Ralph Waldo Emerson, successfully integrated American unitarian values (individualism, personal responsibility, and the drive to get ahead) with Eastern idealistic metaphysics and passed the integration on to Theosophy. Emanuel Swedenborg developed metaphysical notions of out-of-body astral experiences and the existence of an invisible spiritual world; Franz Anton

Mesmer advanced ideas of the healing power of sacred spiritual energy. These ideas were developed by the Spiritualists, who talked of the relationship between cosmology and healing and the use of self-induced trances to permit communication between the living and the dead, as well as of healing by the entranced (Braude, 1989). Mary Baker Eddy combined Emerson's monism and Mesmer's healing imperative into Christian Science. Theosophy took the ideas one step further: "If people can contact the dead, utilize the healing power, and know the metaphysical world enough to use it for health, wealth, and happiness, then occult metaphysicians should be able to fill in all the pieces of our knowledge. Inner exploration should reveal the structures and powers of the spiritual universe and detail the great panorama of life and history, even provide a picture of the future" (Melton et al., 1990, p. xxv).

Many occult organizations developed as offshoots from Theosophy, which also nurtured a reborn astrology and provided the channel through which Hinduism and Buddhism moved into the West to reinforce the occult/metaphysical tradition. By the time of the upsurge of the 1960s there was a large and receptive audience that was tapped, after the Asian Exclusion Act was rescinded in 1965, by a wave of teachers and gurus who brought additional strands of Eastern thought to America. "The last days of the 1960s saw the launching of a major missionary thrust by the Eastern religions toward the West" (Melton, 1986b, p. 110).

What emerged was the New Age Movement, which had jelled by 1971, providing services, spokespersons, and periodicals like *New Age*. The primary focus of the movement was on the profound personal transformation of the individual. From the individual, New Agers projected such transformation to the community, the culture, and humanity at large. There was a millenarian vision. The emphasis was on imminence: emergence of the transformation in this generation.

The key movement concept was that of personal spiritual-psychological transformation akin to religious experience. This transformative experience was unique to each individual, with belief systems that remained malleable, but shared several characteristics:

Rejection of orthodox modes of thought, dysfunctional relationships, purposelessness and hopelessness.

The commonality of transformation to open egalitarian relationships, new vitality and health, and a sense of meaning and purpose.

The accompaniment of transformation by profound metaphysical experience that has occurred cumulatively over a period of time and the subordination of all beliefs to this experience.

The expectation of continuing transformation through adoption of particular life-styles, diets, and religious/spiritual practices, ultimately permitting the discovery of Truth, which can only be experienced.

New Agers believe that the New Age will have one universal religion that draws from all present traditions and that gains new insights from both nature and inner experience; that each person chooses a *sadhana* (path of transformation) that can only be realized via reincarnation and the law of karma, the rule by which the universe metes out rewards and punishments for behavior and thus serves as the moral arbiter; that the motive power for spiritual transformation comes from universal energy, the force that is released by meditation and that promotes psychic healing; that the transformative goal is higher mystical consciousness or self-awareness of the Ultimate Unifying Principle that binds the whole together and provides the power that gives it a dynamic. People participate as individualized manifestations of the principle and as channels delivering the universal energy to the world. Teachers (masters) appear at frequent intervals to instruct individuals about the goal of awareness and techniques for self-realization.

The New Age social vision thus embodies

Holism, the interdependence of all systems.
Earth awareness, the interdependence of all things on earth, including humankind.[3]
Human rights, the rights of individuals to choose their *sadhana* and live transformative lives.

Expressions of this vision are to be seen today in the holistic health movement, which calls for broadening orthodox medicine to include psychic healing, biofeedback, and other techniques designed to address stress via psychological-physical linkages; in the upsurge of environmentalism's concerns for nuclear and chemical hazards, destruction of ecosystems, and other threats to the global environment; and in the drive for women's rights.

New Age activism occurred in the 1960s and 1970s at a variety of levels that mirrored previous millenarian experiences. Some saw the New Age as imminent, and called for mass movements to organize its structures. Others argued that the New Age will be a cosmic event, a convergence of natural forces symbolized by the stars and planets that will introduce the Aquarian Age. The most typical response of the 1965–75 decade was, however, to build communes.

Some older communes were among the first to identify with New Age ideas, much as the Brook Farmers adopted Fourierism. A prominent example is the Lama Foundation, which was established by Steve Durkee

Table 13

Group	Spiritual leader
HINDU	
Transcendental Meditation	Maharishi Mehesh Yogi
Rajneesh Foundation Int.	Bhagwan Rajneesh
Hanuman Foundation	Baba Ram Dass
Krishnamurti Foundation	Krishnamurti Jeddu
Siddha Yoga Dham of America	Swami Muktananda
Johannine Daist Community	Da (Bubba) Free John
Self Realization Society	Pamahansa Yogananda
Vedanta Society	Ramakrishna Vivekananda
Tantric yoga groups	
BUDDHIST TAOIST	
Zen Buddhism	
Tibetan Buddhism (Naropa Institute)	Trungpa Rinpoche
The Farm	Stephen Gaskin
SIKH	
Sikh Dharma	Yogi Bhajan
Divine Light Mission	Guru Maharaj Ji
Ruhani Satsang	Kirpal Singh
Movement for Inner Spiritual Awareness	John-Roger Hinkins
ISLAMIC	
Sufi Order	Pir Vilayet Khan
Arica Institute	Oscar Ichazo
Friends of Meher Baba	Meher Baba
THEOSOPHICAL-OCCULT	
Arcane School (World Goodwill)	Alice Bailey
Tara Center	Benjamin Creme
Association for Research and Enlightenment	Edgar Cayce
Church Universal and Triumphant	Elizabeth Clare Prophet (Guru Ma)
SPIRITUALIST-PSYCHIC GROUPS	
Emissaries of Divine Light	
Urantia Foundation (Urantia Book)	
Erhard Training Seminars (EST)	Werner Erhard
NEW THOUGHT METAPHYSICS	
Unity School of Christianity	
Church of Religious Science (Science of Mind)	

in 1968 at San Cristobal, near Taos, New Mexico, and still exists. It was originally a community based on spiritual and environmental values. The original members were joined in 1969 by Harvard professor Richard Albert, who, after experimenting with drugs alongside Timothy Leary, went to India, became a guru, took the name Baba Ram Dass and started a meditative ashram. Members were chosen because of their independent incomes, enabling them to "explore inner space." By 1973 the community was self-supporting and had a vigorous educational program for visitors. Baba Ram Dass became a leading movement spokesman via his Hanuman Foundation.

Most of the Eastern teachers promoted communal living and nurtured communes within their organizations. There were myriad offshoots: "Northern New Mexico became dotted with communes as formerly placid villages from Truchas to Placitas found strange and wonderful visitors descending on them in search of community. Some of the communards had clear notions about what that meant, while others believed it could be found by settling within fifty miles of the Sangre de Cristos and the Taos Pueblo" (Fogarty, 1980). Even Warwick, Rhode Island, had the Brotherhood of the Spirit, "teachers of the Aquarian Age sixth plane when Karmic energy enables you to escape to the astral plane."

Leading New Age groups and teachers, including many of those previously classified as "cults," include those shown in Table 13 (Melton, 1986b, pp. 120–21). The New Age movement they represent is "an updating of the long-standing occult and metaphysical tradition in American life" (ibid., p. 116), yet as the 1970s passed, it encountered major obstacles (Melton et al., 1990, pp. xxx–xxxi), including scientific challenges to its metaphysics, the fragmentation of religions in the 1980s, the attraction of entrepreneurs providing many of the same services as communards ill-prepared to function in the competitive marketplace, and concerted attack by both evangelical Christians and a skeptical press and public. These countervailing forces may have been sufficient to blunt New Age expansion in favor of the greater freedom of choice offered by the Intentional Communities movement, discussed in Chapter 20.

A Capitalist–Socialist Dialectic

It is now time to draw the strands together. Frank Manuel (1966) argues that utopian critiques may well be the most sensitive of the indicators of the anguish of an age (p. 70). Communal experiments have been reactions to capitalism in times of crisis, material expressions of a continuing capitalist–socialist dialectic. Each utopian surge has involved an attempt to abandon existing society and to realize an alternative in which the deepest yearnings of the critics can come to fulfillment. Utopian plans thus are both escapes and creations—escapes from crises, real or imagined, and attempts to realize alternative ideals.

The earliest American critiques were religious, sharing patterns with other fundamentalisms in their understanding of history and eschatology, seeing the past as movement that proceeds inevitably toward a catastrophic future. The view in such critiques has been one of a history that is regressing and a society that is deteriorating. The problematic was one of evil and immorality; the utopian solution—Manuel (1966) calls them "utopias of calm felicity" (p. 71)—included a preeminence of spiritual ideals.

Later in the nineteenth century and on into the twentieth century the critiques became politicoeconomic. The problematic centered on the factory system and industrial capitalism; the solutions included social arrangements in which equality takes precedence—Manuel's "dynamic socialist and historically determinist utopias."

In contrast, the utopian wave of the 1960s was based less on politicoeconomic formulations than on "a psychological critique [that] revolves around alienation and loneliness, both social isolation and inner fragmentation" (Kanter, 1972, p. 7). Rejecting society's emphasis on material achievement, the new communards—"children of prosperity" (Gardner, 1978)—adopted as their credo "self-actualization" and "personal growth."

Their vision revolved around liberating situations conducive to intimacy and psychological health, particularly those framed by New Age beliefs. Manuel (1966) borrows Abraham Maslow's term "eupsychia" to characterize their new psychological and philosophical utopias.

Each utopian response "thus appears as a complex product of sustained dissatisfaction, disappointment and eventual despair of the religious and social condition of the world" (Whitworth, 1975, p. 225). The trigger is a long-wave economic crisis, when downwave psychologies induce millenarian excitement.

This link between millennial commitment and social change, running through an intermediate period in which disorders and excesses may appear psychopathological, is suggested but not explored by Foster (1981) in his work on the emergence of alternative sexual norms and marriage forms among the Shakers, Oneidans, and Mormons. Frank and Fuentes (1988) go further, suggesting that a wide range of social reform movements have surged in rhythms running counter to the long wave in the past two centuries. These include revolutionary (national) liberation movements, labor movements, women's movements, and Marxist socialism. The strength of their demands for liberty, equality, and fraternity, has, they say, been much stronger in Kondratiev downward phases, as criticisms of polity, economy, and society have mounted. They have peaked in deflationary depressions, especially among those whose way of life is being pushed aside by a technology transition. Hartmann (1952) locates the psychological nexus of their discontent in frustration over unmet needs.

Surprisingly, Frank and Fuentes (1988) do not include utopian communities on their list, perhaps because Marx denigrated the "critical utopias" that preceded scientific socialism. Yet alienation from the principal norms of society, resulting from the psychological depression occurring during downwave crises, is exactly what has led groups to take refuge in countercultural alternatives that have shared a number of commonalities:

Rejection of the established order as sinful, unjust, or unhealthful.

Stressing the possibility of perfection through restructuring social institutions to produce an idealized social life.

Returning to the land as the pathway to this perfection, to an isolated location offering protection against evil, to a community offering the possibility of recreating a lost harmony between person and God, person and person, or within the self.

Committed to order in contradistinction to a larger society viewed as chaotic, uncoordinated, and wasteful.

Stressing brotherhood through community of property and group rituals reinforcing the coherence and uniqueness of the group.

Marx was concerned with promoting "scientific" socialism, and he therefore gave only grudging acknowledgment to the earlier communal experiments in *The Communist Manifesto*. In his view, the development of socialism fell into two chief phases, the utopian and the scientific socialist. Utopian socialism was, in turn, marked by two phases, that of religious communism and that which was secular in nature. The phases represented, he said, evolution in the nature of the class struggle as the proletariat contended first with feudalism and then with changes in capitalism on their inevitable march toward a socialist state: "The first direct attempts of the proletariat to obtain its own ends, made in times of universal excitement, when feudal society was being overthrown . . . failed. . . . The revolutionary literature that accompanied those first movements . . . inculcated universal asceticism and social leveling in its crudest form" (Karl Marx, *The Communist Manifesto*, reprinted in Tucker, 1978, pp. 498–99). Despite this failure, the work of the utopians "contained also a critical element . . . full of the most valuable materials for the enlightenment of the working class. The practical measures proposed in them . . . point . . . to the disappearance of class antagonisms." But scientific socialists should not be beguiled:

The significance of Critical-Utopian Socialism and Communism bears an inverse relation to historical development. In proportion as the modern class struggle develops and takes definite shape, [the utopians' proposals] lose all practical value. . . . [They] dream of experimental realization of their social Utopias, . . . [but] to realise [them] they are compelled to appeal to the feelings and purses of the bourgeois. By degrees they sink into the category of the reactionary conservative socialists . . . [who] violently oppose all political action on the part of the working class. (Ibid.)

Marx argued that each proletarian reaction arose in a time of *crisis*. Each response was *critical*, proposing ways of life antithetical to the existing economic and social order. The *causation* ran from an economy in crisis to a proletarian alternative, and the responses *evolved* as the referent economic system changed. Consistent with this construct, "chronologically in the United States . . . utopian socialism has for the most part preceded Marxian socialism, while religious utopianism [has] tended to precede the secular varieties" (Egbert and Persons, 1952, p. 99). This is illustrated by Figure 36, which graphs Okugawa's (1980) data in another way. These "religious utopian, secular utopian, and scientific stages of socialism reflect in the socialist tradition three stages of Western cultural consciousness which are testified in one way or another in almost every philosophy of history since the seventeenth century" (Egbert and Persons, 1952, p. 99).

The setting for the first utopian wave was "an evangelical and rural

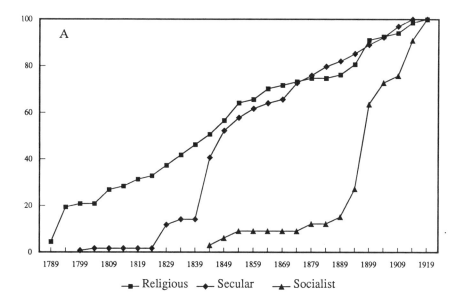

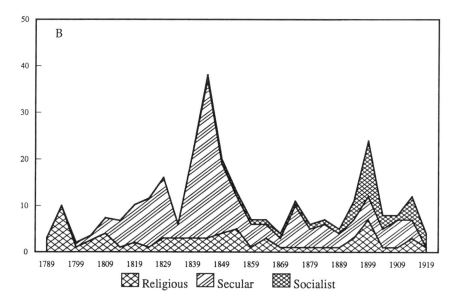

Figure 36. The Evolution of Utopian Experiments. This pair of graphs reveals the successive surges of religious, secular, and socialist community building. The cumulative distributions (*A*) emphasize the differences between successive deflationary depressions. The numerical distributions (*B*) reveal the changing mix of utopian activity. In (*A*) the vertical axis measures the cumulative percentage of communities of each type established between 1787 and 1919. In (*B*) the vertical axis measures number of communities.

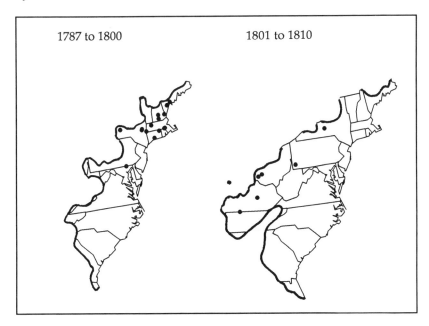

Figure 37. The First Wave of Utopian Development. In this pair of maps, utopian communities are located relative to the frontiers of settlement in 1800 and 1810, respectively. Before 1800 the utopians sought out backwoods locations in New England, but in the first decade of the nineteenth century the locus of initiative shifted to the western frontier of settlement.

society in which the theological doctrines and moral precepts of the Calvinist tradition had already made a firm alliance with a flourishing agrarian capitalism" (Persons, 1952, p. 127). This society was disrupted by the revolutionary war and the depression that followed. In the 1780s the atmosphere of agricultural crisis precipitated by downward movements of prices and deflation of asset values was intensified by a succession of evangelical revivals that encouraged millenarian expectations. Heretical doctrines of direct inspiration and perfect sanctification became widespread. There began to emerge a new complex of religious ideas antithetical to the Calvinism that had dominated the colonial epoch. Millennialist expectations served to sustain believers in the hope that with Christ's speedy return the devil would be chained and sin destroyed. America's first utopians thus were the religious sectarians who formed small agricultural communities on the frontiers of northern settlement (Fig. 37). In these communities goods were produced collectively and held in common, putting into effect in microcosm theories of a good society free from the vicissitudes of the competitive economy.

Figure 38. Utopian Development in the Primary Trough of the 1820s. The principal thrust of the utopian initiatives during the decade (including Robert Owen's first ventures) was in areas where the settlement system was stabilizing, after the frontier had moved through in the previous decade. The frontier shown is that of 1820.

The long-wave trough that followed saw a surge of the brand of secular presocialism formulated by Robert Owen in response to the misery accompanying early British industrialism. In America, Owenism initially attracted those frustrated by the depression of 1819, including those who still had not recovered from the depression and probably never would. The dissatisfied remnant had seen the defeat of Jacksonian democracy in the election of 1824. Owenism was their protest against the Old Guard that dominated state and national politics and the wealthy and powerful who ran business. Most of the settlements established in this surge located close to the Ohio and Indiana frontier (Fig. 38).

The next crisis was precipitated by the Panic of 1837, which brought to an end a speculative boom, especially in cotton and public land. It started with the July 1836 governmental requirement that public lands be purchased only in specie and the Bank of England's refusal in 1837 to accept American paper. A fall in the price of cotton led to defaults in American debts secured by cotton, to a general contraction of credit, runs on banks as business collapsed, and rapid deflation leading to the depression of the early 1840s. Prices in fact fell more from 1839 to 1843 than they did from

Figure 39. Reactions to the Capitalist Crisis of the 1840s. Instead of clustering close to the western frontier, the utopian reaction of the 1840s was generalized throughout the North, tracing out the later configuration of the American manufacturing belt, as communards reacted to the United States' first major capitalist crisis. The frontier shown is that of 1850.

1929 to 1933: 42 percent as opposed to 31 percent. By 1830 many eastern farmers were heavily mortgaged, having borrowed to acquire more land to raise crops for sale in burgeoning urban markets. The transition had been made to a market economy. The collapse of urban markets and of agricultural prices led to a widespread depression and massive farm failures, which produced, in turn, a feeling of "loss of control . . . exacerbated by the mysterious character of a boom and bust economy, for one's fate now seemed determined by incomprehensible forces" (Barkun, 1986, p. 117).

The panic created a new class of discontented, especially among the laborers whose local unions and parties had been destroyed. Reactions were twofold. Millerite millenarianism appealed to distressed backwoods farmers. Reforms stimulated by evangelical revivalism split into moderate and extremist wings. Into this revivalist and reformist atmosphere, Albert Brisbane introduced Fourierism, which appealed in particular to urbanites and intellectuals "and was well adapted to the American spirit of reform, to secular, universalist, and liberal Christianity, and to millenial revivalism" (Bassett, 1952, p. 175). Simultaneously, Noyes introduced his particular brand of Perfectionism, the Transcendentalists sparked moves toward both organic philosophies and the Social Gospel, and Joseph Smith, Jr., moved from Kirtland, Ohio, to Missouri and thence to Nauvoo. The Fourierists argued that the social organism was diseased. The depression of the 1840s, a genuine capitalist crisis, was marked in particular by the settlements they designed to provide basic needs in small-scale communal settings that offered equality and security in self-sufficient havens that were detached from the market economy yet were scattered throughout the North rather than retreating to the frontier (Fig. 39). The evils were to be solved by recasting concepts of work and of private property.

American secular utopians tried or suggested many of the alternatives that Marxian socialists have adopted. Bestor (1950) speaks of the nineteenth-century communes as reflecting societal inventiveness—places "where various types of improved social machinery were hopefully demonstrated" (p. 230). The utopians' analysis of capitalism never approached the systematic, comprehensive, and more empirical treatment of Marx, however (Bassett, 1952). Marxism did stir Icaria in the 1870s. In the depression years after the primary trough of 1873, when the locus of utopianism again switched westward (Fig. 40) and Brigham Young sought safety for Mormons by launching the communal United Order, the community at Corning, Iowa, looked for a time as if it would become one of the centers of the First International in the United States.

The next major utopian wave crested toward the end of the depression of the 1890s. Utopian communities were established throughout the nation's settled area (Fig. 41). Crop failures, falling prices, and poor marketing and credit facilities had led to the emergence of Farmers' Alliances throughout the West and the South in the 1880s, and these in turn produced the Populist movement—essentially agrarian-oriented, demanding an increase in the circulating currency (to be achieved by unlimited coinage of silver), government ownership of the railroads, selective protective tariffs, and a variety of measures to give farmers economic parity with business and industry. At the same time, intellectuals and social reformers were decrying the plight of the urban poor. Henry George had written *Progress and Poverty* when the economic crisis of the 1870s brought the post–Civil War growth surge to an end. In *Looking Backward, 2000–1887* (1888), Edward Bellamy described a future United States under an idyllic socialist system. Among other things, he called for nationalization of public services. During the election campaign of 1892 the Populist party depicted a lost agrarian Eden with redemption blocked by a con-

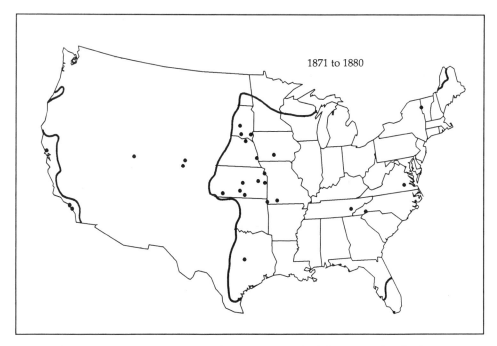

Figure 40. Utopian Initiatives in the Primary Trough of the 1870s. After the distinctive reaction of the 1840s the locus of utopian development shifted west again in the 1870s, close behind the frontier of settlement. Note the absence of utopian communities in the areas in which new settlements had concentrated in the 1840s, reflecting shifts of concerns and utopian ideology. The frontier shown is that of 1880.

spiracy of international capital, and they called for drastic economic re-structuring. After the Crash of 1893, the utopian surge that followed was dominated by the pursuit of the Social Gospel and by experimentation with cooperative colonies and socialist communes.

The following primary trough was that of the Great Depression, plunged to new depths by federal intervention and pulled to recovery by Roosevelt's New Deal. Again, there was a millenarian upswell precipitated by despair amid crisis. The federal government took the lead in building alternative settlements, and the Social Gospel penetrated Catholic and black America. Rexford Tugwell's corporatist flirtation with state socialism was a reaction to the perceived ills of monopoly capitalism, while the religious organizations offered services to the urban poor.

The next Kondratiev trough was quite different from those that preceded it. New Deal stabilization, price-support and safety-net programs had combined with Keynesian deficit spending to produce a trough that was free of deflation. The sense of loss of control, of being at the mercy

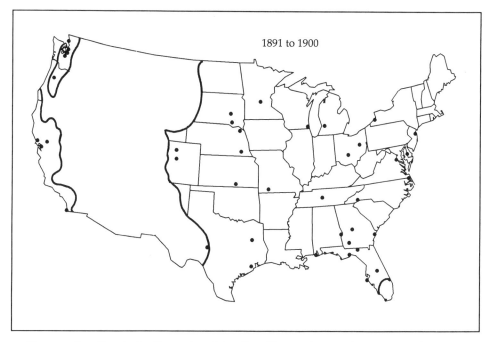

Figure 41. Reactions to the Depression of the 1890s. The utopian reaction was generalized throughout the settled areas of the United States. For the first time since destruction
of the distinctive planter society of the South during the Civil War, utopian experiments
were attempted in that region. The frontier shown is that of 1890.

of a mysterious boom-and-bust economy, had waned. No longer were
basic needs at issue. Yet what began to unfold was an epoch of unprecedented political and social turbulence against a backdrop of anxiety, malaise, and lack of confidence related to triple images of apocalypse: nuclear
Armageddon, natural disaster, and the continuing belief of radicals in
an impending terminal capitalist crisis. The epoch culminated not simply
in a utopian upsurge but also in the emergence of many new cults and
the rebirth of religious Fundamentalism in the Fourth Great Awakening
(McLoughlin, 1978). The counterculture threatened patriotism, the traditional work ethic, family values, and gender rules. Its utopian communities emphasized combinations of Eastern mysticism and of perfection
to be achieved through personal growth, culminating in the New Age
Paradigm. A resurgent Fundamentalism, on the other hand, offered a return to an imagined lost mainstream dominated by traditional American
Christian values. What was shared by New Agers and Fundamentalists
alike was the belief that the alternatives should be communal.

Barkun (1986) offers a crisis-centered model to explain the millenarian process and its relation to the long wave (pp. 143ff.). Millenarian upwellings begin, he says, when the environment prevents individuals from meeting their desires. They are under stress. Such stress may remain individual, or it may become collective, affecting entire communities. When there is a widespread feeling of vulnerability, fear of decline and doom predominate. Those affected must develop coping mechanisms. They first attempt damage control: the consequences of stress must be ameliorated, and future stress may be prevented. If damage control does not work, it is followed by development of a theory of mistakes that explains why it did not work. Such theories have traditionally been housed in religion, involving theological speculation on sin and suffering, but since the eighteenth century have also included an increasing array of secular elements, unexpected and beyond the community's control. If a theory of mistakes is insufficiently persuasive, it is followed by the development of alternative world views. When collective stress is high, there is, Barkun argues, great sympathy for deviant belief systems: religious heterodoxy; spiritualism, magic, and the occult; as well as political radicalism. The competing versions of reality may include the interpretation of disasters as intimations of divine judgement, or they may see the causes of suffering to be in human will and institutions, offering the hope that a new society can be constructed around such alternative moral principles as equality of wealth and social status, equality of the sexes, or the preeminence of community rights and obligations over those of the individual.

A theory of the utopian cycle goes one step beyond Barkun's model of the millenarian process by building in long-wave triggers to utopian activity. Long waves bring capitalist crises at regular intervals. Major deflationary depressions occur roughly each half-century. Midway between these depressions are stagflation crises, each followed by a primary deflationary trough. Downwave crises occur in the deflationary depressions and primary troughs and are characterized by declining prices, asset values, and real wealth and also by clusters of innovations that simultaneously ease the economy out of its crisis and widen the differences between rich and poor. For many, the losses are catastrophic. Yet catastrophes, as S. M. Prince (1920) has suggested, may be a precondition for social change. Some of those who are adversely affected by declining asset values look to havens organized on countervailing economic and social principles. Utopian communities offer escapes to the disillusioned. By so doing, they provide a safety valve for the society at large, as well as suggestions for longer-run social change.

Crises soon pass. The long-wave triggers explain not only the timing but also the brevity of most utopian waves. As the crisis ends and economic opportunities reemerge, the prospect of personal freedom and individual gain draws many of the communards back to the mainstream, along with those social innovations that seem worthy of wider application. The few utopian communities that have survived for any length of time have been those that have been able to isolate themselves from the recovering mainstream by careful selection of members, socialization of recruits to produce a high level of commitment to the community's work and values, development of organizational forms and a system of governance that transcend the life span and authority of particular leaders, with proficient mechanisms for seeking out and eliminating deviance and with rituals to assure continuing rededication to the central beliefs of the group. Kanter's (1972) sociological analysis emphasizes members' commitment to the enterprise: communitarians detached from their precommunal lives and given a new sense of identity, living in detached communities that are able to control factional struggles. This explains the greater life span of the non-English-speaking immigrant communes than those that recruited domestically in times of crisis. It also explains the greater life span of religious communes than of the secular experiments. Americans can easily move back into the mainstream, but immigrant communards may face a difficult process of acculturation.

In *Long-Wave Rhythms*, I argued that long waves are self-regulating fluctuations around the mainstream's path of development as growth surges overshoot society's technological needs, resulting in crises of oversupply and revolutionary epochs of technology transition. Periodic utopian surges are sympathetic reactions to these long waves, reflecting a continuing tension between capitalist and socialist ideals. Socialism flourishes when capitalism sags, especially during periods when older technologies are in trouble and their successors have yet to achieve dominance. Utopian surges provide evidence that when there is a worsening of economic conditions, some will interpret the downturn in catastrophic terms and that among those who see catastrophe some will seek refuge in communities constructed around principles antithetical to those of the mainstream. That such communities have never worked as well as the mainstream, despite its vicissitudes, tells us much about the strengths of capitalism and the inability to create effective socialist alternatives even (or perhaps especially) when the state takes over. As technology transitions have run their course and as new economic opportunities have emerged, when individuals are given the choice between experimental utopia and individual gain, gain has always prevailed.

The Wave of the 1990s

What of the next quarter-century? Following the stagflation crisis of 1980–81, we experienced an epoch of rapid technological change such as occurred after the stagflation crises of 1815, 1865, and 1920. Simultaneously, we experienced a plunge of relative prices and real asset values into another primary trough. Has there been a millenarian response? Do we see another upsurge of utopianism? If so, exactly how has the utopian alternative been formulated with respect to a capitalist system that continues to transform?

Some have argued that the linking mechanisms between millenarianism and utopianism have been blunted. Before the utopian surge of the 1960s, Egbert and Persons (1952), wrote that while the institution of revivalism had been able to survive in the twentieth century in part by adapting itself to an urban culture, it had undergone a radical change (p. 151). The old millennialist expectation, they thought, was still occasionally apparent but was generally associated with a catastrophic judgment upon the world rather than with the realization of personal salvation through reconstruction of social institutions. They missed the entire New Age experience. Fundamentalists were mobilized during the 1970s, forming political action groups, because they believed that secular forces were threatening to unravel the country's moral fabric. For them the period 1963 (when the Supreme Court banned prayer in public schools) to 1973 (when the Court permitted abortion on demand) was a "decade of crisis" in which secular humanism was seen to infiltrate the public school curriculum to produce sexual promiscuity, pornography, and drug abuse, to destroy national confidence during the Vietnam War, and to corrupt political institutions. Without preemptive action traditional American values would not survive. The nation had to be organized to protect the Judeo-Christian tradition against the humanists' assault.

Growing out of this mobilization, apocalyptic millenarianism also has become a strongly resurgent force as fundamental religionists argue that the final holocaust now is drawing near. With the outbreak of the Gulf War, a second edition of *Armageddon: Oil and the Middle East*, by Dallas Theological Seminary's chancellor, John F. Walvoord, sold 1.5 million copies from Christian bookstores in barely two months. Walvoord predicts an overall Middle East peace settlement imposed by a ten-nation alliance led by the Antichrist, to be followed by the "Rapture," when true believers depart to join Jesus in heaven. There will then be persecutions by the Antichrist, followed by famines, natural disasters, and demonic torment, and finally, by the battle of Armageddon. But, he writes, Jesus will return at the climax of World War III, establish Jerusalem as the capital of the New World Kingdom, wipe out the economic, political, and spiritual decay of the world, and reign for a thousand years of peace before he sits in final judgment. Evangelist Billy Graham, who still sees the revival as the place where sinners can seek salvation, ordered more than three hundred thousand copies of Walvoord's book for his followers.

This resurgent apocalyptic religiosity has been paralleled by the emergence of secular prophets of doom. In San Francisco the Society for Secular Armageddonism maintains a twenty-four-hour "Hotline of Doom" to warn callers about the coming apocalypse. The secular Armageddonists point to a frightening array of evidence that the end of the world is near: nuclear proliferation, chemical weapons, deforestation, AIDS, global warming, ozone depletion, acid rain, poisoning of waters, rising racism, species loss on a large scale, global famine, rampant greed, toxic waste, exploding population and worldwide complacency. They say they believe that the final battle will be between Ignorance and Awareness, not between the Antichrist and Jesus. The only hope for delaying the inevitable is direct action now. As one of the society's press releases says, "Ignoring the world around us and burying your head in fundamentalist dogma doesn't do anything to delay the inevitable. We have reached the same conclusion looking outward, to the world around us."

Among the reactions within the cults, Guru Ma called the members of her Church Universal and Triumphant to their Paradise Valley shelters in 1990 when she had a vision that nuclear Armageddon was imminent.

Reflecting their general sense of malaise about declining morality, groups of Christians, too, now are retreating to rural communes. One example is the Amaeus Road Fellowship, which originated in Colorado. Located on the Brazos River north of Waco in Texas, the fellowship is a large and growing agricultural commune to which increasing numbers of mature professionals are coming after disposing of their material possessions. They share a life-style predicated upon traditional Christian values, removed from what they see as a sinful and corrupting world. Although the fellowship is interdenominational, many of those who have come have been inspired by the new wave of charismatic excitation.

How many communes are there in the United States today, and what are the trends? Many of the cults described in Chapter 18 still exist, with their networks of communes, ashrams, and other living arrangements. The Hutterites continue to reproduce and to hive off new settlements: 391 Hutterite colonies existed in North America in early 1991, 106 of which are in the United States—51 in South Dakota, 40 in Montana, and the rest in North Dakota, Washington, and Minnesota. In addition, the 1991 *Directory of Intentional Communities* (which excludes most but not all of the cults) lists another 335 communities and claims some 75 have chosen not to be listed, for a total in excess of 400 (Fellowship for Intentional Community, 1991). Of the 335, only 20 were formed before 1960, including Koinonia in Georgia (Chapter 17) and Krotona in California (Chapter 12). Another 120 are leftovers from the 1965–75 decade, including The Farm in Tennessee, the Lama Foundation in New Mexico (Chapter 18), Arcosanti in Arizona,[1] Padanaram in Indiana, and Tolstoy Farm in Washington. Some 120 of the 335 intentional communities were founded in the mid- to late 1980s, and, suggestive of an incipient surge, 50 of the listed communities are in the process of formation in 1991.

Three-quarters of the 335 listed communities are secular, and one-quarter are religious. Most are small: only 58 have more than fifty residents. The objectives are diverse, with more explicit New Age themes among the older settlements and a greater range of orientations in the 1980s. Among the stated goals are shared spiritual life, preservation of nature, direct action politics, energy self-sufficiency, feedback and free choice, anthroposophy, ecology, rebirthing, spiritual healing, ecofeminism, universal oneness, environmental consciousness, land stewardship, economic democracy, macrobiotics, psychospiritual growth, meditation, permaculture, and spiritual ecology.

The spatial distribution is shown in Figure 42, revealing clusters along the Boston–Washington corridor, around Puget Sound, San Francisco Bay, and in the Los Angeles Basin, with strings through Appalachia, the Ozarks, the Colorado Front Ranges, and in New Mexico and Arizona. New Age themes predominate in more remote locations, but growing numbers of new living groups, stressing such themes as communal living, collectivity, urban co-ops, philanthropic service, humor, and friendship, lie within the economic sphere of the nation's major cities. Such themes predominate, too, among the communities in process of formation.

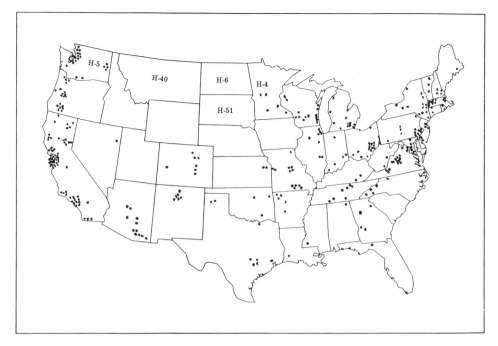

Figure 42. Distribution of Intentional Communities in the United States in 1991. Information for this map was derived from the *1991 Directory of Intentional Communities*
(Fellowship for Intentional Community, 1991). Hutterite communities are indicated by
numbers following the letter *H*.

The Intentional Community Movement

What is at work is the emergence of the "theme of the individual intentionally choosing a life-style of social and environmental responsibility . . .
communicating [their] convictions to others lead[ing] to the formation of
groups, communities, and networks [and] eventually influence[ing] the
larger society" (Fellowship for Intentional Community, 1991, pp. 37–38).

The Intentional Community movement explicitly differentiates itself
from " 'cults'—manipulative, authoritarian mass movements [that] attract . . . young people . . . burned out on drugs, or generally confused
and lost . . . and [that] are still sensationalized in the media. . . . [T]he
element that distinguishes a cult from a healthy, participative community
is the interference with a person's free will rather than the nurturing of
its use" (ibid., p. 31). What the movement sees emerging, in contrast to
the rejection of society by the countercultural communes of the 1960s,
are "*communities [where] members can contentedly enjoy whatever they wish
that mainstream America has to offer while snuggled in the comforting embrace of*

communitarian values" (ibid., p. 27; italics added. For a comparison of the traits of the 1960s and 1980s communes, see McLaughlin and Davidson, 1985, pp. 100–102). The movement's spokespeople continually reiterate the theme of individual choice of life-style, freely made, with both freedom of entry and exit from the communities of choice.[2]

The Tarrytown Group sees ten aspects to the movement's "new utopian vision," reflecting the New Age base while avoiding much of its mysticism:

1. *A dual commitment to transformation*, both personal and planetary: dedication to individual growth and to serving the needs of humanity and society.

2. *Cooperation*: a community based on sharing, pooling of finances and human resources, rather than competition and being "Out for Number One."

3. *A deep respect for the environment*: restoring ecological balance and "living lightly" on the earth; developing organic agriculture; and solar and wind energy.

4. *A spirit of experimentalism* in both work and relationships; committing to "working through" the shadow side of the personality, to confront conflict between individuals and within the self, to bring out the dark side for transformation into affirmative alliances.

5. *A new economics* finding businesses and ways to manage them that put human values on the bottom line and still return a healthy profit.

6. *Common sense*: determination to find practical solutions for conquering society's problems of pollution, inflation, violence and alienation.

7. *A holistic approach to health*: exploring alternative healing—such as herbs, acupuncture, nutrition and massage—and preventive methods aiming at helping people take responsibility for their own health.

8. *Building a positive vision*: creating examples of a better society and striving to live tomorrow's world today—then making their insights available, through outreach programs, to local communities and the world at large.

9. *Self-government by consensus*: working with group process and evoking the intuition of community members in the decision-making process.

10. *A world network*: cooperating with similar communities throughout the world; sharing skills and services, taking political action, and forming the vital nucleus of a new civilization. (Fellowship for Intentional Community, p. 49)

Any resulting "intentional community is, to some degree, a utopian experiment, or attempt to create a new model of association that uses cooperation to create 'a more perfect union' among people. *Any model that holds together, functions harmoniously, and succeeds economically is a potential prototype for future communitarians"* (ibid., pp. 41–42; italics added).

The movement's advocates have a strong sense of appropriateness and timeliness:

It is precisely our diversity of communitarian designs that provides our movement's ability to adapt creatively to changing conditions and opportunities. The potential for communitarian development increases as the level of stress in the wider society rises. With the increase of homelessness, single parent families, violence, ecological degradation, and the potential for economic catastrophe, communitarian models of a human scale society will become more and more relevant. Applying various forms of these models to an ever wider span of urban, suburban, and rural lifestyles in the challenge of the next wave of intentional communities. . . . [We] expect the 1990s to be another time of communitarian growth . . . [and in this] new wave of communitarianism . . . we [should] focus upon building a tradition of individual participation in, and responsibility for, the institutions that control our lives . . . a social tradition which is tolerant of the differences among people, provides a diversity of lifestyle options, and educates individuals for social and environmental responsibility. Communitarianism anticipates, reflects, and quickens the pace of social change." (ibid., p. 39)

After a fifteen-year sag, the utopian urge thus has reappeared amid another primary trough. If the experience of previous primary troughs is any guide, the surge will not be massive, but communities that are being developed will be bellwethers of the utopian surge that will occur in the deflationary depression to come. Owenism in the 1820s heralded the Fourierist surge of the 1840s. Flirtation with cooperatives and socialism in the 1870s presaged the principal thrust of the 1890s. Even the New Deal experiments of the 1930s anticipated the anticapitalist back-to-the-land thrust of the 1960s. Each involved a criticism of capitalism. Each was triggered by downwave despair amid a long-wave crisis. Each was brief, for the crisis soon passed.

If the Fundamentalists' initiatives are to be taken as the latest criticisms of society and economy, then reactions to secularism, greed and licentiousness will be the central axes of the wave to come. If the Intentional Communities movement is correct, the axes will include stress, health, and the environment. In both critiques, there is renewed concern for personal morality and a regenerated sense of "community," combined with a growing sense of collective responsibility for the physical environment.

The Fundamentalists are taking a traditional path—withdrawal from society—but if we learn from two centuries of utopian history, this reactive urge will pass. Economy and society will move in fresh directions, new opportunities will emerge, and the majority of the communards will once again rejoin the mainstream.

What is less certain is whether the goals of the Intentional Communities movement will be so quickly swept away, for their emphasis is on building upon rather than withdrawing from the mainstream. The movement seeks to extend freedom of choice and to multiply rather than to restrict the range of life-styles available to the individual who looks to the mainstream for work and to intentional communities as home.

In *The Human Consequences of Urbanisation* (1973) I concluded that

What appears to have emerged and to be emerging in America is a *mosaic culture*—
a society with a number of parallel and distinctively different life styles. While one
result is divisive tendencies for the society as a whole, at another level, mutual
harmony is produced by . . . withdrawal into homogeneous communities . . . and
isolation from groups with different life styles and values. A mosaic of homogeneous communities maintains different life styles that are internally cohesive and
exclusive, but externally non-aggressive unless threatened. Mobility within the
mosaic leads to a high degree of expressed satisfaction by residents with their communities, and the option for those who are dissatisfied to move to an alternative
that is more in keeping with their life-style requirements. (p. 66)

The goals of the Intentional Communities movement are consistent
with, rather than running counter to, these broader social trends in American society. The experimental communities that they will pioneer in the
long-wave crisis to come will enrich rather than challenge the nation's life-
style mosaic. Offering a synthesis of communitarianism and the market,
their efforts might, in microcosm, sweep away the capitalist–socialist dia-
lectics of the past at the very time that, in macrocosm, societies structured
around the socialist alternative have collapsed.

1. The Spatial Pattern and the Cultural Matrix (pp. 1–15)

1. Thomas Lake Harris, who helped found Mountain Cove, was a mystic who was involved in the development of a succession of theocratic communities, each built on an elaboration of the mythology of sex (Schneider and Lawton, 1942). Born in England in 1823, Harris was brought to New York where, because of his oratorical gifts, he was made a minister of the Universalist church in 1847. He claimed that his preaching began "after angels began putting him in trances and dictating sermons to him." He recorded that he delivered the first of these angelic discourses "in the midst of vibrating intelligence, quivering with love, calm as the stillness of a great night in midsummer; while from eyes to eyes it seemed as if the hushed, melted, audience diffused an atmosphere to hold the dew of tears" (Webber, 1959, p. 323). He left Mountain Cove after the death of his first wife and in 1863 founded a second community, the Brotherhood of the New Life, at Amenia in Dutchess County, New York, with money provided by one Jane Warning. The members were thirty-five followers from his Swedenborgian congregation in New York. However, by 1865, Jane Warning's fortune was consumed. Harris, his wife, and Jane left Amenia and went to England, where he recruited Laurence Oliphant and his mother, Lady Oliphant. With funds from Lady Oliphant and with additional resources provided by prosperous members from the South and New York, he bought sixteen hundred acres of land at Brocton in northern Chautauqua County, near the shore of Lake Erie (Okugawa, 1980, p. 202). Some seventy-five to one hundred members joined his third community, including five clergymen, twenty Japanese of the Samurai class, some American ladies, and Laurence Oliphant with his wife and mother. Harris required the members be celibate, even in marriage. He said that "in serving me these tender hearts believe they are also serving God, working for a kingdom of universal righteousness. They do not think that I rule them, except as aiding to lift and direct them into a larger freedom, wisdom and purity" (Holloway, 1951, p. 285). In practice, however, he was surrounded by gossip concerning his bisexual behavior. In the face of rising criticism, he selected a few members to construct another community at Santa Rosa, Cali-

fornia, in 1875. Other members stayed at Brocton for six years and then moved to California in 1881 (Okugawa, 1980, p. 207). The new community, Fountain Grove, occupied an expensive home on seventeen hundred acres. Referred to by Harris as a "community of theosocialism," it became known for its "divine liquor"—seventy thousand gallons of wine a year. Its thirty-five members included several married but celibate couples. A "Commandery" was built to house one hundred men. The Commandery bathhouse was the focus of sex scandals alleged by Santa Rosa and San Francisco newspapers. Because of the adverse publicity, Harris left for New York in 1892. After his departure, the community became progressively more commercial and was sold off in 1900. When Harris died in New York on 23 March 1906, disciples waited three months, expecting him to rise. When he failed to oblige, the community of the Brotherhood of the New Life was dissolved.

3. Shakerdom (pp. 27–40)

1. Jemima Wilkinson was born in 1752, the eighth child of a Quaker mother and a religiously indifferent father. She was an unexceptional child. Her conversion came in 1774, after she fell into a coma from which she recovered with the conviction that she had died, her original soul had ascended to heaven, and she had returned as a prophet with a new soul, God's Spirit of Life, "to warn a lost and guilty, gossiping and dying world to flee from the wrath to come, and to give an invitation to the last sheep of the House of Israel to come home" (Webber, 1959, pp. 76–77). She changed her name to the Publick Universal Friend. Later, imitating Mother Ann Lee's missionary tours in the eastern states, she began a series of revival meetings.

Her image was dramatic, traveling Massachusetts and Connecticut on a white horse, dressed as a man, wearing a cape and a slouch black hat. She was an attractive woman, tall and graceful, with dark hair and black eyes. Her brothers and sisters and twenty other followers joined her tours in Rhode Island and Connecticut.

Her disciples were called the Apocalyptic Witnesses. She was the risen Savior, like Ann Lee operating in the female line. She thrived on enigma, saying to the disciples, "I have yet many things to say unto you, but you cannot bear them now" and "Who do you say that I am?" When she was asked what the disciples should do to be saved, she said, "Follow me."

As new disciples she targeted the educated classes made wealthy by trade (Holloway, 1951, pp. 78–79). Because she was a successful fund-raiser, she was able to establish three churches in Rhode Island and Connecticut by 1782. She urged converts to leave their families and join her church and was accused of home breaking, of casting out devils with the aid of Beelzebub, and of trying to heal by laying on hands and to raise the dead. Confronted by an increasingly belligerent opposition, she fled to Philadelphia (Webber, 1959, p. 80).

In Philadelphia she was shunned by the Quakers and stoned from some areas because her followers claimed she was Christ. Returning to New England, she determined to build a communal society to install the vanguard of her faith. In 1788 she obtained a large tract of land near Lake Seneca in New York State, funded by followers who sold their property and placed their money in a common fund. After two years she bought more land near Canandaigua, and a benefactor added to it. Finally, they settled the colony of Jerusalem, and initially, they prospered. The fertile land yielded good harvests of wheat. They built a gristmill, a sawmill, and a school. By 1790 the community had 250 to 260 members.

There were no communal dwellings. Instead, community members lived at suitable places within Jerusalem. There was, however, communal sharing of consumption and mutual assistance in production. There was a very strict religious creed that married couples should remain celibate. The unmarried members either lived together or with Jemima Wilkinson in the luxurious house she built for herself. Every member visited her house for religious services or for consultation about his or her problems (ibid., pp. 82–83).

Later in her life, though, greed began to dominate over creed. Jemima, who already was surrounded with the luxuries she had obtained from her members, wanted more gifts, saying, "The Friend hath need of these things." There were many complaints by members who had expected her guidance to prepare them for the millennium (Holloway, 1951, p. 63). Internal dissension began to rise. Their benefactor wanted to withdraw his property and brought suit to regain what he had given her. Even though the courts decided against him, the members began to doubt Jemima's divinity. On the day that she promised to show that she could walk on the water of Lake Seneca, she told her members that she did not need to perform because her friends did not doubt that she could do it (Webber, 1959, pp. 84–85).

Harmful stories were spread as Jemima became old. She became sick with dropsy and died 1 July 1819. Her followers expected that she would rise on the third day, but because it did not come to pass, Jerusalem disintegrated as members withdrew. Some people lived on the communal land until 1863 (Okugawa, 1980, p. 174), when court decisions allowed them to divide the property (Webber, 1959, p. 87).

2. A second community was organized by a former English army officer named Dorril. In 1798 he brought together about forty followers in an area at Leydon, Massachusetts, and Guilford, Vermont, spanning the state line. The organizing theme was strict vegetarianism, hardly sufficient to excite wild or deep, long-term enthusiasm. The group dispersed within a couple of years.

3. The third of the alternative communities built during the Shaker first wave was The Union, established in 1804 between Potsdam and Norwood in St. Lawrence County, New York. Okugawa (1980) says that The Union was the first genuine secular American cooperative experiment (p. 176). A constitution was adopted in 1807, but three years thereafter it was dissolved, overwhelmed by the "virus of self-interest." The 2,427-acre tract of land was divided among its dozen members, most of whom continued to live there. The Shakers thus had no real competitors. The Dorrilites and The Union were short-lived. Jemima Wilkinson imitated Ann Lee. Her community failed to reproduce, living by consuming the wealth of the converts. It vanished when Jemima died because it was committed to a charismatic leader rather than to a set of principles. The Shakers, on the other hand, grew, spread, and transmitted a set of values that endured for 150 years.

4. German Separatists Adjust (pp. 41–55)

1. William Keil was born in Nordhausen, Austria, in 1812. He was a mystic and dealt in magnetism as a curative agent for diseases, working as a physician with some knowledge of botany. He claimed to possess a mysterious volume, written in human blood, that was alleged to contain recipes for curative medicines (Nordhoff, 1965, p. 306). Keil became acquainted with the Rappites while working as a tailor in Pittsburgh. He offered the New Philadelphia group a noncelibate Rappite alternative. Bethel was organized as a paternal, communal family composed of married couples raising children. Although they shared property and labor, private earnings were allowed. Marriage and family support were a religious duty. Those who married outside the community were forced to leave.

A church was one of the first things built in the town, followed by a general store and a post office. There was a distillery, gristmill, sawmill, carding machinery, and woolen mill. There were other machinery trades in the community. The food and clothing came from a common store. Flour and meal were taken from the mill by individual families. The women grew vegetables for their families in their backyard gardens. They were expected to grow surpluses that would be sold in the shop in return for imported goods like sugar, coffee, and tea.

By 1847 dissatisfied persons in the society clamored for privatization of the property. The property was divided. Provision was made for the aged and infirm. Later some sold their property and left the community, while others continued to live in common. After a lawsuit brought by a seceding member to retrieve wages and the property of his parent, a constitution was drawn up. All members signed the constitution, giving up future claims for wages.

In 1849 a branch of Bethel was founded at Ninevah, Adair County, Missouri, on thirteen hundred acres of land. Ninevah (1849–78) replicated Bethel's communal religious life, handicraft activities, and workshops. There were 150 settlers at the peak.

Keil left Bethel in 1856, when the membership was 650. Half of the people went west with Keil and established the Aurora Community in Oregon. The other half remained at Bethel, sharing property and labor. Aurora (1856–81) was founded because of Keil's desire to form a larger communistic society than the one at Bethel. The area they chose was heavily timbered. The town they established had a sawmill, a tan yard, cabinetmakers, carpenters, and a tin shop. There was a gristmill, carding machinery, some looms for weaving, drying houses for fruits, and a supply store for the community. A drugstore was kept by Keil. The society provided a store where members of the society and neighboring farmers could buy goods for cash. Outsiders could work as laborers, or they could, if approved, join the community, putting their resources in the common treasury.

A hotel built in 1863 became one source of the colony's financial prosperity, and during the 1870s substantial dwelling houses were constructed. By 1872 the colony owned twenty-three thousand acres of good land and had a thousand members. Keil remained the dominant force and leading spiritual healer in the community until 1872, when he was pressured into deeding over the community to individual owners. He died in 1877, and the colonists dissolved the communal organization and divided the property.

9. Etienne Cabet's French Communard Icarians (pp. 107–15)

1. Corning produced one group of offshoots, outcomes of the activities of Alcander Longley, whose settlements did attract Americans. After an eight-month stay at Corning, Longley established the Reunion Colony (1868–70) in Jasper County, Missouri. Twenty-seven adult members responded to Longley's call for a "community convention" in *The Communist*, which he published in St. Louis. Mortgage problems forced closure. Longley then moved on to Dallas County, Missouri, and established the Friendship Community (1872–77). Membership grew in the economic turmoil of 1873. Longley closed the settlement after sensing hostility from neighbors.

Meanwhile, William H. Bennett, dissatisfied with Longley's leadership, withdrew from Friendship and established the Bennett Co-operative Colony (1873–77). One determined group of a dozen families, led by N. T. Romaine, created Esperanza (1877–78) in Neosho County, Kansas. They were identified by a local paper as "a branch of the Oneida Community." The community soon vanished.

Longley did not give up. He tried to establish a Liberal Community at St. Louis and at Principia in Polk County before he created the Mutual Aid Community (1883–87) in Bollinger County, Missouri. This 120-acre colony had a constitution identical to that of Friendship. It disbanded because it had too few members and lacked financial support. Longley kept on trying. It seems that his Higby Community in Randolph County (1895–97) and Altruist Community in Jefferson County (1907–11) had only Longley and his family as members.

14. An Epidemic of Socialism? (pp. 162–72)

1. Wattles was not discouraged but moved on. In 1844 he persuaded a group of Spiritualists to form the Union Home on seven hundred acres in Randolph County, Indiana, donated by Hiram Mendenhall, an extensive landowner who resided in Unionsport. This brief socialist experiment, which lasted only until 1846, greatly weakened Mendenhall's financial ability; shortly after its failure he went to California. But Wattles kept on trying. He went on to publish a social reform paper called *The Herald of Progression* in Cincinnati. In May 1846 he and other prominent citizens of Cincinnati organized The Brotherhood (1846–47), a Spiritualist community of agricultural association. About one hundred members rebuilt the building that the Clermont Phalanx had erected on the Ohio River. They also built a large store in Cincinnati to sell their farm produce. The flood of December 1847, which destroyed all of the buildings, ended the life of the community. Despite this ending, Wattles then organized the Grand Prairie Harmonial Institute (1853–54), an "association for educational and social reform purposes." Horace Greeley was one of the trustees to whom Wattles deeded his 350 acres. The experiment, like his two previous ones, lasted little more than a year.

2. William H. Bennett tried again later with the Home Employment Co-operative Colony (1894–1906) in Dallas County, Missouri.

16. The State Takes Over (pp. 178–97)

1. The New Deal communities were not the first experience of the federal government in community building. During World War I, corporations holding contracts for the production of war materiel needed laborers in unprecedented numbers. The workers who flocked to these jobs were frequently unable to find housing, and many quit as a result. The corporations were unable to provide accommodations and turned to the government for help. Two agencies were created to alleviate the problem: the U.S. Housing Authority and the Emergency Fleet Corporation. Together they constructed seventy-two projects in fifty-two separate localities, providing about fifteen thousand units of inexpensive housing for laborers and their families. Despite the hopes of housing reformers that the war housing program might lead to the establishment of a permanent federal housing bureau, Congress was firmly opposed to any continuation of community-building activity. The war agencies were criticized by members of the House and Senate for hiring planners ("college professors and alleged experts in various lines") and allowing them to experiment with innovative design principles. The housing projects were quickly sold to the private sector.

18. Pathways to Self-Realization (pp. 214–27)

1. The countercult movement emerged as evangelical Christian leaders began to realize that there were growing numbers of challenges to the Christian church beginning in the United States. Initially, the focus was on groups such as the Jehovah's Witnesses or the Spiritualists but became more broadly focused with the proliferation of alternatives in the 1960s. Evangelicals view cults as heretical groups, and their countercult ministries try to persuade members to seek salvation by moving back to more orthodox Christian faith: "underlying all Christian countercult literature is a strong belief that cults are Satanic" (Melton, 1986b, p. 224). Christian revivalism surged alongside the proliferation of counterculture communes, and "by 1970, the 'Jesus people' revival was visibly shaking the hippie community from San Diego to Seattle" (ibid, p. 228). The anticult movement fed on the fears of parents whose children had abandoned their families and the American life-style to join religious groups that demanded significant behavior changes and commitment to alternative ideals. A secular action program developed, focusing on "deprogramming" young people removed from the cults and using public information programs to discredit the new groups, successfully creating a negative image of cults and spreading prejudice against a number of visible groups such as the Hare Krishnas, the "Moonies," the Scientologists, and Synanon. Synanon is an organization that features self-help for former drug addicts in communes that have a theology combining Buddhism, Taoism, and the Western mystical traditions of Transcendentalism, combining it with B. F. Skinner's behavioral psychology and

Buckminster Fuller's architecture. Of eight original communities, three survive, two in Badger, California, and one in Houston, Texas.

2. Among the most destructive cults, and contributing to their destructive image, was Jim Jones's ill-fated People's Temple. James "Jim" Jones founded his Christian Assembly of God Church in Indianapolis in 1953, converting it to the People's Temple in 1963. In 1966 seventy families relocated to Ukiah, California, with the Temple after Jones had announced that a nuclear holocaust would occur in 1967. Even though his predictions failed, he still was able to attract a following. In 1970 the People's Temple built churches in San Francisco and Los Angeles, where Jones gained a following of inner-city blacks and radical whites. In 1973 they established a mission in a remote rural area of Guyana. In 1977 nine hundred congregants moved there and started a commune on twenty-seven thousand acres leased from the Guyanese government. Jones was prophet and autocrat but was a man afflicted by progressively more pronounced delusions. A paranoid response to a Congressional investigation in 1978 led to the murder of Congressman Jack Ryan and several accompanying members of the media, followed by the mass suicide of the nine hundred congregants, an event unparalleled in utopian history.

3. An extreme expression is the Gaia hypothesis, which states that earth is a living system and humanity one of part of its life system.

20. The Wave of the 1990s (pp. 240–46)

1. Paolo Soleri's Arcosanti, the nucleus of which was begun a quarter-century ago in the Arizona desert seventy miles north of Phoenix to exemplify the benefits of "arcology"—the peaceful blending of architecture and ecology—hangs on, financed by fifty thousand tourists a year, who pay to visit and who buy the community's only product, Soleri bells. Soleri's architecture has been described by one critic as hovering between the magical and the totalitarian. Built by a rotating force of volunteers, Arcosanti still has not achieved a five-hundred-resident critical mass. Arcosanti's volunteers emphasize the corruptions of urban life and look to the community as pioneering ecologically sound self-contained alternatives in remote locations. This theme reappears in the experimental group that has sealed itself in Biosphere II, a terrarium located near Oracle, Arizona, designed to test a self-contained football-field-size ecological system as a means of survival. Critics allege that the financer, Fort Worth billionaire Ed Bass, views this experimental haven from ecological Armageddon as a major profit-making tourist attraction ("Profits of Doom," *The Dallas Observer*, 10 Oct. 1991).

2. Both private developers and cults are aware of the possibilities, as a staff report in the 4 February 1990 *Dallas Morning News* reveals. Charter Development Group has developed a master plan for a community to be called City of Immortals, located southwest of Austin in the Texas hill country. It is to be built by their affiliate, the Heaven on Earth Development Company. The master plan, they say, derives from the precepts of Maharishi Mahesh Yogi, guru of transcendental meditation (TM). The Maharishi and his disciples envision a worldwide movement to fashion harmonious, largely self-contained residential areas, free

from pollution, crime, and anxiety. The Heaven on Earth Development Company, based in Malibu, California, and tied financially to the Maharishi, is in contact with developers to locate additional Cities of Immortals near Houston, Denver, San Francisco, Los Angeles, San Diego, Washington, D.C., Toronto, Montreal, and in southeastern Iowa.

The Austin development has been preceded by a subdivision called Radiance, located next to the City of Immortals site. There, practitioners of TM meet twice daily in their meditation center. Their rituals are said to foster calm, creativity, and spiritual well-being.

Building on this experience, the larger community is to be equipped not simply with a TM center but also with a community health facility, so as to be able, according to the promotional materials, to restore "balance to the whole person— mind, body, behavior, and environment." "The goal . . . is to prevent disease and promote perfect health and longevity, creating a disease-free individual and a disease-free society." The city also will have its own expanded Maharishi School of the Age of Enlightenment, with a curriculum including TM and study of the Maharishi's Science of Creative Intelligence. Individual residents and the entire community are to be designed according to the Maharishi's *Sthapatya-Ved*, the "science of building in accord with natural law," which outlines designs supposed to reduce stress and criminal behavior. Use of nontoxic materials, energy-efficient construction, and ample green space are featured. "The proper placement of fountains, ponds, lakes, gardens and wooded areas all play a role in purifying the atmosphere and mitigating the effects of any build up of stress, thus providing an environment conducive to maintaining good health," according to Heaven on Earth materials. In addition, they note that homes will be "oriented with respect to the different positions of the sun throughout the day. In this way, the quality of energy produced by the sun promotes the success of the activity being performed."

Albanese, Catherine L. 1988. *The Spirituality of the American Transcendentalists.* Macon, Ga.: Mercer University Press.

Albertson, Ralph. 1936. "A Survey of Mutualistic Communities in America." *Iowa Journal of History and Politics* 3:374–444.

Allen, James B., and Glen M. Leonard. 1976. *The Story of the Latter-day Saints.* Salt Lake City, Utah: Deseret Book Company.

Alyea, Paul E., and Blanche Alyea. 1956. *Fairhope, 1894–1954: The Story of a Single Tax Colony.* Birmingham: University of Alabama Press.

Andelson, Robert V., ed. 1979. *Critics of Henry George: A Centenary Appraisal of Their Structures on Progress and Poverty.* Cranbury, N.J.: Associated University Presses.

Andrews, Edward Deming. 1933. *The Community Industries of the Shakers.* Albany: University of the State of New York.

Andrews, Edward Deming. 1953. *The People Called Shakers: A Search for the Perfect Society* New York: Oxford University Press.

Arndt, Karl J. R. 1965. *George Rapp's Harmony Society, 1785–1847.* Philadelphia: University of Pennsylvania Press.

Arno Press. 1972. *Cooperative Communities: Plans and Descriptions: Eleven Pamphlets, 1825–1847.* New York: Arno Press.

Arnold, Joseph L. 1971. *The New Deal in the Suburbs: A History of the Greenbelt Town Program 1935–1954.* Columbus: Ohio State University Press.

Arrington, Leonard J. 1966. *The Great Basin Kingdom: An Economic History of the Latter-Day Saints, 1830–1900.* Lincoln: University of Nebraska Press.

Arrington, Leonard J., and David Bitton. 1979. *The Mormon Experience: A History of the Latter-day Saints.* New York: Alfred A. Knopf.

Arrington, Leonard J., Feramorz Y. Fox, and Dean L. May. 1976. *Building the City of God: Community and Cooperation Among the Mormons.* Salt Lake City, Utah: Deseret Book Company.

Ayres, Robert U. 1990. "Technological Transformations and Long Waves: Part 1." *Technological Forecasting and Social Change* 37:1–37.

Backus, Charles K. 1955. *The King of Beaver Island*. Los Angeles: Westernlore Press.

Barker, Charles Albro. 1955. *Henry George*. New York: Oxford University Press.

Barkun, Michael. 1984. "Communal Societies as Cyclical Phenomena." *Communal Societies* 4:35–48.

Barkun, Michael. 1985. "The Awakening-Cycle Controversy." *Sociological Analysis* 46:425–43.

Barkun, Michael. 1986. *Crucible of the Millennium: The Burned-Over District of New York in the 1840s*. Syracuse, N.Y.: Syracuse University Press.

Barthel, Diane L. 1984. *Amana: From Pietist Sect to American Community*. Lincoln: University of Nebraska Press.

Bassett, T. Seymour. 1952. "The Secular Utopian Socialists." In *Socialism and American Life*, edited by Donald Drew Egbert and Stow Persons, 1:155–211. Princeton, N.J.: Princeton University Press.

Beckman, Robert. 1983. *The Downwave, Surviving the Second Great Depression*. Portsmouth, England: Milestone Publications.

Beckman, Robert. 1988. *Into the Upwave: How to Prosper from Slump to Boom*. Portsmouth, England: Milestone Publications.

Beecher, Jonathan. 1986. *Charles Fourier: The Visionary and His World*. Berkeley: University of California Press.

Beecher, Jonathan, and Richard Bienvenu. 1971. *The Utopian Vision of Charles Fourier: Selected Texts on Work, Love, and Passional Attraction*. Boston: Beacon Press.

Bennett, David H. 1969. *Demagogues in the Depression: American Radicals and the Union Party, 1932–1936*. New Brunswick, N.J.: Rutgers University Press.

Bercovitch, Sacvan. 1967. "Typology in Puritan New England: The Williams-Cotton Controversy Reassessed." *American Quarterly* 19:166–91.

Berry, Brian J. L. 1973. *The Human Consequences of Urbanisation: Divergent Paths in the Urban Experience of the Twentieth Century*. London and Basingstoke: Macmillan Press.

Berry, Brian J. L. 1991. *Long-Wave Rhythms in Economic Development and Political Behavior*. Baltimore: Johns Hopkins University Press.

Besant, Annie [1897] 1969. *The Ancient Wisdom: An Outline of Theosophical Teachings*. Adyar, India: Theosophical Publishing House.

Bestor, Arthur. 1950. *Backwoods Utopias: The Sectarian and Owenite Phases of Communitarian Socialism in America, 1663–1829*. 2d ed. Philadelphia: University of Pennsylvania Press.

Blavatsky, H. P. 1966. *An Abridgement of the Secret Doctrine*. Edited by Elizabeth Preston and Christmas Humphreys. London: Theosophical Publishing House.

Boorstin, Daniel J. 1958. *The Americans: The Colonial Experience*. New York: Vintage Books.

Brandes, Joseph, and Martin Douglas. 1977. *Immigrants to Freedom: Jewish Communities in Rural New Jersey since 1882*. Philadelphia: University of Pennsylvania Press.

Braude, Ann. 1989. *Radical Spirits: Spiritualism and Women's Rights in Nineteenth-Century America*. Boston: Beacon Press.

Brewer, Priscilla J. 1986. *Shaker Communities, Shaker Lives.* Hanover, N.H.: University Press of New England.

Brinkley, Alan. 1982. *Voices of Protest: Huey Long, Father Coughlin, and the Great Depression.* New York: Alfred A. Knopf.

Brisbane, Albert. 1840. *Social Destiny of Man: Or Association and Reorganization of Industry.* Philadelphia: C. F. Stollmeyer.

Brodie, Fawn M. 1945. *No Man Knows My History: The Life of Joseph Smith.* New York: Alfred A. Knopf.

Carden, Maren Lockwood. 1969. *Oneida: Utopian Community to Modern Corporation.* Baltimore: Johns Hopkins Press.

Carden, Maren Lockwood. 1976. "Communes and Protest Movements in the U.S., 1960–1974: An Analysis of Intellectual Roots." *International Review of Modern Sociology* 6:13–22.

Carter, Kate B. 1960. *The Mormons: Their Westward Trek.* Salt Lake City, Utah: Utah Printing Co.

Cohen, Joseph J. 1957. *In Quest of Heaven: The Story of the Sunrise Co-operative Farm.* New York: Sunrise History Publications.

Cohn, Norman. 1970. *The Pursuit of the Millenium: Revolutionary Millenarians and Mystical Anarchists of the Middle Ages.* New York and Oxford: Oxford University Press.

Conkin, Paul K. 1959. *Tomorrow a New World: The New Deal Community Program.* Ithaca, N.Y.: Cornell University Press for the American Historical Association.

Conkin, Paul K. 1983. *Two Paths to Utopia: The Hutterites and the Llano Colony.* Westport, Conn.: Greenwood Press.

Cord, Stephen B. 1965. *Henry George: Dreamer or Realist?* Philadelphia: University of Pennsylvania Press.

Cross, Whitney R. 1950. *The Burned-Over District: The Social and Intellectual History of Enthusiastic Religion in Western New York, 1800–1850.* New York: Harper.

Cutler, Phoebe. 1985. *The Public Landscape of the New Deal.* New Haven, Conn.: Yale University Press.

Dare, Philip N. 1990. *American Communes to 1860: A Bibliography.* New York and London: Garland.

Davidson, Gabriel. 1943. *Our Jewish Farmers and the Story of the Jewish Agricultural Society.* New York: L. B. Fisher.

Davidson, Rondel Van. 1988. *Did We Think Victory Great? The Life and Ideas of Victor Considerant.* Lanham, Md.: University Press of America.

de Mille, Anne George. 1950. *Henry George, Citizen of the World.* Chapel Hill: University of North Carolina Press.

Desroche, Henri. 1971. *The American Shakers: From Neo-Christianity to Pre-Socialism.* Amherst: University of Massachusetts Press.

Dictionary of American Biography. 1971. s.v. "Sidney Rigdon. Religious Reformer."

Doan, Ruth Alden. 1987. *The Miller Heresy, Millennialism, and American Culture.* Philadelphia: Temple University Press.

Duss, John Samuelson. 1972. *The Harmonist: A Personal History.* Philadelphia: Porcupine Press.

Easton, Lloyd D. 1966. *Hegel's First American Followers: The Ohio Hegelians.* Athens: Ohio University Press.

Egbert, Donald D., and Stow Persons, eds. 1952. *Socialism and American Life.* Princeton, N.J.: Princeton University Press.

Eliade, Mircea. 1966. "Paradise and Utopia: Mythical Geography and Eschatology." In *Utopias and Utopian Thought,* edited by Frank E. Manuel, 260–80. Boston: Houghton Mifflin.

Emlen, Robert P. 1987. *Shaker Village Views: Illustrated Maps and Landscape Drawings by Shaker Artists of the Nineteenth Century.* Hanover, N.H., and London: University Press of New England.

Engels, Friedrich. (1845). "Beschreibung der in Neuerer Zeit enstandenen und noch bestehenden Kommunitischen Anseidlungen." *Deutsches Bürgebuch für 1845* 1 (4): 351–66.

Erikson, Kai T. 1966. *Wayward Puritans: A Study in the Sociology of Deviance.* New York: John Wiley & Sons.

Fairfield, Richard. 1972. *Communes USA: A Personal Tour.* Baltimore: Penguin Books.

Fellman, Michael. 1973. *The Unbounded Frame: Freedom and Community in Nineteenth Century American Utopianism.* Westport, Conn.: Greenwood Press.

Fellowship for Intentional Community. 1991. *Directory of Intentional Communities.* Rutledge, Mo.: Communities Publications Cooperative.

Fischer, David Hackett. 1989. *Albion's Seed: Four British Folkways in America.* New York and Oxford: Oxford University Press.

Fischer, Ernest G. 1980. *Marxists and Utopias in Texas.* Burnet, Tex.: Eakin Press.

Flanders, Robert Bruce. 1965. *Nauvoo: Kingdom on the Mississippi.* Urbana: University of Illinois Press.

Fogarty, Robert S. 1980. *Dictionary of American Communal and Utopian History.* Westport, Conn.: Greenwood Press.

———. 1990. *All Things New: American Communes and Utopian Movements, 1860–1914.* Chicago and London: University of Chicago Press.

Foster, Lawrence. 1981. *Religion and Sexuality: Three American Communal Experiments of the Nineteenth Century.* New York: Oxford University Press.

Foster, Lawrence. 1991. *Women, Family, and Utopia: Communal Experiments of the Shakers, the Oneida Community, and the Mormons.* Syracuse, N.Y.: Syracuse University Press.

Fourier, Charles. 1971. *Design for Utopia: Selected Writings of Charles Fourier.* New York: Schocken Books.

Frank, Andre Gunder, and Marta Fuentes. 1988. "Social Movements in Recent World History" Paper presented at the Second International Karl Polanyi Conference, November 10–13, Montreal.

Freeman, C., and C. Perez. 1990. *Structural Crisis of Adjustment: Business Cycles and Investment Behavior.* In *Technical Change and Economic Theory,* edited by G. Dosi et al., 38–66. London: Pinter Publishers.

Gardner, Hugh. 1978. *The Children of Prosperity: Thirteen Modern American Communes.* New York: St. Martin's Press.

Gaston, Paul M. 1984. *Women of Fairhope*. Athens: University of Georgia Press.

Geiger, George Raymond. 1933. *The Philosophy of Henry George*. New York: Macmillan.

George, Henry. 1879. *Progress and Poverty: An Inquiry into the Cause of Industrial Depressions, and of Increase of Want with Increase of Wealth; the Remedy*. New York: Random House Modern Library.

George, Henry, Jr. 1930. *The Life of Henry George*. New York: Doubleday, Doran.

Goddard, Harold Clarke. 1960. *Studies in New England Transcendentalism*. New York: Hillary House.

Green, Calvin, and Seth Y. Wells. 1848. *Summary View of the Millenial Church, or the United Society of Believers, Commonly Called Shakers: Comprising the Rise, Progress and Practical Order of the Society, Together with the General Principles of Their Faith and Testimony*. 2d ed. Albany, N.Y.: C. Van Benthuysen.

Greenough, Horatio. 1855. "Fourier et Hoc Genus Oyne." *The Crayon* 1:371–72.

Guarneri, Carl J. 1991. *The Utopian Alternative: Fourierism in Nineteenth-Century America*. Ithaca, N.Y., London: Cornell University Press.

Harrison, John F. C. 1969. *Quest for the New Moral World: Robert Owen and the Owenites in Britain and America*. New York: Scribner.

Harrison, John F. C. 1979. *The Second Coming: Popular Millenarianism, 1780–1850*. New Brunswick, N.J.: Rutgers University Press.

Hartmann, George W. 1952. "The Psychology of American Socialism." In *Socialism and American Life*, edited by Donald Drew Egbert and Stow Persons, 1:557–98. Princeton, N.J.: Princeton University Press.

Hayden, Dolores. 1976. *Seven American Utopias: The Architecture of Communitarian Socialism, 1790–1975*. Cambridge, Mass.: M.I.T. Press.

Heingram, John, and Anson Shupe. 1985. *The Mormon Corporate Empire*. Boston: Beacon Press.

Hendricks, Robert J. 1971. *Bethel and Aurora*. New York: AMS Press.

Hernstadt, Richard L., ed. 1969. *The Letters of A. Bronson Alcott*. Ames: Iowa State University Press.

Herrscher, Uri D. 1981. *Jewish Agricultural Utopias in America, 1880–1910*. Detroit: Wayne State University Press.

Hill, Marvin, C. Keith Rooker, and Larry T. Wimmer. 1977. *The Kirtland Economy Revisited: A Market Critique of Sectarian Economics*. Ogden, Utah: Brigham Young University Press.

Hinds, William Alfred. [1878] 1975. *American Communities and Cooperative Colonies*. Philadelphia: Porcupine Press.

Hine, Robert V. 1953. *California's Utopian Colonies*. San Marino, Calif.: The Huntington Library.

Holloway, Mark. 1951. *Heavens on Earth: Utopian Communities in America 1680–1880*. New York: Literary Publishers.

Holloway, Mark. 1966. "Shaker Societies." In *Strange Cults and Utopias of 19th Century America*, edited by John H. Noyes, 64–79. New York: Dover.

Hopkins, Charles H. 1940. *The Rise of the Social Gospel in American Protestantism, 1805–1915*. New Haven, Conn.: Yale University Press.

Hostetler, John. 1974. *Hutterite Society*. Baltimore: Johns Hopkins University Press.

Huntington, Charles White. 1934. *Enclaves of Economic Rent, 1933*. Harvard, Mass.: Fiske Warren.

Jackson, Richard H., ed. 1978. *The Mormon Role in the Settlement of the West*. Provo, Utah: Brigham Young University Press.

Jackson, Richard H., and Robert L. Layton. 1976. "The Mormon Village: Analysis of a Settlement Type." *The Professional Geographer* 28:136–41.

Jaher, Frederic Cople. 1964. *Doubters and Dissenters: Cataclysmic Thought in America, 1885–1918*. New York: The Free Press of Glencoe.

James, Bartlett B. 1899. *The Labadist Colony in Maryland*. Baltimore: Johns Hopkins University Press.

Jinarajadasa, C. [1921] 1963. *First Principles of Theosophy*. Adyar, India: Theosophical Publishing House.

Judah, J. Stillson. 1967. *The History and Philosophy of the Metaphysical Movements in America*. Philadelphia: Westminster Press.

Kamenka, Eugene. 1987. *Utopias: Papers from the Annual Symposium of the Australian Academy of the Humanities*. Melbourne, Australia: Oxford University Press.

Kanter, Rosabeth Moss. 1972. *Commitment and Community: Communes and Utopias in Sociological Perspective*. Cambridge, Mass.: Harvard University Press.

Kanter, Rosabeth Moss. 1973. *Communes: Creating and Managing the Collective Life*. New York: Harper and Row.

Kephart, William M. 1987. *Extraordinary Groups: An Examination of Unconventional Life-Styles*. 3d ed. New York: St. Martin's Press.

Kern, Louis J. 1981. *An Ordered Love: Sex Roles and Sexuality in Victorian Utopias: The Shakers, the Mormons, and the Oneida Community*. Chapel Hill: University of North Carolina Press.

Klein, Walter C. 1942. *Johann Conrad Beissel, Mystic and Martinet, 1690–1768*. Philadelphia: University of Pennsylvania Press.

Kondratiev, Nikolai D. [1926] 1935. "The Long Waves in Economic Life." Translated by W. F. Stolper. *Review of Economic Statistics* 17:105–15.

Layton, Eunice, and Felix. 1967. *Theosophy: Key to Understanding*. Wheaton, Ill.: Theosophical Publishing House.

Leone, Mark P. 1979. *Roots of Modern Mormonism*. Cambridge, Mass.: Harvard University Press.

LeWarne, Charles P. 1975. *Utopias on Puget Sound, 1885–1915*. Seattle: University of Washington Press.

Lockwood, George B. 1971. *The New Harmony Communities*. New York: AMS Press.

Lord, Russell, and Paul H. Johnstone, eds. 1942. *A Place on Earth: A Critical Appraisal of Subsistence Homesteads*. Washington, D.C.: U.S. Department of Agriculture, Bureau of Agricultural Economics.

Mandelker, Ira L. 1984. *Religion, Society and Utopia in Nineteenth-Century America*. Amherst: University of Massachusetts Press.

Manuel, Frank E. 1966. "Toward a Psychological History of Utopias." In *Utopias and Utopian Thought*, edited by Frank E. Manuel. Boston: Houghton Mifflin.

Maslow, Abraham H. 1962. *Toward a Psychology of Being*. Princeton, N.J.: D. Van Nostrand.

McCloskey, Herbert, and John Zaller. 1984. *The American Ethos: Public Attitudes Towards Capitalism and Democracy*. Cambridge, Mass.: Harvard University Press.

McLaughlin, Corinne, and Gordon Davidson. 1985. *Builders of the Dawn: Community Lifestyles in a Changing World*. Walpole, N.H.: Stillpoint Publishing.

McLoughlin, William G. 1978. *Revivals, Awakenings and Reform: Essays on Religion and Social Change in America, 1607–1977*. Chicago: University of Chicago Press.

McNemar, Richard. 1807. *The Kentucky Revival; or, A Short History of the Late Extraordinary Outpouring of Spirit of God in the Western States of America*. Cincinnati, Ohio: John W. Browne.

Meinig, Donald W. 1965. "The Mormon Culture Region: Strategies and Patterns in the Geography of the American West, 1847–1964." *Annals of the Association of American Geographers* 55:191–220.

Melcher, Marguerite F. 1968. *The Shaker Adventure*. Cleveland, Ohio: Press of Case Western Reserve University.

Melton, J. Gordon. 1986a. *Biographical Dictionary of American Cult and Sect Leaders*. New York and London: Garland.

Melton, J. Gordon. 1986b. *Encyclopedic Handbook of Cults in America*. New York and London: Garland.

Melton, J. Gordon. 1989. *The Encyclopedia of American Religions*. 3d ed. 2 vols. Wilmington, N.C.: McGrath Publishing.

Melton, J. Gordon, Jerome Clark, and Aidan A. Kelly. 1990. *New Age Encyclopedia*. Detroit: Gale Research.

Melville, Keith. 1972. *Communes in the Counter Culture: Origins, Theories, Styles of Life*. New York: William Morris.

Mensch, Gerhard. 1979. *Stalemate in Technology: Innovations Overcome the Depression*. Cambridge, Mass.: Ballinger.

Mikkelsen, Michael Andrew. 1892. *The Bishop Hill Colony, a Religious Communistic Settlement in Henry County, Illinois*. Baltimore: Johns Hopkins University Press.

Miller, Perry. 1949. *Jonathan Edwards*. New York: William Sloane Associations.

Miller, Perry. 1950. *The Transcendentalists: An Anthology*. Cambridge, Mass.: Harvard University Press.

Miller, Perry, and Thomas H. Johnson, eds. 1938. *The Puritans*. New York: American Book Company.

Miller, Timothy. 1990. *American Communes, 1860–1960: A Bibliography*. New York: Garland.

Moment, Gairdner B., and Otto F. Kraushaar. 1980. *Utopias: The American Experience*. Metuchen, N.J.: Scarecrow Press.

Morgan, Arthur. 1944. *Edward Bellamy*. New York: Columbia University Press.

Myerson, Joel, ed. 1984. *The Transcendentalists: A Review of Research and Criticism*. New York: Modern Language Association of America.

Niebuhr, H. Richard. [1937] 1959. *The Kingdom of God in America*. New York: Harper & Row.

Nordhoff, Charles. 1965. *The Communistic Societies of the United States*. New York: Schocken.

Noyes, John Humphrey. 1870. *History of American Socialisms*. Philadelphia: Lippincott.

Noyes, John Humphrey. 1966. *Strange Cults and Utopias of 19th-Century America* (formerly titled *History of American Socialisms*). New York: Dover.

Numbers, Ronald L., and Jonathan M. Butler. 1987. *The Disappointed: Millerism and Millenarianism in the Nineteenth Century*. Bloomington: Indiana University Press.

O'Brien, Michael. 1979. *The Idea of the American South, 1920–1941*. Baltimore: Johns Hopkins University Press.

Okugawa, Otohiko. 1980. "Annotated List of Communal and Utopian Societies, 1787–1919." In *Dictionary of American Communal and Utopian History*, edited by Robert S. Fogarty, 173–233. Westport, Conn.: Greenwood Press.

Oved, Ia'acov. 1988. *Two Hundred Years of American Communes*. New Brunswick, N.J.: Transaction Books.

Owen, Robert. 1967. *The Life of Robert Owen*. New York: A. M. Kelley.

Parker, Robert Allerton. [1935] 1973. *A Yankee Saint: John Humphrey Noyes and the Oneida Community*. Hamden, Conn.: Anchor Books.

Persons, Stow. 1952. "Christian Communitarianism in America." In *Socialism and American Life*, edited by Donald Drew Egbert and Stow Persons, 1:125–51. Princeton, N.J.: Princeton University Press.

Peters, John L. 1956. *Christian Perfection and American Methodism*. New York: Abingdon Press.

Peters, Victor. 1965. *All Things Common: The Hutterian Way of Life*. Minneapolis: University of Minnesota Press.

Piehl, Mel. 1982. *Breaking Bread: The Catholic Worker and the Origin of Catholic Radicalism in America*. Philadelphia: Temple University Press.

Pitzer, Donald E., ed. 1972. *Robert Owen's American Legacy: Proceedings of the Robert Owen Bicentennial Conference*. Indianapolis: Indiana Historical Society.

Popenoe, Cris, and Oliver Popenoe. 1984. *Seeds of Tomorrow: New Age Communities That Work*. San Francisco: Harper & Row.

Porter, Philip W., and Fred E. Lukermann. 1976. "The Geography of Utopia." In *Geographies of the Mind: Essays in Historical Geography in Honor of John Kirtland Wright*, edited by David Lowenthal and Martyn J. Bowden, 197–223. New York: Oxford University Press.

Powell, J. M. 1971. "Utopia, Millenium and the Co-operative Ideal: A Behavioral Matrix in the Settlement Process." *The Australian Geographer* 11:606–18.

Prince, S. M. 1920. *Catastrophe and Social Change: Based upon a Sociological Study of the Halifax Disaster*. New York: Columbia University Press.

Quaife, Milo M. 1930. *The Kingdom of Saint James: A Narrative of the Mormons*. New Haven, Conn.: Yale University Press.

Rexroth, Kenneth. 1974. *Communalism: From Its Origins to the Twentieth Century*. New York: Seabury Press.

Riasanovsky, Nicholas V. 1969. *The Teaching of Charles Fourier*. Berkeley: University of California Press.

Robertson, Constance Noyes. 1977. *Oneida Community Profiles*. Syracuse, N.Y.: Syracuse University Press.

Rogers, L. W. 1929. *Elementary Theosophy*. Wheaton, Ill.: Theosophical Publishing House.

Rose, Anne C. 1981. *Transcendentalism as a Social Movement, 1830–1850*. New Haven, Conn. and London: Yale University Press.

Rose, Edward J. 1968. *Henry George*. New York: Twayne.

Sams, Henry W. 1958. *Autobiography of Brook Farm: A Book of Primary Source Materials*. Englewood Cliffs, N.J.: Prentice-Hall.

Sandeen, Ernest R. 1970. *The Roots of Fundamentalism: British and American Millenarianism, 1800–1930*. Chicago: University of Chicago Press.

Sanford, Charles L. 1961. *The Quest for Paradise: Europe and the American Moral Imagination*. Urbana: University of Illinois Press.

Schlesinger, Arthur M., Jr. 1960. *The Politics of Upheaval*. Vol. 3 of *The Age of Roosevelt*. Boston: Houghton Mifflin.

Schneider, Herbert W., and George Lawton. 1942. *A Prophet and a Pilgrim: Being the Incredible History of Thomas Lake Harris and Lawrence Oliphant; Their Sexual Mysticisms and Utopian Communities Amply Documented to Confound the Skeptic*. New York: Columbia University Press.

Schumpeter, Joseph A. 1939. *Business Cycles: A Theoretical, Historical, and Statistical Analysis of the Capitalist Process*. 2 vols. London: McGraw-Hill.

Schwartz, Gary. 1970. *Sect Ideologies and Social Status*. Chicago: University of Chicago Press.

Sears, Clara Endicott. 1915. *Bronson Alcott's Fruitlands*. Boston: Houghton Mifflin.

Shambaugh, Bertha M. 1908. *Amana, The Community of True Inspiration*. Iowa City: The State Historical Society of Iowa.

Shaw, Albert. 1884. *Icaria, A Chapter in the History of Communism*. New York: G. P. Putnam's Sons.

Shields, Steven L. [1975] 1982. *Divergent Paths of the Restoration: A History of the Latter Day Saint Movement*. 3rd ed. Bountiful, Utah: Restoration Research.

Shipps, Jan. 1985. *Mormonism: The Story of a New Religious Tradition*. Urbana and Chicago: University of Illinois Press.

Smith, David E. 1965. "Millenarian Scholarship in America." *American Quarterly* 17:535–49.

Sowell, Thomas. 1985. *Marxism: Philosophy and Economics*. New York: Quill.

Spann, Edward. 1989. *Brotherly Tomorrows: Movements for a Cooperative Society in America, 1820–1920*. New York: Columbia University Press.

Spence, Clark C. 1985. *The Salvation Army Farm Colonies*. Tucson: University of Arizona Press.

Spencer, Michael C. 1981. *Charles Fourier*. Boston: Twayne.

Starr, Kevin. 1985. *Inventing the Dream: California Through the Progressive Era*. New York: Oxford University Press.

Starr, Kevin. 1986. *Americans and the California Dream, 1850–1915*. New York: Oxford University Press.

Sternsher, Bernard. 1964. *Rexford Tugwell and the New Deal*. New Brunswick, N.J.: Rutgers University Press.

Swift, Lindsay. 1961. *Brook Farm: Its Members, Scholars, and Visitors*. New York: Corinth Books.

Taylor, Barbara. 1983. *Eve and the New Jerusalem: Socialism and Feminism in the Nineteenth Century*. London: Virago Press.

Teeple, John B. 1985. *The Oneida Family: Genealogy of a 19th Century Perfectionist Commune*. Oneida, N.Y.: Oneida Community Historical Committee Mansion House.

Thomas, John L. 1983. *Alternative America: Henry George, Edward Bellamy, Henry Demarest Lloyd, and the Adversary Tradition*. Cambridge, Mass.: Belknap Press.

Thomas, Robert David. 1977. *The Man Who Would Be Perfect: John Humphrey Noyes and the Utopian Impulse*. Philadelphia: University of Pennsylvania Press.

Tucker, Robert C. 1978. *The Marx-Engels Reader*. New York: W. W. Norton.

Tugwell, Rexford. 1937. "The Future of National Planning." *The New Republic*, 9 Dec.

Tugwell, Rexford. 1955. *A Chronicle of Jeopardy, 1945–1955*. Chicago: University of Chicago Press.

Tuveson, Ernest Lee. 1949. *Millennium and Utopia: A Study in the Background of the Idea of Progress*. Berkeley: University of California Press.

Tuveson, Ernest Lee. 1968. *Redeemer Nation: The Idea of America's Millennial Role*. Chicago: University of Chicago Press.

Tyler, Alice Felt. 1944. *Freedom's Ferment: Phases of American Social History from the Colonial Period to the Outbreak of the Civil War*. New York: Harper & Row.

Van Duijn, J. J. 1983. *The Long Wave in Economic Life*. London: George Allen & Unwin.

Van Noord, Roger. 1988. *King of Beaver Island: The Life and Assassination of James J. Strang*. Urbana, Ill.: University of Illinois Press.

Veysey, Laurence. 1978. *The Communal Experience: Anarchist and Mystical Communities in Twentieth-Century America*. Chicago: University of Chicago Press.

Wagner, Jon. 1982. *Sex Roles in Contemporary American Communes*. Bloomington: Indiana University Press.

Walters, Ronald G. 1978. *American Reformers, 1815–1860*. New York: Hill & Wang.

Webber, Everett. 1959. *Escape to Utopia: The Communal Movement in America*. New York: Hastings House.

Weber, Timothy P. 1979. *Living in the Shadow of the Second Coming: American Premillennialism, 1875–1925*. New York: Oxford University Press.

Weisbrot, Robert. 1983. *Father Divine and the Struggle for Racial Equality*. Urbana: University of Illinois Press.

Whicher, George F. 1949. *The Transcendentalist Revolt Against Materialism*. Boston: D. C. Heath.

White, Anna, and Leila Taylor. [1904] 1971. *Shakerism, Its Meaning and Its Message: Embracing an Historical Account, Statement of Belief and Spiritual Experience of the Church from Its Rise to the Present Day*. New York: AMS Press. Reprint. Columbus, Ohio: Press of F. J. Heer.

Whitworth, John McKelvie. 1975. *God's Blueprints: A Sociological Study of Three Utopian Sects*. London: Routledge & Kegan Paul.

Williams, Aaron. 1886. *The Harmony Society at Economy, Pennsylvania: Founded by George Rapp A.D. 1805*. Pittsburgh, Pa: W. S. Haven.

Wilson, Bryan R. 1963. "Typologie des sectes dans une perspective dynamique et comparative." *Archives de Sociologie des Religions* 16:49–63.

Young, Arthur Nichols. 1916. *The Single Tax Movement in the United States*. Princeton, N.J.: Princeton University Press.

Young, Benjamin Seth. 1856. *Testimony of Christ's Second Appearing*. 4th ed. Albany, N.Y.: The United Society, Called Shakers.

Zablocki, Benjamin. 1971. *The Joyful Community: An Account of the Bruderhof, a Communal Movement Now in Its Third Generation*. London: Penguin Books.

Zablocki, Benjamin. 1980. *Alienation and Charisma: A Study of Contemporary American Communes*. New York: The Free Press.

Zicklin, Gilbert. 1983. *Countercultural Communes: A Sociological Perspective*. Westport, Conn.: Greenwood Press.

UNIVERSITY PRESS OF NEW ENGLAND publishes books under its own imprint and is the publisher for Brandeis University Press, Brown University Press, University of Connecticut, Dartmouth College, Middlebury College Press, University of New Hampshire, University of Rhode Island, Tufts University, University of Vermont, and Wesleyan University Press.

Library of Congress Cataloging-in-Publication Data

Berry, Brian Joe Lobley, 1934–
    America's utopian experiments : communal havens from long-wave crises / Brian J. L. Berry.
        p.   cm. — (The Nelson A. Rockefeller series in social science and public policy)
    Includes bibliographical references and index.
        ISBN 0–87451–589–0.—ISBN 0–87451–590–4 (pbk.)
    1. Utopias—History.   2. Collective settlements—United States—History.   3. Sects—United states—History.   4. Socialism—United States—History.   5. Social movements—United States—History.
    I. Title.   II. Series.
    HX83.B44   1992
    335′.973—dc20   92–10001

    ⊚